DICTIONARY OF CHEMISTRY

PARAMESHWAR HEDGE

Gaurav Book Centre
4832/24, Prahlad Lane.S-207 Ansari
Road, Daryaganj, Delhi-110002

Publisher
Gaurav Book Centre
4832/24, Prahlad Lane, S-207 Ansari Road,
Daryanganj, Delhi-110002
Ph. : 43570976, 23278261

Edition : 2013

ISBN : 978-93-80317-25-0

Laser Typesettingh
Vinood Bhardwaj
Delhi

Price : 295.00

Printed in India
Published - Gaurav Book Centre, Delhi

PREFACE

Chemistry (from Egyptian *keme* (chem), meaning "earth" is the science concerned with the composition, behavior, structure, and properties of matter, as well as the changes it undergoes during chemical reactions It is a physical science for studies of various atoms, molecules, crystals and other aggregates of matter whether in isolation or combination, which incorporates the concepts of energy and entropy in relation to the spontaneity of chemical processes. Modern chemistry evolved out of alchemy following the chemical revolution (1773).

Disciplines within chemistry are traditionally grouped by the type of matter being studied or the kind of study. These include inorganic chemistry, the study of inorganic matter; organic chemistry, the study of organic matter; biochemistry, the study of substances found in biological organisms; physical chemistry, the energy related studies of chemical systems at macro, molecular and submolecular scales; analytical chemistry, the analysis of material samples to gain an understanding of their chemical composition and structure. Many more specialized disciplines have emerged in recent years, e.g. neurochemistry the chemical study of the nervous system.

Chemistry is the scientific study of interaction of chemical substances that are constituted of atoms or the subatomic particles: protons, electrons and neutrons Atoms combine to produce molecules or crystals. Chemistry is often called "the central science" because it connects the other natural sciences such as astronomy, physics, material science, biology, and geology

Energy and entropy considerations are invariably important in almost all chemical studies. Chemical substances are classified in terms of their structure, phase as well as their chemical compositions. They can be analysed using the tools of chemical analysis, e.g. spectroscopy and chromatography.

Chemistry is an integral part of the science curriculum both at the high school as well as the early college level. At these levels, it is often called "general chemistry" which is an introduction to a wide variety of fundamental concepts that enable the student to acquire tools and skills useful at the advanced levels, whereby chemistry is invariably studied in any of its various sub-disciplines.

Present Chemistry Dictionary Provides maximum number of words belongs to chemistry, which are very useful for students, teachers, research scholars and alsofor common people.

I would like to express my sincere thanks to the publishers for their continued interest in bringingout this edition.

Parameshwar Hegde
M.Sc.,M.A.

Sirsi[N.K.]
Karnataka

A

Ab initio. From first principles.

Abscissa. The name given to the horizontal axis in a set of two-dimensional coordinates. Commonly referred to as the x-axis.

Absolute Entropy (of a substance). The increase in the entropy of a substance as it goes from a perfectly ordered crystalline form at 0 °K (where its entropy is zero) to the temperature in question.

Absolute Zero. The zero point on the absolute temperature scale; -273.15°C or 0 K; theoretically, the temperature at which molecular motion ceases.

Absorption filter. Filter which allow all light through except for that in a narrow region; this is caused by the light being absorbed by the filter material.

Absorption Spectrum. Spectrum associated with absorption of electromagnetic radiation by atoms (or other species) resulting from transitions from lower to higher energy states.

Accuracy. How closely a measured value agrees with the correct value.

Acid . A substance that produces H+(aq) ions in aqueous solution. Strong acids ionize completely or almost completely in dilute aqueous solution. Weak acids ionize only slightly.

Acid Anhydride. The oxide of a nonmetal that reacts with water to form an acid.

Acid Anhydride. Compound produced by dehydration of a carbonic acid; general formula is R—C—O—C—R

Acidic Salt. A salt containing an ionizable hydrogen atom; does not necessarily produce acidic solutions.

Ac arc. A method of vaporization and excitation in emission spectroscopy, using voltages of less than 5000 V. Results with this method are more reproducible than that possible with a dc arc.

Ac spark. Put a charge of 40,000V across two electrodes; the electrons which flow between them will ionize the sample.

Acceleration slits. Positively charged ions produced in an ionization chamber of a mass spectrometer are passed into the analyzer by the accleration slits. Generally, two acceleration slits are used; one has a slight negative potential with respect to the ionization chamber in order to attract the positive ions, and the other slit has an extremely high voltage which accelerates that ions to up to half the speed of light.

ACF. Activated carbon fibers

Activation Energy. Amount of energy that must be absorbed by reactants in their ground states to reach the transition state so that a reaction can occur.

Active Metal .Metal with low ionization energy that loses electrons readily to form cations.

Activity (of a component of ideal mixture). A dimensionless quantity whose magnitude is: equal to molar concentration in an ideal solution; equal to partial pressure in an ideal gas mixture; and defined as 1 for pure solids or liquids.

Activity Series. A listing of metals (and hydrogen) in order of decreasing activity

Actual Yield. Amount of a specified pure product actually obtained from a given reaction. Compare with Theoretical Yield.

Actinides. Elements 90 to 103 (after actinium)

Acyl Group. Compound derived from a carbonic acid by replacing the —OH group with a halogen (X), usually —Cl; general formula is O R—C—X

Addition Reaction. A reaction in which two atoms or groups of atoms are added to a molecule, one on each side of a double or triple bond

Adhesion. The force between unlike molecules.

Adhesive Forces. Forces of attraction between a liquid and another surface.

Adsorption. Adhesion of a species onto the surfaces of particles .

A*/E. Low-field absorption/high-field emission with net absorptive character.

Aerosols. Dispersions of liquids in gases and solids in gases.

Afocal system. Where both the object and image are focused at infinity. Primarily used in magnification, or when a beam needs to be expanded but not focused.

AIMD. ab inito molecular dynamics.

Alcohol. Hydrocarbon derivative containing an —OH group attached to a carbon atom not in an aromatic ring.

Aldehyde. Compound in which an alkyl or aryl group and a hydrogen atom are attached to a carbonyl group and a hydrogen atom are attached to a carbonyl group; general formula, O-R-C-H

Alkali Metals. Metals of Group IA (Na, K, Rb).

Alkaline Battery. A dry cell in which the electrolyte contains KOH.

Alkaline Earth Metals. Group IIA metals

Alkenes(Olefins). Unsaturated hydrocarbons that contain one or more carbon-carbon double bonds.

Alkyl Group. A group of atoms derived from an alkane by the removal of one hydrogen atom.

Alkyl benzene.A compound containing an alkyl group bonded to a benzene ring.

Alkynes. Unsaturated hydrocarbons that contain one or more carbon-carbon triple bonds.

Allomorph. Any of two or more crystalline forms of a substance

ALON. Also known as Raytran, Al23O27N5, a glass used in IR spectroscopy

Allotropes. Different forms of the same element in the same physical state.

Allotropic Modifications (Allotropes). Different forms of the same element in the same physical state.

Alloying. Mixing of metal with other substances (usually other metals) to modify its properties.

Alpha Particle.A helium nucleus.

Alpha (a) Particle. Helium ion with 2+ charge; an assembly of two protons and two neutrons.

Alpha-AgI. A form of silver iodide which is stable at high temperatures. It acts as a superionic material, conducting electricity effectively through ionic transport. Degrades below 147 C to beta-AgI.

Alpha-electron. An electron in which the spin is +1/2

Alpha particles. The helium nucleus.

Alums. Hydrated sulfates of the general formula M+M3+(SO4) 2.12H2).

Aluminosilicates. Silicates with aluminum occupying some of the silicon sites.

A-MCMB's. Activated meso-carbon microbeads. Show ferromagnetism at low temperatures

Ambident. Describing a chemical species that has two alternative reactive centres such that reaction at one centre stops or inhibits reaction ar the other. An example is the enolate ion in which electrophilic attack can occur at either the oxygen atom or at the beta-carbon atom.

Amide. Compound containing the O-C-N group. Compound that can be considered a derivative of ammonia in which one or more hydrogens are replaced by a alkyl or aryl groups.

Amine. Derivatives of ammonia in which one or more hydrogen atoms have been replaced by organic groups.

AmineComplexes. Complex species that contain ammonia molecules bonded to metal ions.

Amino Acid. Compound containing both an amino and a carboxylic acid group.The —NH2 group.

Ammeter. A device that measures current

Amorphous Solid. A noncrystalline solid with no well-defined ordered structure.

Ampere. Unit of electrical current; one ampere equals one coulomb per second.

Ampere hour. A practical unit of electric charge equal to the charge flowing in one hour through a conductor passing one ampere. It is equal to 3600 coulombs.

Ampere turn . The Sl unit of magnetomotive force equal to the magmetomotive force produced when a current of one ampere flows through one turn of a magnetzing coil.

Ampholyte. A substance that may act as either an acid or a base

Amphiprotism. Ability of a substance to exhibit amphiprotism by accepting donated protons.

Amphiphilic. Describing a molecule that has both hydrophilic and hydrophobic parts, as in detergents.

Ampholyte. A substance that can act as either an acid, in the presence of a strong base, or a base, when in the presence of a strong acid.

Amphoterism. The ability to react with both acids and bases.Ability of substance to act as either an acid or a base.

Amylopectin. A polysaccharide comprising highly branched chains of glucose molecules. It is one of the constituents (the other being amylose) of starch.

Amylose. A polysaccharide consisting of linear chains of between 100 and 1000 linked glucose molecules. Amylose is a constituent of starch. In water, amylose reacts with iodine to give a characteristic blue colour.

Analyzer tube. A part of a mass spectrometer in which positive ions are separated according to their mass/charge ratios. In TOF, this part is straight, in others, curved.

Anhydrous. Denoting a chemical compound lacking water; applied particularly to salts lacking their water of crystallization.

Anion. A negative ion; an atom or goup of atoms that has gained one or more electrons.

Anode. In a cathode ray tube, the positive electrode. Electrode at which oxidation occurs.

Angstrom. 10^{-10} meters.

Anion photoelectron spectroscopy. What you do is hit a sample with a laser and create anions. A carrier gas takes the anions down to a magnetic-bottle time-of-flight photoelectron analyzer, where you can characterize them.

Anisotropy. When something is not isotropic; you look at how much something is not random, and the measure of this non-randomness is the anisotropy.

Annealing. The tempering of glass or metals by heat. Can also be used as a treatment for thin films to give them the desired properties.

Annealing point. The temperature at which residual strain or stress in a glass will relieve itself in a few minutes.

Annulation. A type of chemical reaction in which a ring is fiused to a molecule by formation of two new bonds. Sometimes the term annelation is used.

Annulene. Totally conjugated hydrocarbon

Antiferromagnetism. Where there is no net magnetic moment because the spin magnetic moments are randomly oriented, canceling them.

Antiknock agent. A petrol additive that inhibits preignition ('knocking') in internal-combustion engines. Antiknock agents work by retarding combustion chain reactions. The commonest, lead (IV) tetraethyl, causes environmental pollution, and its use is being discouraged.

Antinodes. Points of constructive interference between two waves

Antireflection coating. Increases energy transmitted through optical surfaces by reducing Fresnel reflection losses. The criteria for such a coating are that the refractive index of the material must be equal to the square root of the substrate index when the substrate is in air; also, the phase difference between the incident wave and reflected wave must be an odd multiple of pi.

Anti-Stokes fluorescence. although most fluorescence complies with the Stokes law, a weak fluorescence is found at a shorter wavelength than the exciting wavelength. This additional energy is gained from excited vibrational levels within the ground state.

Antibonding Orbital. A molecular orbital higher in energy than any of the atomic orbitals from which it is derived; lends instability to a molecule or ion when populated with electrons; denoted with a star (*) superscript or symbol.

Appearance potential. The potential required to get fragmentation ions in a mass spectrometer. Generally, this value is 1-4 eV greater than the value for the ionization energy of the corresponding molecular ion.

Aquation. The process in which water molecules solvate or form coordination complexes with ions.

Aqueous. Describing a solution in water.

Aquo ion. A hydrated positive ion present in a crystal or in solution.

AR. Antireflective coating.

Archimedes principle. The buoyant force on a body immersed in a fluid is equal to the weight of the fluid displaced by that object.

Arenes. Atomatic hydrocarbons, such as benzene, toluene, and naphthalene.

Armature. Where the coils of wire are mounted on an electric motor.

Argentic compounds. Compounds of silver in its higher (+2) oxidation state; e.g. argentic oxide is silver (II) oxide (AgO).

Argentous compounds. Compounds of silver in its lower (+1) oxidation state; e.g. argentous chloride is silver (1) chloride.

Aromaticity. The property characteristic of aromatic compounds.

Aromatic Hydrocarbons. Benzene and its derivatives.

Arsenic trisulfide. Material used in IR windows (0.6-11 microns)

Arsenous acid. H3AsO3

Artificial Transmutation. An artificially induced nuclear reaction caused by the bombardment of a nucleus with subatomic particiles or small nucei.

Aryl Group. Group of atoms remaining after a hydrogen atom is removed from the aromatic system.

Aryne. A compound that can be regarded as formed from an arene by removing two adjacent hydrogen atoms to convert a double bond into a triple bond. Arynes are transient intermediates in a number of reactions. The simplest example i s benzyne.

ASED. Atom superposition and electron delocalization: a method used in extended-Huckel calculations.

Asphaltanes. Heavy polyaromatics which are insoluble in n-hydrocarbon solvents, produced in oil refineries from the vacuum distillation of virgin crude oils and processed petroleum. They form unit sheets which are arranged in stacks; the number of unit sheets which join together and the height of these sheets is strongly solvent dependant.

Associated Ions. Short-lived species formed by the collision of dissolved ions of opposite charges.

Astigmatism. When the lens is focused in one plane, but not in the plane 90 degrees to it.

Asymmetric induction. The preferential formation of one particular enantiomer or diastereoisomer in a reaction as a result of a chiral element in one of the reactants or in the catalyst used.

ATLEED (automated tensor low energy electron diffraction). A form of LEED (low energy electron diffraction) in which the information obtained can readily be stored and analysed using a computer.

Atmolysis. The separation of a mixture of gases by means of their different rates of diffusion. Usually, separation is effected by allowing the gases to diffuse through the walls of a porous partition or membrane.

Atmosphere. A unit of pressure; the pressure that will support a column of mercury 760 mm high at 0 °C.

Atom. The smallest particle of an element

Atomic clock. An apparatus for standardizing time based on periodic phenomena within atoms or molecules.

Atomic absorption spectroscopy (AAS). Ionize a sample, and then hit the ions with light and see where absorptions take place.

Atomic emission spectroscopy (AES). Heat a sample and it ionizes; measure the wavelengths of the relaxations of these ions.

Atomic fluorescence spectroscopy (AFS). Same as AAS, but you measure the wavelengths that pass through without being absorbed.

Atomic Mass Unit (amu). One twelfth of a mass of an atom of the carbon12 isotope; a unit used for stating atomic and formula weights; also called dalton.

Atomic Number. Integral number of protons in the nucleus; defines the identity of element.

Atomic Orbital. Region or volume in space in which the probability of finding electrons is highest.

Atomic Radius. Radius of an atom.

Atomic Weight. Weighted average of the masses of the constituent isotopes of an element; The relative masses of atoms of different elements.

Attenuator. Used in e.s.r, the attenuation of the microwave power passing along a waveguide is achieved by means of a metal plate placed along the axis of the waveguide. The degree of attenuation increases as the plate is moved away from the wall of the waveguide toward the center. In IR and UV spectroscopy, the attenuator is a toothed comb, grid, or star arrangement introduced into one beam of a spectrometer, operated either automatically through an electronic servosystem, or manually to balance the radiation in both beams.

Auer burner. one source of radiation for far-IR spectroscopy. Consists of a thorium oxide mantle heated to ~2000K by a burning gas. Optimum wavelength is ~50 microns.

Auger effect. the emission of a second electron after high energy radiation has expelled another.

Auger electron spectroscopy. The use of the Auger effect to determine orbital energies and structure of the molecule.

Aufbau ('building up') Principle. Describes the order in which electrons fill orbitals in atoms.

autoprotolysis. solvent dissociation into anion and proton.

Autoionization. An ionization reaction between identical molecules.

auxochrome. a saturated group with nonbonded electrons which, when attached to a chromophore, alters both the wavelength and intensity of an absorption.

Avogadro's Amedeo. Italian chemist and physicist. In 1811 he published his hypothesis, which provided a method of calculating molecular weights from vapour densities.The importance of the work remained unrecognized, however, until championed by Stanislao Cannizzaro in 1860.

Avogadro's Law. At the same temperature and pressure, equal volumes of all gases contain the same number of molecules.

Avogadro's Number. The number (6.022x10^23) of atoms, molecules or particles found in exactly 1 mole of substance.

Aza crown ethers . Crown ethers containing ring nitrogen.

Azeotrope. Some composition of a binary mix in which the two portions cannot be separated by distillation.

Azeotropic distillation. It two substances have similar boiling points or form an azeotrope, separation by fractional distillationis either very difficult or impossible. The method of azeotropic distillation consists of adding a third substance which forms AZEOTROPIC MIXTURES with the other two ; these azeotropes are then further treated to obtain pure compounds. Used in separating ethanol and water using benzene.

Azidodithiocarbonates. Compound containing the SCSN3 group. A pseudohalide.

Azidothymidine (AZT). Anti-viral drug used against HIV.

Azines. Compounds containing C=N-N=C groups prepared from C=O compounds and hydrazine. Also used for compounds containing multiple N2 groups and azine dyes.

Azoic dyes. Water-insoluble azo dyes, also known as ice colours and ingrain colours. In use they are formed within the fibre.

Azophenols. Compounds obtained by compling a diazonium salt with a phenol.

B

Babbit metal. Any of a group of related alloys used for making bearings. They consist of tin containing antimony (about 10%) and copper (1-2%), and often lead. The original alloy was invented in 1839 by the US inventor Isaac Babbit (1799-1862).

Babo's law. The vapour pressure of a liquid is decreased when a solute is added, the amount of the decrease being proportional to the amount of solute dissolved. The law was discovered in 1847 by the German chemist Lambert Babo (1818-99).

Back donation. A form of chemical bonding in which a ligand forms a sigma bond to an atom or ion by donating a pair of electrons, and the central atom donates electrons back by overlap of its dorbitals with empty p-or d-orditals on the ligand. It occurs, for example, in metal carbonyls.

Back e.m.f. An electromotive force that opposes the main current flow in a circuit. For example, in an electric cell, polarization causes a back e.m.f. to be set up by chemical means.

Background Radiation. Ratiation extraneous to an experiment. Usually the low-level natural radiation form cosmic rays and trace radioactive substances present in our environment.

Background region. The region of low transmission of a pass filter.

Back titration. A technique in volumetric analysis in which a known excess amount of reagent is added to the solution to be estimated. The unreacted amount of the added reagent is then determined by titration, allowing the amount of substance in the original test solution to be calculated.

Bacteriocidal. Capable of killing bacteria. Common bacteriocides are some antibodies, antiseptics, and disinfectants.

Bakelite. A trade name for certain phenol-formaldehyde resins, first introduced in 1909 by the Belgian US chemist Leo Hendrik Baekeland (1863-1944).

Band. A series of very closely spaced, nearly continuous molecular orbitals that belong to the crystal as a whole.

Banana bond. Informal name for the type of electron-deficient three centre bond holding the B-H-B bridges in boranes and similar compounds.

Band of Stability. Band containing nonradioactive nuclides in a plot of number of neutrons versus atomic number.

Band Theory of Metals. Theory that accounts for the bonding and properties of metallic solids.

Bar. 100 kPa

Barrier-layer cell. A photoelectric detector which is made of iron coated with a semiconductor film; when light from 250-750nm hits this cell, you get a current; this is a cell which is mainly good for intense light sources, because there is not a huge signal enhancement.

Barrel. A measurement of volume, widely used in the chemical industry, equal to 35 UK gallons (approximately 159 litres).

Bartlett, Neil. (1932-) British inorganic chemist who prepared oxygen hexachlo-roplatinate in 1961 and, in 1962, xenon hexachloroplatine the first compound of a noble gas.

Barometer. A device for measuring pressure.

Barytes (barite). An orthorhombic mineral form of barium sulphate, BaSO4; the chief ore of barium. It is usually white but may also be yellow. grey, or brown. Large deposits occur in Andalusia, Spain, and in the USA.

Basalt. A fine-grained basic igmeous rock. It is composed chiefly feldspar and pyroxene; other minerals present may be olivine, megnetite, and apatite. Basalt is the commonest type of lava.

Base. A substance that produces OH (aq) ions in aqueous solution. Strong soluable bases are soluble in water and are completely dissociated. Weak bases ionize only slightly.

Base metal. A common relatively inexpensive metal, such as iron or lead, that corrodes, oxidizes, or tarnishes on exposure to air, moisture, or heat, as distinguished from precious metals, such as gold and silver.

Base pairing. Pairing of nucleotide bases by hydrogen bonding. Base pairing holds together the two strands in the double helix structure of DNA. The purine adenine pairs with the pyrimidine thymine and the purine guanine pairs with the pyrimidine cytosine.

Basic. 1. Describing a compound that is a base. 2. Describing a solution containing an excess of hydroxide ions; alkaline.

Basic Anhydride. The oxide of a metal that reacts with water to form a base.

Basic Salt. A salt containing an ionizable OH group.

Basis set truncation error. The error you get in computational methods from not expanding an infinite series all the way to infinity. the more terms you use, the less basis set truncation error you get.

Beta Particle. Electron emitted from the nucleus when a neuton decays to a proton and an electron.

Bathochromic shift. Shift of an absorption to a longer wavelength due to substitution or solvent effect (red shift).

Bayer process. Used to obtain aluminum from bauxite

Beckmann rearrangement. The chemical conversion of a ketone oxime into an amide, usually using sulphuric acid as a catalyst. The reaction, used in the manufacture of nylon and other polyamides, is named after the German chemist Ernst Beckmann (1853-1923).

Becquerel. Symbol Bq. The Sl unit of activity. The unit is named after the discoverer of radioactivity A.H. Becquerel.

BEEQ mass spectrometer. A type of mass spectrometer, where the B stands for the magnetic sector, E stands for the electric sector, and Q stands for the quadropole mass filter. All of these letters stand for devices which can be used to separate the ionic products into the desired types.

Bell metal. A type of bronze used in casting bells. It consists of 60-85% copper alloyed with tin, often with some zinc an0d lead included.

Benzodiazepines. A group of related psychotic drugs that affect the central nervous system. They are used medically in the treatment of anxiety, insomnia, convulsions, and alcohol withdrawl. All are addictive and avilable only as prescription drugs in the UK. Common examples are diazepam (Valium) and flunitrazepam (Rohypnol).

Benzoylecgonine (BZ). A primary metabolite of cocaine, used in drug testing. It can be detected in the urine up to 48 hours after taking cocaine. BZ is tested for by immunoassay or by gas chromatography/ mass spectrometry.

Beta electron. An electron in which the spin is -1/2.

Beta particle. Electron.

Bequerel. SI unit of radioactivity, equal to one disintegration per second.

Bernoulli's principle. Where the velocity of a fluid is high, the pressure is low, and vice-versa.

Berry mechanism. A mechanism by which ligands in trigonal bipyramidal complexes can interchange between axial and equatorial positions. It involves intermediate formation of. a square pryramidal conformation. It is also known as the Berry pseudorotation.

Biodegradability. The ability of a substance to be broken down into simpler substances by bacteria.

Bifurcation. Division into two parts or branches or where these branches split apart

Bimolecular reaction. A step in a chemical reaction that involves two molecules.

Binary. Describing a compound or alloy formed from two elements.

Binary Acid. A binary compound in which H is bonded to one or more of the more electronegative nonmetals.

Binary Compound. A compound consisting of two elements; may be ionic or covalent.

Binding Energy (nuclear binding energy). The energy equivalent (E = mc^2) of the mass deficiency of an atom.

where: E = is the energy in joules, m is the mass in kilograms, and c is the speed of light in m/s^2.

Binding site. An area on the surface of a molecule that combines with another molecule. Binding sites on enzymes can be active sites or allosteric sites.

Bioactivation. A metabolic process in which a product that is chemically reactive is produced from a relatively inactive precursor.

Bioelement. Any chemical element that is found in the molecules and compounds that make up a living organism. In the human body the most common bioelements are oxygen, carbon, hydroghen, nitrogen, calcium, and phosphorus. Other bio-elements include sodium, potassium, magnesium, and copper.

BIOGRAF. A computer program that allows the user to determine the positions of atoms or ions in biological molecules.

Biomarker. A normal metabolite that, when present in abnormal concentrations in certain body fluids, can indicate the presence of a particular disease or toxicological condition. For example, abnormal concentrations of glucose in the blood can be indicative of diabetes mellitus.

Biomolecule. Any molecule that is involved in the maintenance and metabolic processes of living organisms. Biomolecules include carbohydrate, lipid, protein, nucleic acid, and water molecules; some biomolecules are macromolecules.

Biosynthesis. The production of molecules by a living cell, which is the essential feature of anabolism.

Biotin. A vitamin in the vitamin B complex. It is the coenzyme for various enzymes that catalyse the incorporation of carbon dioxide into various compounds. Adequate amounts are normally produced by the intestinal bacteria; other sources include cereals, vegetables, milk, and liver.

Biotite. An important rock-forming silicate mineral, a member of the mica group of minerals, in common with which it has a sheetlike crystal structure. It is usually black, dark brown, or green in colour.

Biradical. A radical that has two unpaired electrons at different points in the molecules, so that the radical centres are independent of each other.

Birefringence. When a single incident beam is split into two refracted beams. Both of the refracted beams are parallel, with one offset from the other.

Bistability. When a system is able to exist in either of two steady states.

Bittern. The solution of salts remaining when sodium chloride is crystalized from sea water.

Blake, Joseph. (1728-99) British chemist and physician, born in France. He studied at Glasgow and Edinburgh, where his thesis (1754) contained the first accurate description of the chemistry of carbon dioxide. In 1757 he discovered latent heat, and was the first to distinguish between heat and temperature.

Blakedamp (choke damp) . Air left depleted in oxygen following the explosion of firedamp in a mine.

Blasting gelatin. A high explosive made from nitroglycerine and gun cotton (cellulose nitrate).

Blaze wavelength. The wavelength or which the angle of reflection from the groove face of a grating and the diffraction angle are the same.

BLM. Bilayer lipid membrane

Blood pigment. Any one of a group of metal-containing coloured protein compounds whose function is to increase the oxygen-carrying capacity of blood.

Boehmite. A mineral form of a mixed aluminium oxide and hydroxide, AlO.OH. It is named after the German scientist J.Bohm.

Bohr radius. The radius of the n=1 orbital in hydrogen. .529exp(-10) m.

Bohrium. Symbol Bh. A radioactive transactinide element; a.n. 107. It was first made in 1981 by Peter Armbruster and a team in Darmstadt, Germany by bombarding bismuth 209 nuclei with chromium 54 nuclei. Only a few atoms of bohrium have ever been detected.

Boiling Point. The temperature at which the vapor pressure of a liquid is equal to the applied pressure; also the condensation point

Boiling Point Elevation. The increase in the boiling point of a solvent caused by the dissolution of a nonvolatile solute.

Bolometer. An IR detector where changes in temperature of the responsive element due to incident radiation causes a change in conductivity of the element.

Bomb Calorimeter. A device used to measure the heat transfer between system and surroundings at constant volume.

Bond Energy. The amount of energy necessary to break one mole of bonds of a given kind (in gas phase).

The amount of energy necessary to break one mole of bonds in a substance, dissociating the sustance in the gaseous state into atoms of its elements in the gaseous state.

Bond Order. Half the numbers of electrons in bonding orbitals minus half the number of electrons in antibonding orbitals.

Bonding Orbital. A molecular orbit lower in energy than any of the atomic orbitals from which it is derived; lends stability to a molecule or ion when populated with electron

Bonding Pair. Pair of electrons involved in a covalent bond.

Bonded phase chromatography (BPC). Where the stationary phase of the analyte actually bonds to a solid surface; the solid surface usually consists of silica-based particles.

Borax-bead test. A simple laboratory test for certain metal ions in salts. A small amount of the salt is mixed with borax and a molten bead formed on the end of a piece of platinum wire. Certain metals can be identified by the colour of the bead produced in the oxidizing and reducing parts of a Bunsen flame. For example, iron gives a bead that is red when hot and yellow when cold in the oxidizing flame and a green bead in the reducing flame.

Bordeaux mixture. A mixture of copper (II) sulphate and calcium hydroxide in water, used as a fungicide.

Boron Hydrides. Binary compounds of boron and hydrogen.

Born-Haber Cycle. A series of reactions (and accompanying enthalpy changes) which, when summed, represents the hypothetical one-step reaction by which elements in their standard states are converted into crystals of ionic compounds (and the accompanying enthalpy changes.)

Born, Max. (1882-1970) German born British physicist who was awarded the 1954 Nobel Prize for physics (with W.Bothe) for his work on statistical mechanics. With Heisenberg he also developed matrix mechanics.

Born-Oppenheimer approximation. nuclei are so heavy that they stay essentially stationary during the timescale of electron transfer processes.

Boson. A particle or system that obeys Bose-Einstein statistics. Combining quantum mechanics with special relaitivity theory gives a result that a boson has to have an integer spin. A photon is an example of a boson.

Boudouard carbon. A form of carbon which is generated catalytically in the gas phase.

Bound state. A system in which two (or more) parts are bound together in such a way that energy is required to split them. A example of a bound state is a molecule formed from two (or more) atoms.

Boyle's Law. At constant temperature the volume occupied by a definite mass of a gas is inversely proportional to the applied pressure.

Bragg equation. Relates the angles at which X-rays are scattered from a crystal to the spacing between the layers of molecules.

Bragg peak. A peak in the scattering pattern in X-ray diffraction of a crystal. The intensity of Bragg peaks is proportional to the square of the number of the scatterers. If X-ray scattering from a solid produces Bragg peaks this indicates that the solid has long-range order. Bragg peaks are named after Sir William Henry Bragg, who discovered them in 1912. The scattering of X-rays from a set of planes in a crystal that gives rise to Bragg peaks is called Bragg scattering.

Brass. A group of alloys consisting of copper and zinc. A typical yellow brass might contain about 67% copper and 33% zinc.

Bravais lattice. An infinite array of lattice points. A Bravais lattice can have only fourteen space groups divided into seven crystal systems. It is named after Auguste Bravais. (1811-63).

Breeder Reactor. A nuclear reactor that produces more fissionable nuclear fuel than it consumes.

Bremsstrahlung. (German braking radiation) The X-rays emitted when a charged particle, especially a fast electron, is rapidly slowed down, as when it passes through the electric field around an atomic nucleus. The X-rays cover a whole continuous range of wavelength down to a minimum value, which depends on the energy of the incident particles. Bremsst-rahlung are produced by a metal target when it is bombarded by electrons.

Bridge. An atom or group joining two other atoms in a molecule.

Brillouin zone. A cell in a reciprocal lattice. The first Brillouin zone is the cell of smallest volume enclosed by those planes that are perpendicular bisectors of reciprocal lattice vectors. Higher Brillouin zones also exist. Brillouin zones are used in the theory of energy levels in a periodic potential, as in a crystal. They are named after the French physicist Leon Brillouin (1889-1969), who introduced them into the the theory of crystals in 1930.

Brinell hardness. A scale for measuring the hardness of metals introduced around 1900 by the Swedish metallurgist Johann Brinell (1849-1925). A small chromium-steel ball is pressed into the surface of the metal by a load of known weight. The ratio of the mass of the load in kilograms to the area of the depression formed in square millimetres in the Brinell number.

Britannia metal. A silvery alloy consisting of 80-90% iin, 5-15% antimony, and sometimes small percentages of copper, lead, and zinc. It is used in bearings and some domestic articles.

British thermal unit (Btu). The Imperial unit of heat, being originally the heat required to raise the temperature of 1lb of water by 1°F. 1 Btu is now defined as 1055.06 joules.

Brewster angle. Used in laser rod windows, at this angle light polarized in one direction passes through with very little reflection. Can be used to control the polarization of light leaving a laser. Can be calculated using tan (thet a Brewster)=n of the refractive material (where n is the refractive index).

Bromic(l) acid (hypobromous acid). A yellow liquid, HBrO. It is a weak acid but a strong oxidizing agent.

Bromic(V)acid. A colourness liquid, HBrO3, made by adding sulphuric acid to barium bromate. It is a strong acid.

Bromination. A chemical reaction in which a bromine atom is introduced into a molecule.

Bromothymol blue. An acid-base indicator that is yellow in acid solutions and blue in alkaline solutions. It changes colour over the pH range 6-8.

Bronsted Johannes Nicolaus. (1879-1947) Danish physical chemist. He worked on thermochemistry and electrochemistry and is best known for the Lowry-Bronsted theory of acids and bases, which he proposed in 1923.

Bronsted-Lowry Acid. A proton donor.

Bronsted-Lowry Base. A proton acceptor.

Brown-ring test. A test for ionic nitrates. The sample is dissolved and iron (II) sulphate solution added in a test tube. Concentrated sulphuric acid is then added slowly so that it forms a separate layer. A brown ring at the junction of the liquids indicates a positive result.

Brucite. A mineral form of magnesium hydroxide, Mg(OH)2.

Brusselators cells. A theoretical system of oscillatory cells; useful because they can accurately model biological systems.

Buchner funnel. A type of funnel with an internal perforated tray in which a flat circular filter paper can be placed, used for filtering by suction. It is named after the German chemist Eduard Buchner (1860-1917).

Buffer Solution. Solution that resists change in pH; contains either a weak acid and a soluble ionic salt of the acid or a weak base and a soluble ionic salt of the base.

Bulk modulus (K). Defined as the ratio of hydrostatic pressure to fractional decrease in volume.

Bumping. Violent boiling of a liquid caused by superheating so that bubbles form at a pressure above atmospheric pressure. It can be prevented by putting pieces of porous pot in the liquid to enable bubbles of vapour to form at the normal boiling point.

Buret. A piece of volumetric glassware, usually graduated in 0.1-mL intervals, that is used to deliver solutions to be used in titrations in a quantitative (dropwise) manner.

By product. A compound formed during a chemical reaction at the same time as the main product. Commercially useful by-products are obtained from a number of industrial processes. For example, calcium chloride is a by-product of the Solvay process for making sodium carbonate. Propanone is a by-product in the manufacture of phenol.

C

Cadmium sulphide.A water insoluble compound, Cds; r.d.4.82. It occurs naturally as the mineral greenockite and is used as a pigment and in semiconductors and fluorescent materials.

Cage effect. An effect occurring in certain condensed-phase reactions in which fragments areformed and their diffusion is hindered by a surrounding 'cage' of molecules. The initial fragments are consequently more likely to recombine or to react together to form new products.

Calamine. A mineral form of zinc carbonate, ZnCO3, although in the USA the same name is given to a hydrated zinc silicate. The calamine used medicinally in lotions for treating sunburn and other skin conditions is basic zinc carbonate coloured pink with a trace of iron (III) oxide.

Calcination. The formation of a calcium carbonate deposit from hard water.

Calcium hydroxide (slaked lime). A white solid, Ca(OH)2, which dissolves sparingly; r.d. 2.24. It is manufactured by adding water to calcium oxide, a process that evolves much heat and is known as slaking. It is used as a cheap alkali to neutralize the acidity in certain soils and in the manufacture of mortar, whitewash, bleaching powder, and glass.

Calgon. Tradename for a water softening agent.

Calmodulin. A protein, consisting of 148 aminoacid residues, that acts as a receptor for calcium ions in many receptor for calcium ions in many calcium-regulated prcesses in both animal and plant cells. Calmodulin mediates reactions catalysed by many enzymes.

Calorie. The amount of heat required to raise the temperature of one gram of water from 14.5°C to 15.5°C. 1 calorie = 4.184 joules.

Calorimeter. Any of various devices used to measure thermal properties, such as calorific values or heats of chemical reactions.

Calvin, Melvin. (1911-97) US biochemist. After World War II, at the Lawrence Radiation Laboratory, Barkeley, he investigated the light-indepedent reactions of photosynthesis. Using radioactive carbon 14 to label carbon dioxide he discovered the Calvin cycle, for which he was awarded the 1961 Nobel Prize for chemistry.

Calx. A metal oxide formed by heating an ore in air.

Canada balsam. A yellow-tinted resin used for mounting specimens in optical microscopy. It has similar optical properties to glass.

Canal Ray. Stream of positively charged particles (cations) that moves toward the negative electrode in cathode ray tubes; observed to pass through canals in the negative electrode.

Canonical form. One of the possible structures of a molecule that together form a resonance hybrid.

Capacitor. A device for storing electric charge; consists of two conducting objects placed near each other but not touching; typically, when there is a voltage gradient between them, the energy can be kept stored until it needs to be discharged or until the voltage grows high enough that it spontaneously discharges.

Capillary. A tube having a very small inside diameter.

Capillary Action. The drawing of a liquid up the inside of a small-bore tube when adhesive forces exceed cohesive forces, or the depression of the surface of the liquid when cohesive forces exceed the adhesive forces.

Carot. 1. A measure of fineness of gold. Pure gold is described as 24-carat gold. 14-carat gold contains 14 parts in 24 of gold, the remainder usually being copper. 2. A unitof mass equal to 0.200 gram, used to measure the masses of diamonds and other gemstones.

Carbanion. An organic ion carrying a negative charge on a carbon atom.

Carbon arc. A carbon electrode superheated so that it emits light. Good for producing IR radiation between 10-100 microns.

Carbon assimilation. The incorporation of carbon from atmospheric carbon dioxide into organic molecules. This process occurs during photosynthesis.

Carbon filament atom reservoir. Used in atomic spectroscopy, it enables materials to be examined without the use of highly flammable materials. When the sample is passed through a graphite tube under high voltage, it is atomized.

Carbonation. The solution of carbon dioixde in a liquid under pressure.

Carbon black. A fine carbon powder made by burning hydrocarbons in insufficient air. It is used as a pigment and a filler (e.g. for rubber).

Carbonium ion. An orgainic ion carrying a positive charge on a carbon atom.

Carbonize. To change an organic compound into carbon by heating, or to coat something with carbon in this way.

Carbonyl group. The group >C=O, found in aldehydes, ketones, carboxylic acids, amides, etc., and in inorganic carbonyl complexes.

Carboranes. Compounds similar to the boranes, but with one or more boron atoms replaced by carbon atoms..

Carcinogen. A substance capable of causing or producing cancer in mammals.

Carius method. A method of determining the amount of sulphur and halogens in an organic compoumd, by heating the compound in a sealed tube with silver nitrate in concentrated nitric acid., The compound is decomposed and silver sulphide and halides are precipitated, separated, and weighed.

Carnauba wax. A natural wax obtained from the leaves of the copaibapalm of South America. It is extremely hard and brittle and is used in varnishes and to add hardness and lustre to other waxes in polishes.

Carrageenan. A naturally occurring polysaccharide isolated from red algae. The polymer is composed of Dgalactose units, many of which are sulphated. K-carrageman is a gelling agent with uses similar to those of agar.

Carrier gas. Any gas used in a process which serves as a solvent for the chemical of interest. Useful in GC and other processes.

Cascade process. The procedure for increasing the strength of a weak signal by the progressive build-up of electron displacement in a series of dynode plates in a photomultiplier.

Case hardening. The hardening of the surface layer of steel, used for tools and certain mechanical components. The commonest method is to carburize the surface layer by heating the red hot metal into molten sodium cyanide. Diffusion of nitrogen into the surface layer to form nitrides is also used.

Casein. One of a group of phosphate-containing proteins found in milk. Caseins are easily digested by the enzymes of young mammals and represent a major source of phosphorous.

CASSCRF. Complete active space multicon figuration self-consistent field; something that is incorporated into very complete ab initio molecular dynamics calculations.

Cast iron. A group of iron alloys containing 1.8 to 4.5% of carbon. It is usually cast into specific shapes ready for machining, heat treatment, or assembly. It is sometimes produced direct from the blast furnace or it may be made from remelted pig iron.

Catalysis. The process of changing the rate of a chemical reaction by use of a catalyst.

Catalyst. A substance that speeds up a chemical reaction without being consumed itself in the reaction.

A substance that alters (usually increases) the rate at which a reaction occurs.

Catecholamine. Any of a class of amines that possess a catechol ring. Including dopamine, adrenaline, and noradrenaline, they function as neurotransmitters and/or hormones.

Catenane. A type of compound consisting of two or more large rings that are interlocked like the links of a chain. In a catenane, there is no chemical bonding between the rings; the rings are held together by mechanical bonding.

Catenation. Bonding of atoms of the same element into chains or rings.

The bonding together of atoms of the same element to form chains.

The ability of an element to bond to itself.

Cathode. Electrode at which reduction occurs

In a cathode ray tube, the negative electrode.

Catadiotropic systems. Optical systems which contain both reflecting and refracting elements; handy for correcting aberrations over wide angular fields.

Cathodic Protection. Protection of a metal (making ir a cathode) against corrosion by attaching it to a sacrifical anode of a more easily oxidized metal.

Cathode Ray Tube. Closed glass tube containing a gas under low pressure, with electrodes near the ends and a luminescent screen at the end near the positive electrode; produces cathode rays when high voltage is applied.

Catenation. The linking of like atoms to form chains or rings.

Cathode. Electrode where reduction occurs.

Cation. A positive ion; an atom or group of atoms that has lost one or more electrons.

CBS. Complete basis set.

Cellular plastics. Solid synthetic materials having an open structure. A common example is rigid polystyrene foam used in insulation and packaging.

Celluloid. A transparent highly flammable substance made from cellulose nitrate with a camphor plasticizer. It was formerly widely used as a thermoplastic material, especially for film (a use now discontinued owing to the flammability of celluloid).

Cellulose. A polysaccharide of glucose; the main component of plants.

Cell Potential. Potential difference, Ecell, between oxidation and reduction half-cells under nonstandard conditions.

Cementation. Any metallurgical process in which the surface of a metal is impregnated by sime other substance, especially an obsolete process formaking steel by heating bars of wrought steel by heatingbars of wrought iron to red heat for several days in a bed of charcoal.

Centripetal force. The force which always points from a body in rotation to the center of rotation.

Central Atom. An atom in a molecule or polyatomic ion that is bonded to more than one other atom.

CESR. Conduction electron spin resonance.

Channeltron. A variant of the electron multiplier; used to enhance electron signals.

CHARMM. A computatinal method for simulate protein dynamics in water.

Chain Reaction. A reaction that, once initiated, sustains itself and expands.

This is a reaction in which reactive species, such as radicals, are produced in more than one step. These reactive species, radicals, propagate the chain reaction.

Chain Termination Step. The combination of two radicals, which removes the reactive species that propagate the change reaction.

Chalcedony. A mineral consisting of a microcry-stalline variety of quartz. It occurs in several forms, including a large number of semiprecious gemstones; for example, sard, carnelian, jasper, onyx, chrysoprase, agate, and tiger's-eye.

Chalconides. Binary compounds formed between metals and group

16 elements; i.e. oxides, sulphides, selenides, and tellurides.

Chalk. A very fine-grained white rock composed of the skeletal remains of microscopic sea creatures, such as plankton, and consisting largely of calcium carbonate. It is used in toothpaste and cosmetics. It should not be confused with blackboard 'chalk', which is made from calcium sulphate.

Change of phase. A change of matter in one physical phase (solid, liquid, or gas) into another. The change is invariably accompained by the evolution or absorption of energy.

Charge carrier. The entity that transports electric charge in an electric current. The nature of the carrier depends on the type of conductor: in metals, the charge carriers are electrons; in semiconductors the carriers are electrons or positive holes in gases the carriers are positive ions and and electrons; in electrolytes they are positive and negative ions.

Charle's Law. At constant pressure the volume occupied by a definite mass of gas is directly proportional to its absolute temperature.

Chemical Bonds. The attractive forces that hold atoms together in elements or compounds.

Chemical Change. A change in which one or more new substances are formed.

Chemical Equation. Description of a chemical reaction by placing the formulas of the reactants on the left and the formulas of products on the right of an arrow.

Chemical equivalence. When a nucleus or group of nuclei are related by a symmetry operation of the molecule and have the same chemical shifts.

Chemical Equilibrium. A state of dynamic balance in which the rates of forward and reverse reactions are equal; there is no net change in concentrations of reactants or products while a system is at equilibrium.

Chemical Hygiene Officer (CHO). A person or employee who is qualified by training or experience to provide technical guidance in the development and implementations of the provisions of a Chemical Hygiene Plan (CHP)

Chemical Hygiene Plan (CHP). A written program developed and implemented by an employer designating proceedures, equipment, personal protective equipment, and work practices that are capable of protecting employees from the health hazards presented by hazardous chemicals usid in that particular workplace.

Chemical Kinetics. The study of rates and mechanisms of chemical reactions and of the factors on which they depend.

Chemical oxygen-iodine lasers (COIL). Lasers in which O2(a1deltag) generated chemically spurs the subsequent excitation of iodine atoms. Multi-kilowatt power possible.

Chemical shift. The difference in the absorption spectrum of a particular proton from the absorption position of a reference proton.

Chemical vapor deposition. Use a vapor transport mechanism in which the gaseous reactants decompose and recombine to form some desired thin film. Decomposition and reaction are helped by having a heated substrate.

Chemical Periodicity. The variations in properties of elements with their position in the periodic table.

Choke coil. A coil that has significant self-inductance.

Christiansen filter. Used as a bandpass filter, these filters transmit light where the refractive index of the material matches that of the light. This wavelength changes with temperature, so when using one of these filters the temperature must be kept roughly constant.

Chromatic aberration. When the different wavelengths of light passing through a lens focus at different points. This effect arises from the fact that different wavelengths of light experience different refractive indexes when passing through a material.

Chromophore. Functional groups with characteristic optical absorptions or the molecules which contain them

CIDEP. Chemically induced dynamic electron polarization

Cine-substitution. A type of substitution reaction in which the entering group takes a position on a atom adjacent to the atom to which the leaving group is attached.

Cinnabar. A bright red mineral form of mercury (II) sulphide, HgS, crystallizing in the hexagonal system; the principal ore of mercury. It is deposited in veins and impregnations near recent volcanic impregnations near recent volcanic rocks and hot springs. The chief sources include Spain, Italy, and Yugoslavia.

Circular dichroism (CD). Optically active materials absorb left and right circularly polarized light to different extents.

Cis-. The prefix used to indicate that groups are located on the same side of a bon about which rotation is restricted.

Cis-Trans Isomerism. A type of geometrical isomerism related to the angles between like ligands.

Clathrate. A water cage that forms around a hydrocarbon in solution.

Clay. A class of silicate and aluminosilicate minerals with sheet-like structures that have enormous surface areas that can absorb large amounts of water.

Cleavage. The spliting of a crystal along planes of atoms in the

Cloud chamber. A device which is used to determine which elementary particles are being generated in a nuclear reaction. What happens is that the elementary particles go zipping through a saturated water fog, and the ionized water molecules provide nucleation centers for the condensation of water. From following these tracks, the identities of the particles can be determined.

Club drug. A drug typically used by young people at clubs, parties, etc. Examples are ecstasy, gammahydroxybutyric acid (GHB), and methamphetamines.

Cluster compound. A compound in which groups of metal atoms are joined together by metal-metal bonds. The formation of such compounds is a feature of the chemistry of certain elements, particularly molybdenum and tungsten, but also vanadium, tantalum, niobium, and uranium, Isopoly compounds are ones in which the cluster; heteropoly compounds contain a mixture of different elements.

Coexistance curve. A plot of density versus temperature for some substance. It measures the range over which the liquid and vapor phases can exist in equilibrium.

Coefficient of expansion. The ratio of the change in length or volumen of a body to the original lengthor volume for a unit change in temperature.

Coherence length. How long it is before waves from a light source get out of step. The less wide the spread of radiation leaving the source, the longer the coherence length.

Coherent Raman beat (CRB). An ESR technique in which you monitor the electron resonance using a single, weak microwave field. The purpose is to detect coherences between nuclear transitions that are in hyperfine contact with the unpaired electron spin.

Cohesion. The force between like molecules

Cohesive Forces. All the forces of attraction among particles of a liquid.

Coke. An impure form of carbon obtained by destructive distillation of coal or petroleum.

Cold mirror. Reflects visible and transmits IR light

Colligative Properties. Physical properties of solutions that depend upon the number but not the kind of solute particles present.

Collimated. Forming a highly non-divergent beam

Collision Theory. Theory of reaction rates that states that effective collisions between reactant molecules must occur in order for the reaction to occur.

Colloid. When large numbers of molecules swarm together due to intermolecular forces. The dispersed phase in a colloid has a huge surface area.

Coma. The variation of focal length with aperture.

Combination bands. Describes weak absorptions in IR spectra corresponding to the sum of two or more fundamental vibrational frequencies. These combination modes arise from the anharmonicities of the oscillators which leads to an interaction of the vibrational states in polyatomic molecules.

Combination Reaction. Reaction in which two substances (elements or compounds) combine to form one compound.

Reaction of a substance with oxygen in a highly exothermic reaction, usually with a visible flame.

Combustible. Classification of liquid substances that will burn on the basis of flash points. A cornbustible liquid means any liquid having a flash point at or above 37.8°C (100°F) but below 93.3°C (200°F), except any mixture having components with flash points of 93.3°C (200°F) or higher, the total of which makes up 99 percent or more of the total volume of the mixture.

Common Ion Effect. Suppression of ionization of a weak electrolyte by the presence in the same solution of a strong electrolyte containing one of the same ions as the weak electrolyte.

Compression factor (Z). One way of determining how a gas deviates from ideality; Z=1 for ideal gases.

Complex conjugate. The imaginary portion of some function f(x)

Complex Ions. Ions resulting from the formation of coordinate covalent bonds between simple ions and other ions or molecules.

Composition Stoichiometry. Descibes the quantitative (mass) relationships among elements in compounds.

Compound. A substance of two or more elements in fixed proportions. Compounds can be decomposed into their constituent elements.

Compton effect. The observation that X-rays scattered off of materials have a lower frequency than the incident X-rays. Attributed to collisions between the X-rays and electrons.

Compressed Gas. A gas or mixture of gases having, in a container an absolute pressure exceeding 40 psi at 21.1°C (70°F)

A gass or mixture having in a container, an absolute pressure exceeding 104 psi at 54.4°C (130°F) regardless of the pressure at (21.1°C (70°F)

A liquid having a vapour pressure exceeding 40 psi at 37.8°C (70°F) as determined by ASTM D-323-72.

Concentration. Amount of solute per unit volume or mass of solvent or of solution.

Condensation. Liquefaction of vapor.

Condensed Phases. The liquid and solid phases; phases in which particles interact strongly.

Condensed States. The solid and liquid states.

Conduction. The result of collisions between molecules; when one end of an object is heated, the molecules vibrate faster and the energy is transferred to their neighbors.

Conduction Band. A partially filled band or a band of vacant energy levels just higher in energy than a filled band; a band within which, or into which, electrons must be promoted to allow electrical conduction to occur in a solid.

Conjugate Acid-base Pair. In Bronsted-Lowry terminology, a reactant and product that differ by a proton, H+.

Conformations. Structures of a compound that differ by the extent of rotation about a single bond.

Continuous Spectrum. Spectrum that contains all wavelengths in a specified region of the electromagnetic spectrum.

Control Rods. Rods of materials such as cadmium or boron steel that act as neutron obsorbers (not merely moderaters) used in nuclear reactors to control neutron fluxes and therfore rates of fission.

Conjugated Double Bonds. Double bonds that are separated from each other by one single bond -C=C-C=C-.

Contact Process. Industrial process by which sulfur trioxide and sulfuric acid are produced from sulfur dioxide.

Convection. When heat is transferred by the mass movement of molecules from one place to another.

Continuous flow stirred tank reactors (CSTR). Reactors in which reagents go in, are stirred, and products come out. May also be used for other purposes, such as coupling many reaction chambers to each other in a network.

Copolymer. When two or more monomeric units of different type are strung togther into a polymer.

Coprecipitation. When some precipitate contains an impurity within its bulk.

Cordite. An explosive mixture of cellulose nitrate and nitroglycerin, with added plasticizers and stabilizers, used as a propellant for guns.

Coriolis force. Used in rotating body problems, it is a pseudoforce that explains why bodies at the outer edge of a rotating disk experience higher linear speeds.

Coordinate Covalent Bond. Covalent bond in which both shared electrons are furnished by the same species; bond between a Lewis acid and Lewis base.

Coordinate Covalent Bond. A covalent bond in which both shared electrons are donated by the same atom; a bond between a Lewis base and a Lewis acid.

Coordination Compound or Complex. A compound containing coordinate covalent bonds.

Coordination Isomers. Isomers involving exchanges of ligands between complex cation and complex anion of the same compound.

Coordination Number. In describing crystals, the number of nearest neighbours of an atom or ion.

The number of donor atoms coordinated to a metal.

Coordination Sphere. The metal ion and its coordinating ligands but not any uncoordinated counterions.

Corner-cube prisms. Also called retroreflectors, they have one corner of a cube which collects the light and returns it to the original source.

Cornu mounting. A prism system employed in spectrophotometers in which radiation is passed in through one face of the prism and out through the opposite face. The prism employed for this purpose is formed from two thirty degree quartz prisms, one of right-handed quartz and one of left-handed quartz. Produces very good dispersion but no polarization.

Corrosion. Oxidation of metals in the presence of air and moisture.

COSMOSIL SPYE. A material used in HPLC columns. Good for separating fullerenes.

COSY. Correlated spectroscopy; a two-D NMR technique.

Coulomb. Unit of electrical charge.

Coulometry. The quantitative application of Faraday's Law to the analysis of materials. The current and time are the usual variables measured.

Coulombic attraction. The positive-negative attraction which takes place when you have two charged particles in close proximity.

Coulometric titration. A titration method in which the current passed through the sample is used to indicate completion of the reaction.

Counter ion. An ion of opposite charge to a given ion. For example, in a crystal of sodium chloride, the chloride ions can be regarded as counter ions to the sodium ions. In certain colloids, the charge on the surface of colloidal particles is neutralized by oppositely charged counter ions in the surrounding solution.

Coupling constant. The separation between the peaks of a first-order multiplet produced as a result of spin-orbit coupling. The larger the value of J, the greater the coupling between the nuclei. J is usually measured in Hertz, and is not dependant on the operating frequency of the instrument.

Covalent Bond. Chemical bond formed by the sharing of one or more electron pairs between two atoms.

Covalent crystal. A crystal in which the atoms are held together by covalent bonds. Covalent crystals are sometimes called macromolecular or giant molecular crystals. They are hard high-melting substances. Exam-ples are diamond and boron nitride.

Covalent. Compounds containing predominantly covalent bonds.

CPMAS NMR. Stands for charge polarized magic angle spinning nuclear magnetic resonance. Basically this is a method for taking molecules that have high degrees of spin and imparting some of that spin to molecules that have none. It's handy for getting NMR signals off of atoms that usually do not have signals.

Cracking. The process of breaking down chemical compounds by heat. The term is applied particularly to the cracking of hydrocarbons in the kerosine fraction obtained from petroleum refinig to give smaller hydrocarbon molecules and alkenes. It is an important process, both as a source of branchedchain hydrocarbons suitable for gasoline and as a source of ethene and other alkenes. Catalytic creaking is a similar process in which a catalyst is used to lower the temperature required and to modify the products obtained.

Cresote. 1. An almost colourless liquid mixture of phenols obtained by distilling tar obtained by the destructive distillation of wood. It is used medically as an antiseptic and expectorant. 2. A dark liquid mixture of phenols and cresols obtained by distilling coal tar. It is used for preserving timber.

Critical Mass. The minimum mass of a particular fissionable nuclide in a given volume required to sustain a nuclear chain reaction.

Critical Point. The combination of critical temperature and critical pressure of a substance.

Critical Pressure. The pressure required to liquefy a gas (vapor) at its critical temperature.

Critical state. The state of a fluid in which the liquid and gas phases both have the same density. The fluid is then at its critical temperature, critical pressure, and critical volume.

Critical Temperature. The temperature above which a gas cannot be liquefied; the temperature above which a substance cannot exhibit distinct gas and liquid phases.

Critical volume. The volume of a fixed mass of a fluid in its critical state; i.e. when it is at its critical temperature and critical pressure. The critical specific volume is its volume per unit mass in this state; in the past this has often been called the critical volume.

Crossproduct. A cross B = [A][B] sin(theta)

Crusible. A dish or other vessel in which substances can be heated to a high temperature.

Cryohydrate. A eutectic mixture of ice and some other substance (e.g. an ionic salt) obtained by freezing a solution.

Cryoscopic constant. Used to measure the freezing point depression with the addition of a solvent.

Cryoscopy. The use of depression of freezing point to determine relative molecular masses.

Cry Field Stabilization Energy. A measure of the net energy of stabilization gained by a metal ion's nonbonding d electrons as a result of complex formation.

Crystal defect. An imperfection in the regular lattice of a crystal.

Crystal Field Theory. Theory of bonding in transition metal complexes in which ligands and metal ions are treated as point charges; a purely ionic model; ligand point charges represent the crystal (electrical) field perturbing the metal?s d orbitals containing nonbonding electrons.

Crystal Lattice. A pattern of arrangement of particles in a crystal.

Crystal Lattice Energy. Amount of energy that holds a crystal together; the energy change when a mole of solid is formed from its constituent molecules or ions (for ionic compounds) in their gaseous state.

The energy charge when one mole of formula units of a crystalline solid is formed from its ions, atoms, or molecules in the gas phase; always negative.

Crystalline. Having the regular internal arrangement of atoms, ions, or molecules characteristics of crystals. Crystalline materials need not necessarily exist as crystaline although they are not usually seen as regular geometric crystals.

Crystalline Solid. A solid characterized by a regular, ordered arrangement of particles.

Crystallite. A small crystal, e.g. one of the small crystals forming part of a microcrystalline substance.

Crystalization. The process of forming crystals from a liquid of gas.

Crystallography. The study of crystal form and structure.

Crystal test.A type of presumptive test in which a substance is identified by the formation of characteristic crystals when a certain reagent is added. Usually, such tests are conducted using a microscope. An example is the acetone-chlor-haemin test for blood.

Cubic crystal. A crystal in which the unit cell is a cube. There are three possible packings for cubic crystals; simple cubic, face-centred cubic, and body-centred cubic.

Cupellation. A method of separating noble metals from base metals by melting the mixture with a blast of hot air in a shallow porous dish. The base metals are dioxized, the oxide being carried away by the blast of air absorbed by the porous container.

Cupric compounds. Compounds containing copper in its higher (+2) oxidation state; e.g. cupric chloride is copper (II) chloride (CuCl2).

Cuprite. A red mineral cubic form of copper(I) oxide, Cu2O; an important ore of copper. It occurs where deposits of copper have been subjected to oxidation. The mineral has been mined as a copper are in Chile. Democratic Republic of Congo, Bolivia, Australia, Russia, and the USA.

Cupronickel. A type of corrosion resistant alloy of copper and nickel containig up to 45 % nickel.

Cuprous compounds. Compounds containing copper in its lower (+1) oxidation state; e.g. cuprous chloride is copper(I) chloride (CuCI).

Curare. A resin obtained from the bark of South American trees of the genera Strychnos and Chondrodendron that causes paralysis of voluntary muscle. It acts by blocking the action of the neutrotransmitter acetylcholine ar neuromuscular junctions. Curare is used as an arrow poison by South American Indians and was formerly used as a muscle relaxant in surgery.

Curie (Ci). The basic unit used to describe the intensity of radioactivity in a sample of material. One curie equals 37 billion disintegrations per second or approximately the amount of radioactivty given off by 1 gram of radium.

Curie point. The temperature at which a ferromagnetic substance loses its ferromagnetism and becomes only paramagnetic. For iron the Curie point is 760°C and for nickel 356°C. It is named after Pierre Curie.

Curie temperature. Where a ferromagnetic transition occurs.

Cutting agent. A substance used to dilute illegal drugs such as heroine and cocaine. Examples include flour, starch, sugar and caffeine.

CVD. Chemical vapor deposition

Cyanine dyes. A class of dyes that contain a -CH= group linking two nitrogen-containing heterocyclic rings. They are used as sensitizers in photography.

Cyanoacrylate. A compound formed by the condensation of an alkyl cyanothanoate and methanal. Cyanoacrylates have the the general formula CH2: C(CN)COOR. The methyl and ethyl esters are the basis of various 'superglues', which rapidly polymerize in air (under the action of moisture) to form strong adhesives.

Cyano group. The group-CN in a chemical compound.

Cyanuric acid. A white crystalline water-soluble trimer of cyanic acid, (HNCO)3. It is a cyclic compound having a six-membered ring made of alternating imide (NH) and carbonyl (CO) groups (i.e. three-NH-C(O)- units). It can also exist in a phenolic form (three-N=C(OH)- units).

Cyclic AMP. A derivative of ATP that is widespread in animal cells as a second messenger in many biochemical reactions induced by hormones. Upon reaching their target cells, the hormones activate adenylate cyclase, the enzyme that catalyses cyclic AMP production. Cyclic AMP ultimately activates the enzymed of the reaction induced by the hormone concerned. Cyclic AMP is also involved in controlling gene expression responses, and in nervous transmission.

Cyclic voltammetry. A method for determining the kinetics of electrode processes. Current is monitored as the potential of the electrode is changed.

Cyclization. The formation of a cyclic compound from an open-chain compound.

Cyclo. Prefix designating a cyclic compound, e.g. a cycloalkane or a cyclosilicate.

Cycloaddition. A reaction in which two or more unsaturated compounds form a cyclic adduct or in which a cyclic compounds is formed by addition between unsaturated parts of the same molecule. In cycloaddition, there is no net reduction in bond mltiplicity. The Diels-Alder reaction is an example. Cycloadditions may be step-wise reactions or may be pericyclic reactions.

Cyclobutadiene. A short-lived cyclic diene hydrocarbon, C4H4, with its four carbon atoms in square ring. It is made by degradation of its metal complexes, and has a short lifetime of a few seconds. It undergoes addition reactions with alkynes.

Cyclophane. A compound consisting of one or more atomatic rings forming part of a larger ring system in which aliphatic chains of the CH2 groups link the aromatic rings. Compounds of this type have the suffix phane in their names. Depending on the sizes of the (CH2)n chains, the aromatic rings may not be planar.

Cyclotron. A device for accelerating charged particles along a spiral path.

Cystine. A molecule resultig from the oxidation reaction between the sulphydryl (-SH) groupsof two cysteline molecules. This often occurs between adjacent cysteine residues in polypeptides. The resultant disulphide bridges (-S-S-) are important in stabilizing the structure of protein molecules.

Cytidine. A nucleoside comprising one cytosine molecle linked to a Dribose sugar molecule. The derived nucleotides, cytidine mono-, di-, and triphosphate (CMP, CDP, and CTP respectively) participate in various biochemical reactions, notably in phospholipid synthesis.

Cytochrome. Any of a group of proteins, each with an iron-containing haem group, that form part of the electron transport chain in mitochondria and chloroplasts. Electrons are transferered by reversible changes in the iron atom betweem the reduced Fe(II) and oxidized Fe(III) states.

Cytosine. A pyrimidine derivative. It is one of the principal component bases of nucleotides and the nucleic acids DNA and RNA.

CZE. Capillary zone electrophoresis.

D

D. Deuterium. Also a system of designating configuration of molecules such as monosaccharides by analogy with (+) glyceraldehyde-dessignated D. Molecules analogous to (-) glyceraldehyde are designated 1.

Dalton's law of partial pressures. The total pressure (P) exerted by a mixture of gases is equal to the sum of the partial pressures (p) of the components of the gas mixture. The partial pressure is defined as the pressure the gas would exert if it was contained in the same volume as that occupied by the mixture. Assumes no interaction between the gas molecules.

Daminozide. Herbicide, alkanoic acid derivative.

Damped harmonic motion. When there is friction within an oscillating system, the amplitudes of the oscillation decrease over time due to this damping force.

Dansyl. A Dimethylami-nonaphthalene 1 - sulphonyl derivatives used (e.g. chloride and fluoride) for active site investigations in serine proteinases.

Dark current. The background current that flows in photoemissive and photoconductive detectors when no radiation is falling on the detector. It is a temperature-dependant effect, and can be decreased by many orders of magnitude by operating below -20C.

Dative covalent bond. A co-ordinate bond.

Daughter Nuclide. Nuclide that is produced in a nuclear decay.

Dazomet. Nematocide, fungicide, herbicide, insecticide, thiadiazone derivative.

Dc arc. Put a voltage of 200-300 V across two graphite electrodes separated by about one centimeter; resulting heat causes ionization of the sample. This is commonly used in atomic absorption spectroscopy.

DDT. Formerly an important insecticide, Organo-chlorine derivative.

d-d transition. Electronic transition occurring between non-degenerate d orbitals, e.g. those which have been split by a crystal field. Generally occurs in the visible region but may also occur in the u.v. or near i.r.

Deactivating collision. An intermolecular collision between an 'activated' and a normal molecule, which results in the deactivation of the fo rmer without it undergoing reaction.

Deactivators. Additives used in gasoline to prevent the catalysis of gum formation by metals (e.g. Cu).

Deaeration. Removal of oxygen and other dissolved gases from solvents by physical or chemical means. Carried out on a large scale from boiler feed water with a view to reducing corrosion.

Deasphalting. A single-solvent precipitation process whereby petroleum residues are treated with liquid propane or similar light solvent in a counter-current column. The ASPHALTENES are precipitated and the high-quality lubricating oil stock (bright stock) dissolves in the propane and may be further refined by solvent extraction.

Debye. The unit used to express dipole moments.

Debye temperature. The temperature above which a certain crystal behaves classically; the temperature above which thermal vibrations are more important than quantum effects.

Decantation. The removal of a liquid from a suspension of from an immiscible heavier liquid by pouring while leaving the latter in the original container.

Decoctions. Pharmaceutical solutions made by boiling a drug (often naturally occurring) with water and filtering.

Decomposition point. In a laboratory distillation the thermometer reading coinciding with the first indications of thermal decomposition of the liquid or solid.

Decomposition voltage. The smallest voltage which will cause the electrolysis of an electrolyte. The decomposition voltage or potential depends both upon the nature of the electrolyte and of the electrodes.

Decoupling. Electronic technique used in n.m.r. spectroscopy to remove particular coupling from observation. Hence simplifies observed spectrum.

Degenerate. Of the same energy.

Degeneracy. When one energy level corresponds to two or more states of motion. It arises when the symmetry of a molecule is such that certain fundamental frequencies are equal and is a common feature in IR spectroscopy.

Degree of hydrolysis. The degree of hydrolysis of a salt is defined as the fraction of the total salt hydrolysed by water. Thus, if in a solution of the salt AB, 90% of it is hydrolysed to yield the base AOH and the acid BH, the degree of hydrolysis is 0.90. It may be expressed also as a percentage, i.e. 90%.

Degree of polymerization. Number of monomeric units in an oligomer or polymer.

Dehydrated castor oil (DCO). Polyunsaturated carboxylic acid glyceride, typically a 9,11octadecadienoic acid derivative, prepared by heating castor oil to 250-300°C in the presence of catalyst. Used to form sebacic and capryl derivatives (by cleavage at the C=C bond) and for pains and varnishes.

Dehydro. A prefix for an organic compound indicating the presence of less hydrogen. Often synonymous with ANHYDRO-.

Dehydrocyclization In petroleum CRACKING or REFORMING processes alkanes undergo dehydrocyc-lization yielding aromatics and hydrogen.

Deintercalation. The expulsion of a foreign atom from some crystal lattice where it has been residing (usually in interstitial spaces). The opposite of intercalation.

Deliquescence. The property of having a water vapour pressure lower than that of the surrounding air so that water is absorbed (to give a solution).

Deliquescent substance. A material showing deliquescence.

Delocalization. Of electrons; refers to bonding electrons that are distributed among more than two atoms that are bonded together; occurs in species that exhibit resonance.

The formation of a set of molecular orbitals that extend over more than two atoms; important in species that valence bond theory describes in terms of resonance.

Delphinine. A plant alkaloid related to ACONITINE.

Delta bonding. Lateral overlap between two orbitals (e.g. orbitals) such that there are four regions of overlap.

Deltamethrin. Insecticide, pyrethroid derivative.

Demeton-s-methyl (meta-systox). Insecticide, acaricide, organophosphate derivative.

Demulsibility. The property enabling oils to separate from oil-water emulsions. Good demulsibility is obtained by special refining processes to remove polar compounds not removed in normal refining.

Denaturants. Substances added to dutiable articles to render them unfit for human consumption, e.g. denatured alcohol.

Denaturation. A process pertaining to a change in structure of a protein form regular to irregular arrangement of the polypeptide chains.

Denatured. A commercial term used to describe ethanol that has been rendered unfit for human consumption because of the addition of harmful ingredients to make it sales tax-expempt.

Dendrite. A tree-like crystal formation formed because crystal growth proceeds at different rates in certain directions from the initial crystallization point. Found particularly in alloys, and ice crystals. Many salts can be induced to crystallize as dendrites. Havee advantages over normal forms.

Dendritic salt. NaCl crystallized as dendrites. It is less dense than normal rock salt, does not cake so easily, dissolves more quickly.

Denitrogenation. The removal of nitrogen compounds, particularly from gas oil cracking feedstocks, to prevent the ammonia which would be formed neutralizing the acid catalysts used. Denitrogenation can be effected catalytically.

Dense media separation. Separation of solids of different density by means of a liquid of intermediate density which allows a 'float and sink' separation. Liquids of suitable density can be obtained by suspending finely divided solids in water. Used for separation of mineral products such as coal, ores or aggregates.

Densitometer. An apparatus for measuring the intensities of e.g. lines on a photographic plate. Used in X-ray analysis and spectrometric analysis.

Density. Mass per unit Volume: D=MV.

Density-gradient column. A graduated glass tube, filled with a mixture of solutions such that a density gradient is obtained throughut the length of the tube. Used for rapid determination of densities of small particles of solid which sink to a particular level in the tube.

Density of states. Usd in thermodynamics. The number of states in a energy range divided by the width of the range.

Deodorants. Perfumes that mask odours when natural secretions decompose on the skin. Aluminium compounds (Al(OH)3) absorb the odours.

Depilatories. Materials used for hair removal. The most widely used is calcium thioglycollate in an alkaline medium at pH 12.3.

Depolarization factor. By enclosing the sample tube in polarizing sheets, each line in a Raman spectrum can be split into a horizontal component and a vertical component. The depolarization factor is the ratio of these two components.

Depolarization ratio. Applied to Raman lines. the ratio of the intensity of the scattered light with polarization perpendicular and parallel to the incident radiation. Gives information on the symmetry of the vibration.

Deposition. The direct solidification of a vapor by cooling; the reverse of sublimation.

Depot fat. The reserve of fat in animals, deposited in adipose tissue and which usually undergoes metabolism slowly.

Derivative. A compound that can be imagined to arise from a partent compound by replacement of one atom with another atom or group of atoms. Used extensively in orgainic chemistry to assist in identifying compounds.

Derris. Obtained from the root of the Far Eastern shrub Derris elliptica, and originally used as a fish poison; contains rotenone. It is applied as a dust, and is used as an insecticide.

Dermal toxicity. Adverse health effects resulting from skin exposure ot a substance.

Desensitization. A process used in photography to induce a loss of sensitivity in the silver halide emulsion over part of its spectral sensitivity range Often used during development to allow subsequent processing to be carried out in a bright light but without affecting the latent image or inhibiting development.

Deshielding. NMR effect that has signals at lower field (down field).

Designated area. An area that may be used for work with carcinogens, reproductive toxins, or substances that have a high degree of acute toxicity. A designated area may be the entire laboratory, an area of a laboratory, or a device such as a loboratory hood.

Dess-Martin oxidation. Conversion of primary and secondary alcohols to aldehydes and letones using triacetoxyperiodinone.

Destructive distillation. The distillation of organic solids or liquids in which the substance being heated partly or wholly decomposes during distillation, leaving a solid or viscous liquid in the still. Volatile liquid products are collected after condensation. Typical destructive distillation processes involve the carbonization of coal, peat, wood or oil shale.

Desulphurization. The removal of sulphur compounds from petroleum fractions using hydrogen in the presence a catalyst. Also known as hydrofining, hydrodesulphurization and hydrotreating.

Detergent. A soap-like emulsifer that contains a sulfate, SO_3 or a phosphate group instead of a carboxylate group.

Detoxication. A term for the biochemical transformations which occur during the metabolism of foreign organic compounds by animals. The process does not always result in decreased toxicity.

Deuterium. An isotope of hydrogen whose atoms are twice as massive as ordinary hydrogen;deuterion atoms contain both a proton and a neutron in the nucleus.

Deuteron. The nucleus of the deuterium atom. Used in linear accelerators for bombarding other nuclei.

Devarda's alloy. 50% Cu, 45% Al, 5% Zn; used to reduce inorganic nitrates and nitrites to ammonia.

Development centres. The areas of a silver halide crystal in which exposure to light has induced latent images and where, on development, reduction to metallic silver will start.

Devitrification. The crystallization of a glass (a supercooled liquid) which then becomes opaque.

Dew point. When air containing a given amount of water is cooled, the temperature at which the partial pressure of water equals the saturated vapor pressure.

Dextrins. Intermediate products formed during the hydrolysis of starch to sugars. They are strongly dextrorotatory. Manufactured by the action of heat and hydrolytic agents on wet or dry starch and used as adhesives, for improvement of stability and making taste or odour.

Dextrorotatory. Refers to an optically active substance that rotates the plane of plane polarized light clockwise; also called dextro.

DFT. Density functional theory.

Diagonal relationship. A similarity (in solubility and thermal stability) between compounds of element of the main groups of the Periodic table related to one another diagonally. Results from a similarity in size in combining forms.

Diagonal Similarities. Refers to chemical similarities in the Periodic Table of elements of Period 2 to elements of Period 3 one group to the right; especially evident toward the left of the periodic table.

Dialysis. The separation of small solute particles from colloid particles by means of a semi-permeable membrane.

Diamagnetic. A diamagnetic material has no unpaired spins; when such a material without permanent dipoles has a magnetic field applied to it, the magnetic dipoles induced in the material line up opposite to that of the induced field.

Diamagnetism. Weak repulsion by a magnetic field.

Diamond anvil cell. Device for applying high pressure to samples which are held between two diamonds. Pressure of up to 1 Mbar can be obtained by the turn of a screw.

Diaphragm valve. A valve for controlling the flow of liquids and gases in which a flexible diaphragm is pressed down against a ridge running across the valve body. Only the valve body and the diagram come into contact with the fluid and the valve may thus be made corrosionresistant.

Diastereotopic. Non-interchangeable protons; the chemical shift is not ever equivalent.

Diatomite (kieselguhr). A hydrated silica, the remains of diatoms. The partricles are hollow and the material is used as a filler and an absorbent (nitroglycerine gives dynamite). Other uses are for polishing, filtration, decolorizing and for heat-insulation. Tripolite is a compact form.

Diathermic. Something that allows energy transfer as heat

Dicarboxylic acids. Organic acids containing two carboxyl (-C(O)OH) groups. They form both acidic and neutral salts and esters; some give anhydrides by loss of a molecule of water between the two carboxyl groups. Many occur naturally as the free acid or an ester. They are generally prepared by the oxidation of a glycol, hydroxy-acid or hydroxyaldehyde, or by hydrolysis of a dintrile or cyano-acid.

Dichlorop. Herbicide, alkanoic acid derivative.

Dichlorophen. Acaricide, fungicide, bacteriostat chlorophenol derivative.

Dichlorvos. Insecticide, acaricide, organophosphate derivative.

Dichroism. PLEOCHROISM in a uniaxial crystal.

Dicophos. Insecticide, acaricide, organophosphorous derivative.

Dieldrin. The epoxy derivative of aldrin, now withdrawn.

Diesel fuel. Fuel used for diesel (compression ignition) engines. The composition varies but is near that of GAS OIL. Fuel for diesel-engined road vehicles is commonly known as Derv.

Diethyl sulphate. A colourless liquid with a faint ethereal odour; b.p. 208°C (decomp). Manufactured from ethene and 100% sulphuric acid. Ethylating agent in organic synthesis. Highly toxic, carcinogen.

Differential Scanning Calorimetry (DSC). A technique for measuring the temperature, direction, and magnitude of thermal transitions in a sample material by heating/cooling and comparing the amount of energy required to maintain its rate of temperature increase or decrease with an inert reference material under similar conditions.

Differential Thermal Analysis (DTA). A technique for observing the temperature, direction, and magnitude of thermally induced transitions in a material by heating/cooling a sample and comparing its temperature with that of an inert reference material under similar conditions.

Differential titration. Analysis of a sample which contains two or more similarly reacting species which are differentiated, e.g. use of different bases indicators.

Differential Thermometer. A thermometer used for accurate measurement of very small changes in temperature.

Diffusion pump. A non-mechanical pump used for the production of high vacua. gas molecules are forced through a fine jet by molecular bombardment with a stream of oil or mercury vapour from a boiler. Once through the jet the heavy vapour is condensed and returned to the boiler, while the expelled gas is removed by a mechanical backing pump.

Digestion. The process of ageing (recrystallization) of a precipitate to obtain it in a form more suitable for filtration.

Dilute-spin species. When you have a species that is not very abundant; there is very little chance that there will be more than one magnetically-active isotope in a molecule.

Dilatometer. An apparatus for measuring small changes of volume of a liquid, solution or solid immersed in a liquid. It usually consists of a cylindrical glass bulb-with attached capilarly tube, and charge of volume of the contents of the bulb is noted by observing the movement of the meniscus in the capillary. Dilatometry is useful for determining transition temperatures, rates of reaction, polymerization, etc.

Dilution. Process of reducing the concentration of a solute in solution, usually simply by mixing with more solvent.

Dimethyl sulphite. A colourless liquid with a faint odour; b.p. 126°C. Prepared by boiling methanol with thionyl chloride. Decomposed by boiling water to methanol and SO2. It reacts with organic acids, amines and alcohols to give methyl esters, methyl amines and methyl ethers. Methylating agent in syntheses.

Dimer. Molecule formed by combination of two smaller (identical) molecules.

Diphenyl ether. PhOPh. M.p. 21°C, b.p. 250°C. Prepared from NaOPh and PhCl. Used as a heat-transfer agent for perfuming soaps and as a herbicide.

Dipole. Refers to the separation of charge between two covalently bonded atoms

Dipole-dipole Interactions. Attractive interactions between polar molecules, that is, between molecules with permanent dipoles.

Dipole Moment. The product of the distance separating opposite charges of equal magnitude of the charge; a measure of the polarity of a bond or molecule; a measured dipole moment refers to the dipole moment of an entire molecule.

Dispersion. The spreading of white light into the full spectrum.

Dispersing Medium. The solvent-like phase in a colloid.

Dispersed Phase. The solute-like species in a colloid.

Displacement Reactions. Reactions in which one element displaces another from a compound.

Disproportionation Reactions. Redox reactions in which the oxidizing agent and the reducing agent are the same species.

Dissociation. In aqueous solution, the process in which a solid ionic compound separates into its ions.

Dissociation Constant. Equilibrium constant that applies to the dissociation of a comples ion into a simple ion and coordinating species (ligands).

Distilland. The material in a distillation apparatus that is to be distilled.

Distillate. The material in a distillation apparatus that is collected in the receiver.

Distillation. The separation of a liquid mixture into its components on the basis of differences in boiling points.

The process in which components of a mixture are separated by boiling away the more volitile liquid.

Distortion. Departure of image shape from that predicted by first-order Gaussian optics; one example, when a rectangle is shaped like a pillow.

DOAS (differential optical absorption spectroscopy). Analytical technique used particularly on gases, e.g. pollution measurement.

Dolerite. A widely distributed igneous rock composed essentially of plagioclase feldspar and augite. Used for road metal.

Dolomite, MgCO3. CaCO3. The term is loosely used for all mixtures of the two carbonates in the very common 'dolomite rock' or magnesian limestone, which is used for building purposes and or the basic linings of Bessemer converters and open-hearth steel furnaces. It is one of the most important raw materials for the production of magnesium and its salts.

Domain. A cluster of atoms in a ferromagnetic substance, all of which align in the same direction in the presence of an external magnetic field.

Donnan membrane equilibrium. The distribution of ions on each side of a membrane separating two portions of a solution of an electrolyte, e.g. NaCl, in water; on one side of the membrane a polyelectrolyte, e.g. a protein, the molecules and ions of wich cannot pass through the membrane. The distribution of the NaCl on the two sides of the membrane will be unequal and a membrane potential will be established. Such systems are of importance in biology.

Donor Atom. A ligand atom whose electrons are shared with a Lewis acid.

D-Orbitals. Beginning in the third energy level, aset of five degenerate orbitals per energy level, higher in energy than s and p orbitals of the same energy level.

Dopant. Foreign species implanted into a lattice.

Doppler effect. The phenomena that the frequencies of waves are blue-shifted when the source moves toward the observer and red-shifted when the source moves away from the observer.

Dosimeter. A small, calibrated electroscope worn by laboratory personnel and designated to detect and measure incident ionizing radiation or chemical exposure.

Dot product. A dot B = AB cos (theta).

Double Bond. Covalent bond resulting from the sharing of four electrons (two pairs) between two atoms.

Double refraction. Having different refractive indices in different crystallographic directions.

Double Salt. Solid consisting of two co-crystallized salts.

Doublet. Two peaks or bands of about equal intensity appearing close together on a spectrogram.

Dove prisms. Used to rotate the image in optical systems

Downs Cell. Electrolytic cell for the commercial electrolysis of molten sodium chloride.

Dow process. The process for the extraction of magnesium from sea water by precipitation of Mg(OH)2 by Ca(OH)2 followed by solution of the hydroxide in hydrochloride acid.

Dowtherm. Mixtures of high-boiling organic substances used for purposes of heat exchange.

DP number. The degree of polymerization; the average number of monomer units per polymer unit.

DQ. Duroquinone, also known as tetramethyl-1,4-benzoquinone.

Drier. Plant of equipment for drying a material. Also METALLIC SOAPS and solvents added to plant, solvents and varnishes to hasten drying.

drift region. The length that the charged ions travel through in a TOF mass spec.

Dropping-mercury electrode (DME). An electrode consisting of a column of mercury passing through a fine capillary and emerging in the solution as fine drops to give a continuously fresh surface.Used in POLAROGRAPHY.

Dry Cells. Ordinary batteries (voltaic cells) for flashlights. radios, and so on; many are Leclanche cells.

Drying. Remvoal of small quantities of water from a sample by physical or chemical means. Removal of the water from a solid may be speeded up by warming the sample. Drying may also refer to the removal of solvents other than water.

D -Transition elements (metals). B Group elements except IIB in the periodic table; sometimes called simply transition elements EX. Fe, Ni, Cu, Ti .

Ductility. How much strain a material will take before it breaks.

Dumas Method. A method used to determine the molecular weights of volatile liquids.

Dynamic Equilibrium. An equilibrium in which processes occur continuously, with no net change.

Dynamite. A mixture of nitroglycerine with other substances to make the explosive safer to handle and to have specific explosive properties.

Dynode. The anodes which are used to amplify the signal in photomultiplier tubes.

E

E/A*. Low field emission/high field absorption with net absorptive character.

EAC. Emergency action code.

Earth's atmosphere. The gas that surrounds the earth. The composition of dry air at sea level is; nitrogen 78.08%, oxygen 20.95%, argon 0.93%, carbon dioxide 0.03%, neon 0.0018%, helium 0.0005%, krypton 0.0001%, and xenon 0.00001%. In addition to water vapour, air in some localities containes sulphur compounds, hyrdrogen peroxide, hydrocarbons, and dust particles.

Ebullioscopic constant. Used to measure the boiling point elevation of a solvent with the addition of a solute.

Ebullioscopy. The use of elevation of boiling point to determine relative molecular masses.

Echelon. A form of interferometer consisting of a stack of glass plates arranged stepwise with a constant offset. It gives a high resolution and is used in spectroscopy to study hyperfine line structure.

Effective Collisons. Collision between molecules resulting in a reaction; one in which the molecules collide with proper relative orientations and sufficient energy to react.

Effective Molality. The sum of the molalities of all solute particles in a solution.

Effective Nuclear Charge. The nuclear charge experienced by the outermost electrons of an atom; the actual nuclear charge minus the effects of shielding due to inner-shell electrons.

Example: Set of dx_2-y_2 and dz_2 orbitals; those d orbitals within a set with lobes directed along the x-, y-, and z-axes.

Effervescence. The formation of gas bubbles in a liquid by chemical reaction.

Efflorescence. The process in which a crystalline hydrate loses water, forming a powdery deposit on the crystals.

Effusion. The rate at which a gas escapes through an orifice or hole.

EHMO. Extended Huckel molecular orbital.

Eigenfunction. In general, a solution of an eigenvalue equation. In quantum mechanics eigenfunctions occur as the allowed wave functions of a system and so satisfy the Schrodinger equation.

Einsel lens. Produces focusing without an overall change in the energy of the transmitted particle. A lens used in TOF mass spec devices.

Einstein. The amount of energy absorbed by one mole of material undergoing a photochemical reaction.

Elastin. A fibrous protein that is the major constituent of the yellow elastic fibres of connective tissue. It is rich in glycine, alanine, proline, and other nonpolar amino acids that are cross-linked, making the protein relatively insoluble. Elastic fibres can stretch to several times their length and then return to their original size. Elastin is particularly abundant in elastic cartilage, blood-vessel walls, ligaments, and the heart.

Elastic deformation. The linear region on a strain versus stress plot where a material will still assume its original shape.

Elastomer. A natural or synthetic rubber or rubberoid material, which has the ability to undergo deformation under the influence of a force and regain its original shape once the force has been removed.

Electret. A permanently electrified substance or body that has opposite chrges at its extremities. Electrets resemble permanent magnets in many ways. An electret can be made by cooling certain waxs in a string electric field.

Electrical Conductivity. Ability to conduct electricity.

Electric-arc furnace. A furnace used in melting metals to make alloys, especially in steel manufacture, in which the heat source is an electric arc. In the direct-arc furnace, such as the Heroult furnace, an arc is formed between the metal and an electrode. In the indirect-arc furnace, such as the Stassano furnace, the arc is formed between two electrodes and the heat is radiated onto the metal.

Electrochemical equivalent. Symbol z. The mass of a given element liberated from a solution of its ions in electrolysis by one coulomb of charge.

Electrochemistry. Study of chemical changes produced by electrical current and the production of electricity by chemical reactions.

Electrocyclic reaction. A type of cyclic rearrangement in which a sigma bond is formed between two terminal carbon atoms of a conjugated molecule, resulting in a decrease of one in the number of pibonds present.

Electrode. A conductor that emits or collects electrons in a cell, thermionic valve, semiconductor device, etc. The anode is the positive electrode and the cathode is the negative electrode.

Electrodeposition. The process of depositing one metal on another by electrolysis, as in electroforming and electroplating.

Electroforming. A method of forming intricate metal articles or parts by electrodeposition of the metal on a removable conductive mould.

Electrolytic cell. An electrochemical cell in which a non-spontaneous reaction is driven by an outside current.

Electrolytic corrosion. Corrosion that occurs through an electrochemical reaction.

Electrolytic gas. The highly explosive gas formed by the electrolysis of water. It consists of two parts hydrogen and one part oxygen by volume.

Electrodes. Surfaces upon which oxidation and reduction half-reactions; occur in electrochemical cells.

Electrode Potentials. Potentials, E, of half-reactions as reductions versus the standard hydrogen electrode.

Electrolysis. Process that occurs in electrolytic cells.

Electrolyte. A substance whose aqueous solutions conduct electricity.

Electrolytic Cells. Electrochemical cells in which electrical energy causes nospontaneous redox reactions to occur.

An electrochemical cell in which chemical reactions are forced to occur by the application of an outside source of electrical energy.

Electrolytic Conduction. Conduction of electrical current by ions through a solution or pure liquid.

Electromagnetic Radiation. Energy that is propagated by means of electric and magnetic fields that oscillate in directions perpendicular to the direction of travel of the energy.

Electromotive Series. The relative order of tendencies for elements and their simple ions to act as oxidizing or reducing agents; also called the activity series.

Electron. A subatomic particle having a mass of 0.00054858 amu and a charge of 1-.

Electron Affinity. The amount of energy absorbed in the process in which an electron is added to a neutral isolated gaseous atom to form a gaseous ion with a 1- charge; has a negative value if energy is released.

Electron Configuration. Specific distribution of electrons in atomic orbitals of atoms or ions.

Electron Deficient Compounds. Compounds that contain at least one atom (other than H) that shares fewer than eight electrons

Electron flow. The transfer of electrons along a series of carrier molecules in the electron transport chain.

Electron gun. Use a controlled beam of electrons striking a surface to elevate a local area to evaporation temperature; often used in manufacture of films by vapor deposition.

Electron impact (EI). A commonly-used mode in a mass spec where molecules in the vapor phase are bombarded with a high-energy electron beam. These impacts are recorded as a spectrum of positive ions separated on the basis of mass/charge (m/z).

Electron magnetic resonance (EMR). Covers a wide range of experimets including ESE, CRB, and others in the field of ESR.

Electron spin echo (ESE). A method in which you initially hit your sample, and follow that up with other pulses to generate these spin echoes. An ESR technique.

Electron spin echo envelope modulation (ES-EEM). Amethod similar to CRB, except that you typically require three pulses instead of the one required by CRB.

Electron spin resonance (ESR). Also known as electron paramagnetic resonance (EPR), this method is used to determine whether radicals are formed in solution. Although it is very useful at this purpose, the sensitivity toward determination of structure is poor. It is the study of molecules containing unpaired electrons by observing the magnetic fields at which they come into resonance with monochromatic radiation. The radiation is in the microwave region, and the magnetic fields are about .3 Tesla. It can be used to study radicals generated either through chemical reactions or radiation, as well as d-metal complexes and molecules in triplet states.

Electron volt. Corresponds to the energy acquired by an electron accelerated through a potential difference of one volt. 1eV corresponds to 1.602exp(-19)J.

Electroorganic reaction. An organic reaction produced in an eletrolytic cell. Electroorganic reactions are used to synthesize compounds that are difficult to produce by conventional techniques. An example of an electroorganic reaction is Kolbe's method of synthesizing alkanes.

Electronic Transition. The transfer of an electron from one energy level to another.

Electronegativity. A measure of the relative tendency of an atom to attract electrons to itself when chemically combined with another atom.

Electronic Geometry. The geometric arrangement of orbitals containing the shared and unshared electron pairs surrounding the central atom of a molecule or polyatomic ion.

Electrophile. Positively charged or electron-deficient.

Electrophoresis. A technique for separation of ions by rate and direction of migration in an electric field.

Electroplating. Plating a metal onto a (cathodic) surface by electrolysis.

Electroosmosis. The process by which charged particles will tend to migrate toward a less charged area. Generally, when we think of this, we think of an electrolysis process where cations move in one direction, anions move in the other, and the net movement over the sample is zero. However, commonly there are areas of higher charge density, and the electroosmotic effect can greatly affect the behavior of the liquid.

Electrophilic addition. An addition reaction in which the first step is attack by an electrophile (e.g. a positive ion) on an electron-rich part of the molecule. An example is addition to the double bonds in alkenes.

Electrophilic substitution. A substitution reaction in which the first step is attack by an electrophile. Electrophilic substitution is a feature of reactions of benzene (and its compounds) in which a positive ion approaches the delocalized pi electrons on the benzene ring.

Electrophoretic deposition. A technique for coating a material making it an electrode in a bath containing a colloidal suspension of charged particles. Under suitable conditions, the particles are attached to, and deposited on, the electrode. Electrophoretic deposition is used extensively in industry; for example, in applying paint to metal components.

Electrophoretic effect. The effect in which the mobility of ions in solution moving under the influence of an applied electric field is affected by the flow of ions of opposite charge in the opposite direction.

Electroplating. A method of plating one metal with another by electrodeposition. The articles to be plated are made the cathode of an electrolytic cell and a rod or bar of the plating metal is made the anode. Electroplating is used for covering metal with a decorative, more expensive, or corrosion-resistant layer of another metal.

Electropositive. Describing elements that tend to lose electrons and form positive ions. The alkali metals are typical electropositive elements.

Electrospray ionization (ESI). A technique for producing ions for mass spectrometry, used especially for obtaining ions from large molecules, which would be likely to produce fragment ions in electronimpact impact ionization sources. The sample is dissolved in a volatile solvent, which may also contain volatile acids or bases so that the sample exists in an ionic from. The solution is forced through a charged metal capillary tube and forms an aerosol. Evaporation of the solvent results in single ions of the sample, which are analyzed by the mass spectrometer. Electrospray ionization is the ionization technique often used in chromatography-mass spectrometry.

Electrostatics. The study of charges at rest.

Element. A substance that cannot be decomposed into simpler substances by chemical means.

Elementary particle. One of the fundamental particles of which matter is composed, such as the electron, proton, or neutron.

Elementary reaction. A reaction with no intermediates; i.e. one that takes place in a single step with a single transition state.

Elimination reaction. A reaction in which one molecule decomposes into two, one much smaller than the other.

Elinvar. Trade name for a nickelchromium steel containing about 36% nickel, 12% chromium, and smaller proportions of tungsten and manganese. Its elasticity does not vary with temperature and it is therefore used to make hairsprings for watches.

Eluant or eluent. The solvent used in the process of elution, as in liquid chromatography.

Eluate. Solvent (or mobile phase) which passes through a chromatographic column and removes the sample components from the stationary phase.

Elution. The process of removing an absorbed material (adsorbate) from an adsorbent by washing it in a liquid (eluent). The solution consisting of the adsorbate dissolved in the eluent is the eluate. Elution is the process used to wash components of a mixture through a chromatography column.

Elutriation. The process of suspending finely divided particles in an upward flowing stream of air or water to wash and separate them into sized fractions.

Emanation. The former name for the gas radon, of which there are three isotopes: Rn-222 (radium emanation), Rn-220 (thoron emanation), and Rn-219 (actinium emanation).

Emerald. The green gem variety of beryl: one of the most highly prized gemstones. The finest specimens ocur in the Muzo mines. Colombia. Other occurrences include the Ural Mountains, the Transvaal in South Africa, and Kaligunan in India. Emeralds can also be successfully synthesized.

Emery. A rock composed of corundum with magnetite, haematite, or spinel. It occurs on the island of Naxos (Greece) and in Turkey. Emery is used as an abrasive and polishing material and in the manufacture of certain concrete floors.

Emission Spectrum. Spectrum associated with emission of electromagnetic radiation by atoms (or other species) resulting from electronic transitions from higher to lower energy states.

Empirical. Denoting a result that is obtained by experiment or observation rather tha from theory.

Emulsification. The breakdown of fat globules in the duodenum into tiny droplets, which provides a larger surface area on which the enzyme pancreatic lipase can act to digest the fats into fatty acids and glycerol. Emulsification is assisted by the action of the bile salts in bile.

Emulsifying Agent. A sustance that coats the particles of the dispersed phase and prevents coagulation of colloidal particles; an emulsifier.

Emulsion. A colloid in which small particles of one liquid are dispersed in another liquid. Usually emulsions involve a dispersion of water in an oil or a dispersion of oil in water, and are stabilized by an emulsifier. Commonly emulsifiers are substances, such as detergents, that have lyophobic and lyophilic parts in their molecules.

En. The symbol for ethylene diamine (1,2-diaminoe-thane) functioning as a bidentate ligand used in formulae.

Enantiomeric pair. A pair of molecules consisting of one chiral molecule and the mirror image of this molecule. The molecules making up an enantiomeric pair rotate the plane of polarized light in equal, but opposite, directions.

Enantiomer. One of the two mirror-image forms of an optically active molecule.

Enantiotopic. Protons that are interchangeable through any symmetry operation (except rotation). The chemical shift is the same for these protons in an achiral environment.

Endo. Prefix used to designate a bridged ring molecule with a substituent on the ring that is on the same side as the bridge. If the substituent is one the opposite side the compound is designated exo.

ENDOR. Electron nuclear double resonance; an ESR technique.

Endothermic. Describes processes that absorb heat energy.

Endothermicity. The absorption of heat by a system as the process occurs.

End Point. The point at which an indicator changes colour and a titration is stopped.

Energy. The capacity to do work or transfer heat.

Enolate ion. A negative ion obtained from an enol, by removal of a hydrogen atom. Enolate ions can have two forms: one with a single C-C bond and the negative charge on the beta carbon atom and the other with a double C-C bond and the negative charge on the oxygen atom.

Enols. Compounds containing the group -CH=C(OH)- in their molecules.

Enrichment. The process of increasing the abundance of a specified isotope in a mixture of isotopes. It is usually applied to an increase in the proportion of U-235, or the addition of Pu-239 to natural uranium for use in a nuclear reactor or weapon.

Enthalpy. The heat content of a specific amount of substance; defined as E= PV.

Entropy. A thermodynamic state or property that measures the degree of disorder or randomness of a system.

Enyl complex. A type of complex in which there is a link between the metal atom or ion and the pi electrons of a double bond, Zeise's salt was the first known example.

Enzyme. A protein that acts as a catalyst in biological systems.

Epimerism. A type of optical isomerism in which a molecule has two chiral centres; two optical isomers differ in the arrangement about one of these centres.

Epitaxial. The growth of one layer of crystals on another such that they have the same structure.

Epoietin (EPO). A hormone that regulates the production of red blood cells in the body. The drug is used medically to treat anemia, and is aso used illegally by athletes participating in endurance events.

Epoxides. Compounds that contain oxygen atoms in their molecules as part of a three-membered ring.

Equation of State. An equation that describes the behavior of matter in a given state; the van der Waals equation describes the behavior of the gaseous state.

Equilibrium or Chemical Equilibrium. A state of dynamic balance in which the rates of forward and reverse reactions are equal; the state of a system when neither forward or reverse reaction is thermodynamically favored.

Equilibrium Constant. A quantity that characterizes the position of equilibrium for a reversible reaction; its magnitude is equal to the mass action expression at equilibrium. K varies with temperature.

Equivalence Point. The point at which chemically equivalent amounts of reactants have reacted.

Equivalent Weight. An oxidizing or reducing agent, who's mass gains (oxidizing agents) or loses (reducing agents) 6.022×10^{23} electrons in a redox reaction.

The mass of an acid or base that furnishes or reacts with 6.022×10^{23} H_3O+ or OH- ions.

Ergosterol. A sterol occurring in fungi, bacteria, algae, and plants, It is converted into vitamin D2 by the action of ultraviolet light.

Escape depth. The maximum depth under a surface from which ionized electrons come.

Essential Oil. A natural oil with a distinctive scent secreted by the glads of certain aromatic plants. Terpenes are the main constituents. Essential oils are extracted from plants by steam distillation, extraction with cold neutral fats or solvents, or pressing and used in perfumes, flavourings, and medicine. Examples are citrus oils, flower oils (e.g. rose, jasmine), and oil of cloves.

Ester. A Compound of the general formula R-C-O-R1 where R and R1 may be the same or different, and may be either aliphatic or aromatic.

Ether. Compound in which an oxygen atom is bonded to two alkyl or two aryl groups, or one alkyl and one aryl group.

Eudiometer. An apparatus for measuring changes in volume of gases during chemical reactions. A simple example is a graduated glass tube sealed at one end and inverted in mercury. Wires passing into the tube allow the gas mixture to be sparked to initiate the reaction between gases in the tube.

Eutectic mixture. A solid solution consisting of two or more substances and having the lowest freezing point of any possible mixture of these components. The minimum freezing point for a set of component is called the eutectic point. Low-melting-point alloys are usually eutectic mixtures.

Eutectic temperature. The temperature in a 2-component mixture where a liquid solution and both pure solids exist at a fixed pressure.

Eutrophication. The undesirable overgrowth of vegetation caused by high concentrates of plant nutrients in bodies of water.

Evanescent wave. A wave on the other side of a surface from a total internal reflection; decays exponentially with distance.

Evaporation. The change of state of a liquid into a vapour at a temperature below the boiling point of the liquid, Evaporation occurs at the surface of a liquid, some of those molecules with the highest kinetic energies escaping into the gas phase. The result is a fall in the average kinetic energy of the molecules of the liquid and consequently a fail in its temperature.

Evaporization. Vaporization of a liquid below its boiling point.

Evaporation Rate. The rate at which a particular substance will vapourize (evaporate) when compared to the rate of a known substance such as ethyl ether. This term is especially useful for health and fire-hazard considerations.

Even function. A function in which f(x)=f(-x).

EXAFS. Extended X-ray absorption fine structure.

Excimer. A combination of two atoms which survives only in an excited state and which dissolves as soon as the excitation has been lost.

Excimer laser. A laser which is used to pump another laser, usually dye, laser.

Exciplex. A combination of two different atoms that exists only in an excited state. When an exciplex emits a photon of electromagnetic radiation, it immediately dissociates into the atoms, rather than reverting to the ground state. A similar transient excited association of two atoms of the same kind is an excimer. An example of an exciplex is the species XeCl (the asterisk indicates an excited state), which can be formed by an electric discharge in xenon and chlorine. This is used in the exciplex laser, in which a population inversion is produced by an electrical discharge.

Excitation. A process in which a nucleus, electron, atom, ion, or molecule acquires energy that raises it to a quantum state (excited state) higher that that of its ground state. The difference between the energy in the ground state and that in the excited state is called the excitation energy.

Excited State. Any state other than the ground state of an atom or molecule.

Exothermic. Describes processes that release heat energy.

Exothermicity. The release of heat by a system as a process occurs.

Exotic atom. A species in which some other charged particle replaces the electron or nucleon. An example is an atom in which an electron has been replaced by another negatively charged particle, such as a muon or meson. In this case the negative particle eventually collides with the nucleus with the emission of X-ray photons. Another system is one in which the nucleus of an atom has been replaced by a positively charged meson. An association of an electron and a position is also regarded at an exotic atom (known as positronium).

Expanded plastic. A plastic in the form of a rigid solid foam. Polystyrene, used as a packing material, is a common example.

Expectation value. Equal to the integral of (complex conjugate of psi)A(psi) d(tau). Gives the most probable value for that operator.

Explosive. A chemical or compound that causes a sudden, almost instantaneous release or pressure, gas, heat and light when subjected to sudden shock, pressure, high temperature or applied potential.

Explosive limits. The range of concentrations over which a flammable vapour mixed with proper ratios of air will ignite or explode if a source of ignitions is provided.

Extender. An inert substance added to a product (paint, rubber, washing powder, etc.) to dilute it (for economy) or to modify its physical properties.

Extensive Property. A property that depends upon the amount of material in a sample.

Extensive variable. A quantity in a macroscopic system that is proportional to the size of the system. Examples of extensive variables include the volume, mass, and total energy. If an extensive variable is divided by an arbitrary extensive variable, such as the volume, an intensive variable results. A macroscopic system can be described by one extensive variable and a set of intensive variables.

External conversion. A process in which molecules in electronically excited states pass to a lower electronic state (which is frequently the ground state) by colliding with other molecules. In this process the electronic energy is eventually converted into heat. Since this process involves collisons, the rate at which it occurs depends on how frequently collisons occurs. As a result, this process occurs much faster in liquids than in gases. It is sometimes called collision quenching.

Extraction. The separation of a component from its mixture by selective solubility.

Extractive distillation. A distillation techniques in which a solvent is added to the mixture in order to separate two closely boiling components. The added solvent is usually nonvolatile and is selected for its ability to have different effects on the volatilities of the components.

Extraordinary ray. The beam that is deviant on being split by a birefringent crystal. It is parallel to the ordinary ray.

Extrapolate. To estimate the value of a result outside the range of a series of known values. Technique used in standard additions calibration procedure.

F

FAD (flavin adenine dinucleotide). A coenzyme important in various biochemical reactions. It comprises a phosphorylated vitamin B2 (riboflavin) molecule linked to the nucleotide adenine monophosphate (AMP). FAD is usually tightly bound to the enzyme forming a flavoprotein. It functions as a hydrogen acceptor in dehydrogenation reactions, being reduced to $FADH_2$. This in turn is oxidized to FAD by the electron transport chain, thereby generating ATP (two molecules of ATP per molecule of $FADH_2$).

Fahrenheit, Gabriel Daniel. German physicist, who became an instrument maker in Amsterdam. In 1714 he developed the mercury in glass thermometer, and devised a temperature scale to go with it.

Fahrenheit scale. A temperature scale in which (by modern definition) the temperature of boiling water is taken as 212 degrees and the temperature of melting ice as 32 degrees. It was invented in 1714 by G.D. Fahrenheit, who set the zero at the lowest temperature he knew how to obtain in the laboratory (by mixing ice and common salt) and took his own body temperature as 96°F. The scale is no longer in scientific use. To convert to the *Celsius scale the formula is C=5(F-32)9.

Faraday. One faraday of electricity corresponds to the charge on 6.022 x 10^{23} electrons, or 96,487 coulombs.

Faraday cap. Used as a collector for the direct detection of a current of charged particles.

Faraday's Law of Electrolysiss. One equivalent weight of a substance is produced at each electrode during the passage of 96,487 coulombs of charge through an electrolytic cell.

Fast Neutron. A neutron ejected at high kinetic energy in a nuclear reaction.

Fat. Solid triester of glycerol and (mostly) saturated fatty acids.

Fatty Acids. An aliphatic acid; many can obtained from animal fats.

f-block elements. The block of elements in the periodic table consisting of the lanthanoid series (from cerium to lutetium) and the actinoid series (from thorium to lawrencium). They are characterized by having two selectrons in their outershell (n) and felectrons in their inner (n-1) shell.

FEP. Free energy perturbation.

Fermentation. A form of anaerobic respiration occurring in certain microorganisms, e.g. yeasts. Alcoholic fermentation comprises a series of biochemical reactions by which pyruvate (the end product of glycolysis) is converted to ethanol and carbon dioxide. Fermentation is the basis of the baking, wine, and beer industries.

Fermi level. The energy in a solid at which the average number of particles per quantum state is1/2; i.e. one half of the quantum states are occupied. The Fermi level in conductors lies in the conduction band, in insulators it lies in the valence band, and in semiconductors it falls in the gap between the conduction band and the valence band. At absolute zero all the electrons would ocupy energy levels up to the Fermi level and no higher levels would be occupied. It is named after the Italian-born US physicist Enrico Fermi (1901-54).

Fermion. An elementary particle (or bound state of an elementary particle, e.g. an atomic nucleus or an atom) with half-integral spin; i.e. a particle that conforms to FermiDirac statistics.

Fermium. Symbol Fm. A radioactive metallic transuranic element belonging to the actinoids; a.n. 100; mass number of the most stable isotope 257 (half-life 10 days). Ten isotopes are known. The element was first identified by A. Ghiorso and associates in debris from the first hydrogen-bomb explosion in 1952. It is named after Enrico Fermi.

Fermi resonance. The term given to accidental degeneracy arising in polyatomic molecules in which two different vibrational states accidentally possess approximately the same energy and interact with each other.

Ferric chloride test. A presumptive test for morphine. The reagent is a 10% solution of ferric chloride (iron (III) chloride, Fe Cl3) in water. With morphine a blue-green coloration occurs, changing to green.

Ferroalloys. Alloys of iron with other elements made by smelting mixtures of iron ore and the metal ore; e.g. ferrochromium, ferrovanadium, ferromanganese, ferrosilicon, etc. They are used in making alloy steels.

Ferroelectric materials. Ceramic dielectrics, such as Rochelle salt and barium titanate, that have a domain structure making them analogous to ferromagnetic materials. They exhibit hysteresis and usually the piezoelectric effect.

Ferromagnetism. The ability of a substance to become permanently magnetized by exposure to an external magnetic field.

Fertilizer. Any substance that is added to soil in order to increase its productivity. Fertilizers can be natural origin, such as composts, or they can be made up of synthetic chemicals, particularly nitrates and phosphates. Synthetic fertilizers can increase crop yields dramatically, but when leached from the soil by rain, which runs into lakes, they also increase the process of eutrophication. Bacteria that can fix nitrogen are sometimes added to the soil to increase its fertility; for example, in tropical countries the cyanobacterium Anabaena is added to rice paddies to increase soil fertility.

Field-ionization microscope. A type of electron microscope that is similar in principle to the field-emission microscope, except that a high positive voltage is applied to the metal tip, which is surrounded by low pressure gas (usually helium) rather than a vaccum. The image is formed in this case by field ionization: ionization at the surface of an unheated solid as a result of a strong electric field creating positive ions by electron transfer from surrounding atoms or molecules. The image is formed by ions striking the fluorescent screen. Individual atoms on the surface of the tip can be resolved and, in certain cases, absorbed atoms may be detected.

Filler. A solid inert material added to a synthetic resin or rubber, either to change its physical properties or simply to dilute it for economy.

Film badge. A small patch of photographic film worn on clothing to detect and measure accumulated incident ionizing radiation.

Filter. A device for separating solid particles from a liquid or gas. The simplest laboratory filter for liquids is a funnel in which a cone of paper is placed. Special containers with a porous base of sintered glass are also used.

Filter pump. A simple laboratory vacuum pump in which air is removed from a system by a jet of water forced through a narrow nozzle. The lowest pressure possible is the vapour pressure of water.

Filtrate. The clear liquid obtained by filtration.

Filtration. The process of separating solid particles using a filter. In vacuum filtration, the liquid is drawn through the filter by a vacuum pump. Ultrafiltration is filtration under pressure.

Fine chemicals. Chemicals produced industrially in relatively small quantities and with a high purity e.g. dyes and drugs.

Fineness of gold. A measure of the purity of a gold alloy, defined as the parts of gold in 1000 parts of the alloy by mass. Gold with a fineness of 750 contains 75% gold, i.e. 18 carat gold.

Fine structure. Closely spaced spectral lines arising from transitions between energy levels that are split by the vibrational or rotational motion of a molecule or by electron spin. They are visible only at high resolution. Hyperfine structure, visible only at very high resolution, results from the influence of the atomic nucles on the allowed energy levels of the atom.

Finger domain. A finger-shaped structure produced in a protein when a series of the constituent amino acids combines with a metal atom.

First Law of Thermodynamics. The total amount of energy in the universe is constant (also known as the Law of Conservation of Energy) energy is neither created nor destroyed in ordinary chemical reactions and physical changes.

Fischer, Hans. (1881-1945) German organic chemist who worked mainly in Munich. He worked on porphyrins, synthesizing haemin in 1927.Fischer worked also on chlorophyll, showing that it was a porphyrin containing magnesium. In 1944 he synthesized bilirubin. He was awarded the 1930 Nobel Prize for chemistry.

Fischer projection. A type of projection in which a molecule is drawn with horizontal bonds representing bonds coming out of the page and vertical bonds representing bonds in the plane of the page or behind the page. It is named after Emil Fischer.

Fission-track dating. A method of estimating the age of glass and other mineral objects by observing the tracks made in them by the fission fragments of the uranium nuclei that they contain. By irradiating the objects with neutrons to induce fission and comparing the density and number of the tracks before and after irradiation it is possible to estimate the time that has elapsed since the object solidified.

Fixed point. A temperature that can be accurately reproduced to enable it to be used as the basis of a temperature scale.

Flame. A hot luminous mixture of gases undergoing combustion. The chemical reactions in a flame are mainly free-radical chain reactions and the light comes from fluorescence of excited molecules or ions or from incandescence of small solid particles (e.g. carbon).

Flame test. A simple test for metals, in which a small amount of the sample (usually moistened with hydrochloric acid) is placed on the end of a platinum wire and held in a Bunsen flame. Certain metals can be detected by the colour produced: barium (green), calcium (brick red), lithium (crimson),potassium (lilac), sodium (yellow), strontium (red).

Flammable. A liquid as defined by NFPD and DOT as having a flash point below 37.8°C (100°F).

Flame emission spectroscopy (FES). Burn the sample and measure the spectral lines emitted from the elements. This method is only good for doing an elemental analysis on elements that are easily excited.

Flame ionization detector. When you burn the gas coming out of a GC, any organics present will be ionized. Through the use of electrodes in a detector, the current caused from the presence of these ions can be measured with high sensitivity.

Flow injection analysis (FIA). When streams of reagents are mixed together and cause a chemical reaction which quickly passes into a detector; mostly handy for studying the dynamics of a reaction that happens on a microsecond timescale or more.

Flash Point. The temperature at which a liquid will yield enough flamable vapour to ignite. There are various recognized industrial testing methods; therefore the method used must be stated.

Flavonoids. A group of naturally occurring phenolic compounds many of which are plant pigments. They include the anthocyanins, flavonols, and flavones.

Flint. Very hard dense nodules of microcrystalline quartz and chalcedony found in chalk and limestone.

Flip-flop. The movement (transverse diffusion) of a lipid molecule from one surface of a lipid bilayer membrane to the other, which occurs at a very slow rate. This contrasts with the much faster rate at which lipid molecules exchange places with neighbouring molecules on the same surface of the membrane (lateral diffusion).

Flocculent. Aggregated in woolly masses; used to describe precipitates.

Flotation. Method by which hydrophobic (water-repelling) particles of an ore are separated from hydrophilic (water-attracting) particles of a metallurgical pretreatment process.

Fluids. Substances that flow freely; gases and liquids.

Fluence. Refers to the energy density from an optical souce impingent on a sample. The higher the energy density, the higher the fluence.

Fluorescein. A yellowishred dye that produces yellow solutions with a green fluorescence. It is used in tracing water flow and as an adsorption indicatior.

Fluoridation. The process of adding very small amounts of fluorine salts (e.g. sodium fluoride, NaF) to drinking water to prevent tooth decay. The fluoride becomes incoporated into the fluoroapatite of the growing teeth and reduces the incidence of dental caries.

Fluorination. A chemical reaction in which a fluorine atom is introduced into a molecule.

Fluorite. A mineral form of calcium fluoride, CaF2, crystallizing in the cubic system. It is variable in colour; the most common fluorites are green and purple (blue john), but other forms are white, yellow, or brown. Fluorite is used chiefly as a flux material in the smelting of iron and steel; it is also used as a source of fluorine and hydrofluoric acid and in the ceramic and opticalglass industries.

Fluorocarbons. Compounds obtained by replacing the hydrogen atoms of hydrocarbons by fluorine atoms. Their inertness and high stability to temperature make them suitable for a variety of uses as oils, polymers, etc.

Fluorolube. A mixture of fluorinated hydrocarbons used as a mulling agent for solids in IR spectroscopy, specially formulated to obtain the spectrum in which Nujol absorption bands appear.

Fluorophor. Any molecule in an excited state which is capable of exhibiting fluorescence.

Fluorescence. Absorption of high energy radiation by a substance and subsequent emission of visible light.

Flux. 1. Substance applied to the surfaces of metals to be soldered to inhibit oxidation. 2. A substance used in the smelting of metals to assist in the removal of impurities as slag.

Fluxional molecule. A molecule that undergoes alternate very rapid rearrangements of it atoms and thus only has a specific structure for a very short period of time. For example, the molecule ClF3 has a T-shape at low temperatures (-60°C); at room temperature the fluorine atoms change position very rapidly and appear to have identical positions.

Foam. A dispersion of bubbles in a liquid. Foams can be stabilized by surfactants. Solid foams (e.g. expanded polystyrene or foam rubber) are made by foaming the liquid and allowing it to set.

Foaming agent. A substance used to produce a liquid or solid foam (e.g. an expanded plastic). Physical agents are compressed gases; chemical foaming agents are substances that release gas under certain conditions (e.g. sodium hydrogencarbonate).

Fokker-Planck equation. An equation in nonequilibrium statistical mechanics that describes a super position of a dynamic friction (slowing-down) process and a diffusion process for the evolution of variable in a system. The Fokker-Planck equation, which can be used to analyse such problems as Brownian movement, is soluble using statistical methods and the theory of probability. It is named after the Dutch physicist Adriaan Fokker (1887-1968) and Max 'Planck).

Folic acid. A vitamin of the vitamin B complex. In its active form, tetrahydrofolic acid, it is a coenzyme in various reactions involved in the metabolism of amino acids, purines, and pyrimidines. It is synthesized by intestinal bacteria and is widespread in food, especially green leafy vegetables. Deficiency causes poor growth and nutritional anaemia.

Food additive. A substance added to a food during its manufacture or processing in order to improve its keeping qualities, texture, appearance, or stability or to enhance its taste or colour. Additives are usually present in minute quantities; they include colouring materials, sweeteners, preservatives, antioxidants, emulsifiers, and stabilizers. In most countries the additives used must be selected from an approved list of such compounds, which have been tested for safety, and they must be listed on the food labels of individual products.

Forbidden Zone. A relatively large energy separation between an insulator's highest filled electron energy band and the next higher energy vacant band. Beginning in the fourth energy level, a set of seven degenerate orbitals per energy level, higher in energy than s, p, and d orbitals of the same energy level.

Force field. A kind of calculation which is used in molecular dynamics. The calculation is semi-empirical, which means that the wavefunctions of the system are not determined.

Formalin. A colourless solution of methanal in water with methanol as a stabilizer; r.d. 1.075-1.085. When kept at temperatures below 25°C white polymer of methanal separates out. It is used as a disinfectant and preserative for biological specimens.

Formal Charge. A method of counting electrons in a covalently bonded molecule or ion; counts bonding electrons as though they were equally shared between the two atoms.

Formula. Combination of symbols that indicates the chemical composition of a substance.

Formula Unit. The smallest repeating unit of a substance. The molecule for nonionic substances

Formula Weight. The mass of one formula unit of a substance in atomic mass units.

Formylation. A chemical reaction that introduce a formyl group (methanoyl,-CHO) into an organic molecule.

Fossil Fuels. Substances consisting largely of hydrocarbons, derived from decay of organic materials under geological conditions of high pressure and temperature (metamorphism) include coal, petroleum, natural gas, peat and oil shale.

Fractional crystallization. A method of separating a mixture of soluble solids by dissolving them in a suitable hot solvent and then lowering the temperature slowly. The least soluble component will crystallize our first, leaving the other components in solution. By controlling the temperature, it is sometimes possible to remove each component in turn.

Fractional Distillation. The process in which a fractioning column is used in distillation apparatus to separate components of a liquid mixture that have different boiling points.

Fractional Precipitation. Removal of some ions from solution by precipitation while leaving other ions with similar properties in solution.

Frankland, Sir Edward (1825-99). British organic chemist who was the first to produce organometallic compounds (zinc dialkyls). He is remembered as the originator of the theory of valency and introducd a method of writing structural formulas.

Frasch Process. Method by which elemental sulfur is mined or extracted. Sulfur is melted with superheated water (at 170°C under high pressure) and forced to the surface of the earth as a slurry.

Fraunhofer, Josef von. (1787-1826) German physicist, who trained as an optician. In 1814 he observed dark lines in the spectrum of the sun. He also studied diffraction.

Fraunhofer lines. Dark lines in the solar spectrum, discovered by Joself von Fraunhofer, that result from the absorption by elements in the solar chromosphere of some of the wavelengths of the visible radiation emitted by the hot interior of the sun.

FRAP. Fluorescence recovery after photobleaching.

Free Energy, Gibbs Free Energy. The thermodynamic state function of a system that indicates the amount of energy available for the system to do useful work at constant T and P.

Free Energy Change. The indicator of spontaneity of a process at constnt T and P. If delta-G is negative, the process is spontaneous.

Free inductance decay (FID). A measure of how fast magnetic relaxations take place; an exponentially decaying sine wave with the frequency equal to the difference between the applied frequency and the resonance frequency for that nucleus.

Free Radical. A highly reactive chemical species carrying no charge and having a single unpaired electron in an orbital.

Freeze drying. A process used in dehydrating food, blood plasma, and other heat-sensitive substances. The product is deep-frozen and the ice trapped in it is removed by reducing the pressure and causing it to sublime. The water vapour is then removed, leaving an undamaged dry product.

Fresnel lens. An aspheric lens whose surface is broken up into many concentric annular rings. Each ring refracts incident rays to a common focus, so that a very large-aperture and small fnumber thin aspheric lens results. Not to be used for precision focusing applications.

Freezing mixture. A mixture of components that produces a low temperature. For example, a mixture of ice and sodium chloride gives a temperature of -20°C.

Freezing Point Depression. The decrease in the freezing point of a solvent caused by the presence of a solute.

Frequency. The number of repeating corresponding points on a wave that pass a given observation point per unit time.

Friedel-Crafts reaction. A type of reaction in which an alkyl group or an acyl group is substituted on a benzene ring. The product is an alkyl benzene or an alkyl aryl ketone. The reactions occur at high temperature (about 100°C) with an aluminium chloride catalyst. The catalyst acts as an electron acceptor for a lone pair on the halide atom. This polarizes the haloalkane or acyl halide, producing a positive charge on the alkyl or acyl group. The mechanism is then electrotrophic substitution. Alcohols and alkenes can also undergo Friedel Crafts reactions. The reation is named after the French chemist Charles Friedel (1832-99) and the US chemist James M.Craft (1839-1917).

Froehde's test. A presumptive test for opiods. **Froehde's reagent** consists of 0.5 gram of sodium molybdate dissolved in 100 ml of concentrated sulphuric acid. LSD gives a blue-green colour, heroin gives purple to olive green, and mescaline gives a greenish colour.

Frontier-orbital theory. A theory of the reactions of molecules that emphasizes the energies and symmetries of frontier orbitals. Frontier orbital theory was developed by the Japanese chemist Kenichi Fukui in the 1950s and is an alternative approach to the Woodward-Hoffmann rules. It has been very successful in explaning such reactions as the Diels-Alder reaction.

Froth flotation. A method of separating mixtures of solids, used industrially for separating ores from the unwanted gangue. The mixture is ground to a powder and water and a frothing agent added. Air is blown through the water. With a suitable frothing agent, the bubbles adhere only to particles of ore and carry them to the surface, leaving the gangue particles at the bottom.

Fructose 1,6 bisphosphate. An intermediate formed in the initial stage of glycolysis by the phosphorylation of glucose using ATP.

Fuel. A substance that is oxidized or otherwise changed in a furnace or heat engine to release useful heat or energy. For this purpose wood. vegetable oil, and animal products have largely been replaced by fossil fuels since the 18th century.

The limited supply of fossil fuels and the expense of extracting them from the earth has encouraged the development of nuclear fuels to produce electricity.

Fuel Cells. Voltaic cells in which the reactants (usually gases) are supplied continuously.

A voltaic cell that converts the chemical energy of a fuel and an oxidizing agent directly into electriacl energy on a continuous basis.

Fullerene onions. Round fullerenes whith several layers of carbon on top of one another.

Fullerenes. Also called buckyballs, these are an elemental form of carbon consisting of some closed surface with no degrees of unsaturation. The most well-known of these is buckminsterfullerene, C60. Related to carbon nanotubes.

Functional Group. A group of atoms that represents a potential reaction site in an organic compound.

Fundamental constants. Those parameters that do not change throughout the universe. The charge on an electron, the speed of light in free space, the Planck constant, the gravitational constant, the electric constant, and the magnetic constant are all thought to be examples.

Furanose. A sugar having a fivemembered ring containing four carbon atoms and one oxygen atom.

Fusel oil. A mixture of high molecular weight alcohols containing also esters and fatty acids, sometimes formed as a toxic impurity in the distillation products of alcoholic fermentation. It is used as a source of higher alcohols and in making paints and plastics.

G

G2 calculations. An ab initio method for determining the entropies and enthalpies of reaction from the Schrodinger equation.

Gabriel's reaction. The conversion of a halogen compound into the corresponding amino compound by treatment with potassium phthalimide and subsequent hydrolysis of the intermediate phthalimido compound. Thus chloroe-thanoic acid gives glycine. Gives a pure primary amine.

Galactans. Polysaccharides which on hydrolysis give galactose. They occur in wood and in many algae. The most important galactan is AGAR.

Galena. PbS. A common lead ore, black or bluish-grey with a metallic lustre. It has the NaCl structure.

Gallium arsenide. GaAs. Important semiconductor material. Used in light-emitting diodes.

Galvanic cell. A cell that producess electricity through a chemical reaction.

Galvanizing. The coating of steel with Zn for protection by dipping into molten Zn or by electrodeposition (cold galvanizing). Corrosion occurs preferentially at the Zn.

Galvanometer. Consists of a coil of wire suspended in the magnetic field of a permanent magnet. When current flows through this coil of wire, the magnetic field exerts a torque on the loop, which is opposed by a spring. When you attach a pointer to this coil, you get an analog readout of the current.

Gamma Ray. High energy electromagnetic radiation.

A highly penetrating type of nuclear radiation similar to x-ray radiation, except that it comes from within the nucleus of an atom and has a higher energy. Energywise, very similar to cosmic ray except that cosmic rays originate from outer space.

Gangliosides. Sphing-olipids composed of sphingosine, fatty acid, at least one sugar and sialic acid. Found in brain, nervous tissues and erythrocytes.

Gangue. Sand, rock, and other impurities surrounding the mineral of interest in an ore.

Gas. The gaseous state is the most diffuse state of matter, in which molecules have almost unrestricted motion. A substance for which the volume increases continuously and without limit as the pressure is continuously reduced. A vapour is distinguished from a gas in that a gas is above the critical temperature of the substance.

Gas absorption. The solution a component of a gaseous mixture in a liquid or the absorption onto a surface. Selective absorption is employed to separate components of mixtures of gases or vapours, e.g. the removal of NH3 from NH3-air mixtures by absorption in water.

Gas adsorption. Adsorption of componentsof a gaseous mixture in a liquid or absorption of a gas on a surface. Of great importance in catalysis.

Gas calorimeter. Equipment for the determination of the CALORIFIC VALUE of a fuel gas by burning at a known rate or, for small amounts of combustible, combustion or explosion of a known volume of gas.

Gas hydrates. Clathrates formed by water with atomic orlow-molecular weight gases and some small organic molecules. Solid water forms open cages with the gases in holes.

Gasification. Conversion of a solid or liquid feedstock to a lower molecular weight gaseous fuel of lower carbon-to-hydrogen ratio.

Gas laws. The laws which describe the behaviour of gases. These are Boyle's law, Charles's law, Gay-Lussac's law of gaseous volumes and Avogadro's hypothesis.

Gas oil. A petroleum distillate fraction intermediate between kerosine and light lubricating oil. It is used as a domestic and industrial fuel oil and as a feedstock for cracking processes. Slightly more viscous grades are used as diesel fuels.

Gattermann Koch reaction. FORMYLATION of an aromatic hydrocarbon to yield the corresponding aldehyde by treatment with CO, HCl and AlCl3; at atmospheric pressure CuCl is also required.

Gatterman's reaction. A variation of the SANDMEYER REACTION; copper powder and/or copper(I) or (II) species and hydrogen halide are allowed to react with the diazonium salt solution and halogen is introduced into the aromatic nucleus in place of an amino group.

Gaussian broadening. Wwhen broadening comes from the varying Doppler shifts of emitting species in a gas.

Geiger counter. A gas filled tube which discharges electriaclly when ionizing radiation passes through it.

Geisser tubes. Gas discharge tubes constructed to concentrate the discharge in a capillary tube joining two glass bulbs containing the anode and cathode. The tubes are operated by induction coils and produce intense glow discharges when small quantities of gases or vapors are contained inside the tube.

Gel. Colloidal suspension of a solid dispersed in a liquid; a semirigid solid.

Gelatin hardeners. Materials used in hardening gelatin, generally in photography. Photographic material containing gelatin can be hardened during manufacture the process involves cross-linking between the gelatin polypeptide chains induced by the hardener.

Gelignite. A form of dynamite used as an explosive.

GEMC. The Gibbs Monte Carlo computer simulation technique; can use to simulate data on the coexisting vapor and liquid phases of a material at a given temperature.

Geminate. United or arranged in pairs.

Gem-dimethyl group. Two methyl groups of the same carbon atom.

Geodesic. The shortest distance between two points on a sphere.

Gemstones. Materials which because of their appearance and variety are used in jewellery and decoration. Synthetic stones simulate natural gemstones.a-Alumina gives ruby and sapphire. Spinel, titania, $SrTiO3$ are also used but a virtually all artificial. Diamonds can be synthesized but are then mainly used for cutting.

Genome. The total genetic material within a cell or individual.

Geometrical Isomers. Compounds with different arrangements of groups on either side of a bond with restricted rotation, such as a double bond or a single bond in a ring; for example cistrans isomers of certain alkenes.

Stereoisomers that are not mirror images of each other; also known as position isomers.

Getter. A chemical for removing impurities, most often from gases. KF acts as a getter to remove HF. Li will remove O,S, etc. from Cu and Cualloys.

G-factor. A measure of how much the spin magnetic moment interacts with the local magnetic field. Used in ESR.

Gibberellic acid (gibberellins). Plantgrowth regulators, metabolites of Gibberella fujikuroi. Gibberellic acid is the most important member of a family of hormones called gibberellins.

Gibbs' isotherm. The relation between the chemical potential at an interface and the change in surface tension.

Glass electrode. Used for determination of particular ions including pH. An electrode for pH determination contains a buffer and when placed in a solution gives a potential dependent on the pH of that solution.

Glass fibre. Glass filaments in the form of filaments, fabric, chopped fibre, added to thermoset resins to confer strength. Used in building and for insulation.

Glass transition. When a supercooled liquid becomes a glass; this is not a real phase change but represents a slowing down of the fluid relaxational motion to a point where the relaxation time is far greater than the time of observation. Not a sharp transition.

Glass transition temperature. The temperature at which an amorphous solid transforms from the viscous state to a hard and brittle state.

Globin. A protein, belonging to the histone class. Combined with heme it forms the respiratory pigmet haemoglobin.

Globar. Emits radiation from 4-15 microns. Bonded SiC rod five cm. long and 5 mm. diameter operated at 1500K. Accurately simulates a blackbody emitter. mite used as an explosive.

Globular proteins. Proteins arranged so that the lipophilic sides are turned inward to face each other, whist the hydrophilic groups are outside.

Glove box. An enclosed space, generally with a glass or plastic viewing port and gloves, used for the manipulation of moisture, oxygen sensitive or poisonous or hazardous materials.

Gluten. A mixture of proteins obtained from wheat dough by washing out the starch. It contains mostly the two proteins gliadin ad glutelin. Causes intestinal problems in some persons.

Glycerides. Esters of glycerol. Classified as mono-, di-and triglycerides according to the number of acid redicals combined with the three hydroxyl groups. The triglycerides occur naturally in animal and vegetable fats and oils.

Glycerophosphoric acid. Phosphate esters of glycerol. LECITHINS are fatty acid esters of glycerophosphoric acid derivatives. Commercially glycerophosphoric acid is used to prepare the medicinal glycerophosphate salts, e.g. the calcium salt.

Glycine. Crystallizes in colourless prisms; m.p. 260°C (decomp.), turning brown at 228°C. It has a sweet taste, Glycine is the simplest of the amino acids and is a hydrolysis product of proteins; it can be made synthertically by the action of ammonia on chloroethanoic acid and from proteins, such as gelatin, by hydrolysis with acids. Glycine can be synthesized in the animal body. Its sulphate is used in electrolysis.

Glycogen. The reserve carbohydrate of the cell. The molecule is built up of a large numberof short chains of a glucose units joined by 1-4 links, the chains being crosslinked by a 1-6 glucoside links. Molecular mass about 4 million. It is a white amorphous powder with no reducing properties. It is broken down in the digestive system by glucosidases to glucose, but in the cells it is broken down to and built up from glucose-1-phosphate by means of phosphorylases.

Glycollic acid. CH2OH-COOH. Colourless crystals, m.p. 80°C. Occurs in the juice of the sugar cane and beets. Prepared by boiling a concentrated aqueous solution of sodium monochloro-ethanoate. Also produced by electrolytic reduction of oxalic acid. Forms an anhydride when heated at 100°C. Used in textile and leather processing and cleaning (metals and dairy sanitation).

Glycois. Dihydric alcohols derived from aliphatic hydrocarbon by replacement of two hydrogen atoms by hydroxyl groups. They are colourless liquids. 1-2 glycols are obtained by oxidation of olefins with potassium permangate or lead tetraacetate; by heating olefin chlorohydrins with weak alkalis; or by heating alkane dihalides with sodium hydroxide. Of great importance as polymers, e.g. polyethylene glycol.

Glycolysis. The metabolic breakdown of carbohydrates in living organisms. Occurs in the presence of oxygen ('aerobic glycolysis'). Anaerobic glycolysis of glucose ultimately yields two moles of ATP per mole of glucose, together with loctate, which can undergo further energy-yielding degradation in the presence of oxygen. Aerobic glycolysis yields pyruvate, which in turn may give rise to acetyl-coenzyme A for the CITRIC ACID CYCLE. Pyruvate may also undergo other metabolic transformations, e.g. aminations to give alanine.

Glycosidases. Enzymes which split off glucoses (glucosidases) or other sugars from glycosides.

Glycylglycine. Decomposes at 260-262°C. The simplest of the dipeptides, it is formed by the action of glycyl chloride on glycine or by hydrolysing diketopiperazine with hydrochloric acid.

Glyoxylate cycle. An ANAPLEROTIC SEQUENCE supplementing the carboxylic acid cycle in micro-organisms and in plants. Isocitric acid is cleaved to succinate and glyoxylate, the latter being used to form malic acid by combination with acetyl-coenzyme A.

Glyoxylic acid. CH(O)-COOH. A thick syrup, rather difficult to crystallize; m.p. 98°C. Widely distributed in plant and animal tissues. Prepared by electrolytic reduction of oxalic acid. Forms salts of the type (HO)2CHCOOM. Also reacts a aldehyde. Condenses with urea to give allantoin. Reduced to glycollic acid.

Glyphosphate, Herbicide, N-(phosphonomethyl)-glycine.

Gmelin (Handbuch der anorganische Chemie). The definitive reference series in inorganic chemistry, although the complete periodic table is not covered.

Gold, organometallic compounds. Gold(I) compounds RAuL (L=sulphide, phosphine, isocyanide) and gold(III) alkyls, e.g. Me3AuPH3 and are (Me2AuBr2)-known.

Gold, standard. Pure gold is too soft for use as ornaments or for coinage, and is alloyed with copper or silver, or both. The fineness is expressed either in parts per thousand, or in carate. Pure gold is 24 carat fine, and the five standard alloys of 22, 18, 15, 12 and 9 carats, i.e. parts of gold in 24 of alloy, are legalized.

Gold number. A number used to define the efficiency of operation of protective colloids based upon the amount of protective colloid, preventing the colour change of a gold sol from red to blue on coagulation by electrolytes.

Gold oxides. Gold(I) oxide, Au2O, is obtained from [AuBr2] and alkali. It decomposes above 200°C. An ill-defined gold(III) hydroxide is soluble in excess of alkali to give the [Au(OH)4] ion.

Goldschmidt process. The preparation of sodium methanoate by pressurizing CO and NaOH at approx. 200°C. Pyrolysis then gives sodium oxalate.

Goldschmidt reaction. The use of Al powder for the reduction of metal oxides.

Gold sulphides. Grey Au2S and black Au2S3 are formed by the action of H2S on gold derivatives. Both decompose to the metal on heating.

Gonadotropins. Hormones influencing the activity of the sex organs. The term is not applied to the steroid sex hormones. Applied to a variety of peptide hormones, produced in the anterior lobe of the pitutary gland and elsewhere.

Gouy balance. A balance for the determination of magnetic susceptibility. The sample is weighed in and out of a magnetic field and the susceptibility is calculated from the difference in weights.

Graham's salt. A polymeric metaphosphate.

Graft terpolymers. A polymer backbone onto which are grafted two series of chemically dissimilar sidechains. Depending on what these sidechains are, they can either order into periodic forms or remain microscopically mixed.

Gram atom. The quantity of an element numerically equal to the relative atomic mass expressed in grams.

Gram equivalent. The equivalent weight of a substance expressed in grams.

Gramicidin. Family of antibiotics produced by soil bacteria.

Gram molecule. The quantity of a compound, or element, equal numercially to the relative molecular mass expressed in grams. The weight in grams of one mole of a substance.

Granite. An igneous rock extensively used as a building stone and road metal.

Granulation. A general term for any process for producing granules. Granulation is frequently carried out by compacting a fine material and then crushing it, and thus employs techniques of both size enlargement and size reduction.

Graphene sheets. The individual component sheets of graphite. Converted into nanotubes.

Gran plot. Measures the volume of acid or base or any substance to be titrated versus the volume of titrant added.

Graham's Law. The rates of effusion of gases are inversely proportional to the square roots of their molecular weights or densities.

Greenhouse Effect. Trapping of heat at the surface of the earth by carbon dioxide and water vapour in the atmosphere.

Ground State. The lowest energy state or most stable state of an atom, molecule or ion.

Group. A vertical column in the periodic table; also called a family.

Guaiol. C13H26O. crystalline alcohol; m.p. 93°C, obtained from the wood oil of Bulnesia sarmienti, Lorenz. On heating with sulphur it gives guaiazulene.

Gum acacia. Obtained as an exudate from acacia trees. It is the calcium salt of arabin, a complex polysaccharide bult of glucuronic acid, arabinose, rhamnose and galactose units. It is used in pharmacy as an emulsifying and suspending agent and in the manufacture of plasters, in the food industry, and as an adhesive.

Gutta-percha. A naturally occurring polymeric material, isomeric with rubber but having the trans configuration. Obtained from the latex of various topical trees. Insulator, dental cement.

H

Haber Process. A process for the catalyzed industrial production of ammonia from N_2 and H_2 at high temperature and pressure.

Haematin test. A test for blood using the presence of characteristic haematin crystals. It was introduced in 1853 by Ludwig Teichmann.

Haemochromogen test. A test used to confirm the presence of blood. It is a microcrystal test exploting the characteristic appearance of haemochromogen crystals observed under a microscope. The test was introduced in Japan in 1912 Masao Takayama.

Haemoerythrin. A red iron-containing respirtory pigment that occurs in the blood of annelids and some other invertebrates. Its structure is essentially the same as that of haemoglobin except the prosthetic group has a different chemical composition.

Half-Cell. Compartment in which the oxidation or reduction half-reaction occurs in a voltaic cell.

Half-Life. The time required for half of a reactant to be converted into product(s).

The time required for half of a given sample to undergo radioactive decay.

Half-Reaction. Either the oxidation part or the reduction part of a redox reaction.

Half-thickness. The thickness of a specified material that reduces the intensity of a beam of radiation to half its original value.

Half-wave plate. A crystal that rotates the polarization of light by 90 degrees.

Half-width. Half the width of a spectrum line (or in some cases the full width) measured at half its height.

Halite. Naturally occurring sodium chloride (common salt, NaCl), crystallizing in the cubic system. It is chiefly colourless or white (sometimes blue) when pure but the presence of impurities may colour it grey, pink, red, or brown. Halite often occurs in association with anhydrite and gypsum.

Halo. A broad ring appearing in the electron diffraction, neutron diffraction, or X-ray diffraction patterns of materials that are not crystals. Haloes of this type occur in gases and liquids as well as in non-crystalline solids.

Halogens. Group VIIA elements: F, Cl, Br, I

Hardening of oils. The process of converting unsaturated esters of fatty acids into (more solid) saturated esters by hydrogenation using a nickel catalyst. It is used in the manufacture of margarine from vegetable oils.

Hard Water. Water containing Fe^{3+}, Ca^{2+}, and Mg^{2+} ions, which forms precipates with soap.

Harmonic. An oscillation having a frequency that is a simple multiple of a fundamental sinusoidal oscillation. The fundamental frequency of a sinusoidal oscilation is usually called the first harmonic. The second harmonic has a frequency twice that of the fundamental, and so on.

Hassium. Symbol Hs. A radioactive transactinide element; a.n. 108. It was first made in 1984 by Peter Armbruster and a team in Darmstadt, Germany. It can be produced by bombarding. It ca be produced by bombarding lead-208 nuclei with iron-58 nuclei. Only a few atoms have ever been produced. The name comes from the Latinized form of Hesse, the german state where it was first synthesized.

Headspace. The space above a sample held in a sealed container. Headspace analysis is used in forensic science to investigate the volatile constituents of a sample.

Heat. A form of energy that flows between two samples of matter because of their differences in temperature.

Heat engine. A device for converting heat into work. Engines usually work on cycles of operation, the most efficient of which would be the Carnot cycle.

Heat of atomization. The energy required to dissociate one mole of a given substance into atoms.

Heat Capacity. The amount of heat required to raise the temperature of a body (of any mass) one degree Celsius.

Heat of combustion. The energy liberated when one mole of a given substance is completely oxidized.

Heat of Condensation. The amount of heat that must be removed from one gram of a vapor at it's condensation point to condense the vapour with no change in temperature.

Heat of Crystallization. The amount of heat that must be removed from one gram of a liquid at its freezing point to freeze it with no change in temperature.

Heat of dissociation. The energy absorbed when one mole of a given substance is dissociated into its constituent elements.

Heat of formation. The energy liberated or absorbed when one mole of a compound is formed in their standard states from its constituent elements.

Heat of Fusion. The amount of heat required to melt one gram of solid at its melting point with no change in temperature. Usually expressed in J/g. The molar heat of fusion is the amount of heat required to melt one mole of a solid at its melting point with no change in temperature and is usually expressed in kJ/mol.

Heat of neutralization. The energy liberated in neutralizing one mole of an acid or base.

Heat of reaction. The energy liberated or absorbed as a result of the complete chemical reaction of molar amounts of the reactants.

Heat of Solution. The amount of heat absorbed in the formation of solution that contains one mole of solute; the value is positive if heat is absorbed (endothermic) and negative if heat is released (exothermic).

Heat of Vaporization. The amount of heat required to vaporize one gram of a liquid at its boiling point with no change in temperature. Usually expressed in J/g. The molar heat of vaporization is the amount of heat required to vaporize one mole of liquid at its boiling point with no change in temperature and usually expressed ion kJ/mol.

Heavy metal. A metal with a high relative atomic mass. The term is usually applied to common transition metals, such as copper, lead, and zinc. These metals area cause of environmental pollution from a number of sources, including lead in petrol, industrial effluents, and leaching of metal ions from the soil into lakes and rivers by acid rain.

Heavy Water. Water containing deuterium, a heavy isotope of hydrogen.

Hecto. Symbol h. A prefix used in the metric system to denote 100 times. For example, 100 coulombs=1 hectocoulomb (hc).

Heisenberg Uncertainty Principle. It is impossible to determine accurately both the momentum and position of an electron simultaneously.

Helicate. A type of inorganic molecule containing a double helix of bipyridyl-derived molecules formed around a chain of up to five copper(I) ions.

Helmholtz coil. An electromagnet wound around a charged-particle optical detector used to cancel out the effect of the earth's magnetic field. Requires two coils.

Helmholtz, Hermann Ludwig Ferdinand von. (1821-94) German physiologist and physicist. In 1850 he measured the speed of a nerve impulse and in 1851 invented the ophthalmoscope. Helm-holtz discovered the conservation of energy (1847), giving many examples of its application, and also introduced the concept of free energy.

Hemicellulose. A polysaccharide found in the cell walls of plants. The branched chains of this molecule bind to cellulose microfibrils, forming a network of cross-linked fibres.

Hemihedral form. The form of a crystal in which only half the number of faces required for the symmetry are present.

Hemihydrate. A crystalline hydrate containing two molecules of compound per molecule of water.

Henry. Symbol H. The SI unit of inductance equal to the inductance of a closed ciruit in which an e.m.f. of one volt is produced when the electric current in the circuit varies uniformly at a rate of one ampere per second. It is named after the U.S. physicist Joseph Henry (1797-1878).

Henry's Law. The pressure of the gas above a solution is proportional to the concentration of the gas in the solution.

Heparin. A glycosaminoglycan with anticoagulant properties, occurring in vertebrate tissues, especially the lungs and blood vessels.

Heptahydrate. A crystalline hydrate that has seven moles of water permole of compound.

Heptavalent. Having a valency of seven.

Heroin. A highly addictive drug produced by acetylating morphine. It is usually used as the hydrochloride. In the UK it is a class A drug but it can be prescribed as a painkiller under the name diamorphine. The Marquis and Froedhetests are used to give a initial indication of heroin.

Hertz. Symbol Hz. The SI unit of frequency equal to one cycle per second. It is named after Heinrich Hertz.

Hess' Law of Heat Summation. The enthalpy change for a reaction is the same whether it occurs in one step or a series of steps.

Hetero atom. An odd atom in the ring of a heterocyclic compound. For instance, nitrogen is the hetero atom in pyridine.

Heterocyclic Amine. Amine in which the nitrogen is part of a ring.

Heterogeneous. Relating to two or more phases, e.g. a heterogenous catalyst.

Heterogeneous catalysis. A process where you have one material supporting the actual catalyst for a reaction. One common example is where a porous inorganic material (such as a zeolite) supports small metal particles. Through using small particles, you maximize the catalyst surface area, making it more efficient.

Heterolytic fission. The breaking of a bond in a compound in which the two fragments are oppositely charged ions.

Heterogeneous Equilibria. Equilibria involving species in more than one phase.

Heterogeneous Mixture. A mixture that does not have uniform composition and properties throughout.

Heteronuclear. Consisting of different elements.

Heusler alloys. Ferromagnetic alloys containing no ferromagnetic elements. The original alloys contained copper, manganese, and tin and were first made by Conrad Heusler (19th century mining engineer).

Hexacyanoferrate(II). A complex iron-containing anion, used as a solution of its potassium salt as a test for ferric iron (iron(III)), with which it forms a dark blue precipitate of Prussian blue. The sodium salt is used as an anticaking agent in common salt.

Hexahydrate. A crystalline compound that has six moles of water per mole of compound.

Hexanoate. A salt or ester of hexanoic acid.

Hexapole selection. A method by which molecules can be oriented in space; this can be used to set the up-down symmetry.

Hexose. A monosaccharide that has six carbon atoms in its molecules.

HFCC. Hyperfine coupling constant.

Highest occupied molecular orbital HOMO). The orbital in a molecule that has the highest energy level occupied at the temperature of absolute zero. The highest occupied molecular orbital and the lowest unoccupied molecular orbital are the two 'frontier orbitals of the molecule.

High frequency(HF). A radio frequency in the range 3-30 megahertz; i.e. having a wavelength in the range 10-100 metres.

High-performance liquid chromatography (HPLC). A sensitive technique for separating or analysing mixtures, in which the sample is forced throough the chromatography column under pressure.

High-resolution electron-loss spectroscopy (HRELS). A technique for obtaining information about molecules absorbed on a surface by inelastic scattering of electrons.

High-speed steel. A steel that will remain hard at dull red heat and can therefore be used in cutting tools for high-speed lathes. It usually contains 12-22% tungsten, up to 5% chromium, and 0.4-0.7% carbon. It may also contain small amounts of vanadium, molybdenum, and other metals.

High Spin Complex. Crystal field designation for an outer orbital complex; all t2g and eg or bitals are singly occupied before any pairing occurs.

Hildebrand rule. If the density of the vapour phase above a liquid is constant, the molar entropy of vaporization is constant. This law does not hold if molecular association takes place in the liquid or if the liquid is subject to quantum-mechanical effects, e.g. as in superfluidity. The rule is named after the US chemist Joel Henry Hildebrand (1881-1983).

Hill reaction. The release of oxygen from isolated illuminated chloroplasts when suitable electron acceptors (e.g. potassium ferricyanide) are added to the surrounding water. The reaction was discovered by Robert Hill (1899-1991) in 1939; the electron acceptors substitute for NADP, the natural acceptor for the light-dependent reactions of photosynthesis.

Histochemistry. The study of the distribution of the chemical constituents of tissue by means of their chemical reaction. It utilizes such techniques as staining, light and electron microscopy, autoradiography, and chromatography.

Hohlraum. A laboratory device to produce blackbody radiation. Consists of a closed metal tube, blackened on the inside, with a narrow slit cut into one of the flat ends. On heating the tube the radiation escaping from the slit is virtually identical with that expected from a blackbody.

Hole. 1. A vacant electron position in the lattice structure of a solid that behaves like a mobile positive charge carrier. 2. A vacant electron position in one of the inner orbitals of an atom.

Holohedral form. The form of a crystal in which the full number of faces required for the symmetry are present.

HOMCOR. Homonuclear correlated spectroscopy; a 2-D NMR technique.

Homogeneous. Relating to only one phase, e.g. a homogeneous mixture, a homogeneous catalyst.

Homogeneous Catalyst. A catalyst that exists in the same phase (solid, liquid or gas) as the reactants.

Homogeneous Equilibria. Equilibria involving only one species in a single phase. For example, all gases, all liquids or all solids.

Homoleptic compound. A chemical complex with only one type of ligand, as in nickel carbonyl or lead tetraethyl.

Homogeneous Mixture. A mixture which has uniform composition and properties throughout.

Homologous Series. A series of compounds in which each member differs from the next by a specific number and kind of atoms.

Homonuclear. Consisting of only one element.

Homotopic. Protons that are interchangeable through an axis of symmetry. The chemical shift of these protons is the same in any environment.

Hormone. A substance that is manufactured and secreted in very small quantities into the bloodstream by an endocrine gland or a specialized nerve cell and regulates the growth or functioning of a specific tissue or organ in a distant part of the body. For example, the hormone insulin controls the rate and manner in which glucose is used by the body.

Hot mirror. Reflect IR light and transmit visible.

Huckel, Erich(1896-1980). German physicist and theoretical chemist who worked with Peter Debye at Zurich on the theory of electrolysis. Later he moved to Copenhagen to work with Niels Bohr and here he produced his work on bonding in aromatic molecules.

Humectant. A substance used to maintain moisture levels. Humectants are generally hygroscopic.For example, glycerol is employed as a humectant in confectionery, foodstuffs, and tobacco. Other polyhydric alcohols, such as mannitol and sorbitol, are also used as humerctant additives in the foodstuffs industry.

Hund's Rule. All orbitals of a given sublevel must be occupied by single electrons before pairing begins

HWOT. Halfwave optical thickness.

Hyaluronic acid. A glycosaminoglycan that is part of the matrix of connective tissue. Hyaluronic acid binds cells together and helps to lubricate joints. It may play a role in the migration of cells at wounds; this activity ceases when hyaluronidase breaks down hyaluronic acid.

Hybridization. Mixing a set of atomic orbitals to form a new set of atomic orbitals with the same total electron capacity and with properties and energies intermediate between those of the original unhybridized orbitals.

Hydrate. A solid compound that contains a definite percentage of bound water.

Hydrate Isomers. Isomers of crystalline complexes that differ in whether water is present inside or outside the coordination sphere

Hydration. Reaction of a substance with water.

Hydration Energy. The energy change accompanying the hydration of a mole of gase and ions.

Hydride. A binary compound of hydrogen.

Hydrocarbons. Chemical compounds that contain only carbon and hydrogen. A vast number of different hydrocarbon compounds exist, the main types being the alkanes alkenes, alkynes, ad arenes.

Hydrodynamics. The study of fluid in motion.

Hydrogen Bond. A fairly strong dipole-dipole interaction (but still considerably weaker than the covalent or ionic bonds) between molecules containing hydrogen directly bonded to a small, highly electronegative atom, such as N, O, or F.

Hydrogenation. 1. A chemical reaction with hydrogen; in particular, an addition reaction in which hydrogen adds to an unsaturated compound. Nickel is a good catalyst for such reactions. **2.** The process of converting coal to oil by making the carbon in the coal combine with hydrogen to form hydrocarbons.

Hydrogen bromide. A colourless gas, HBr; m.p. -88.5°C; b.p. -67°C. It can be made by direct combination of the elements using a platinum catalyst. It is a strong acid dissociating extensively in solution.

Hydrogencarbonate. A salt of carbonic acid in which one hydrogen atom has been replaced; it thus contains the hydrogencarbonate ion HCO3.

Hydrogen carrier. A molecule that accepts hydrogen atoms or ions, becoming reduced in the process. The electron transport chain, whose function is to generate energy in the form of ATP during respiration, involves a series of hydrogen carriers, including NAD and FAD, which pass on the hydrogen (derived from the breakdown of glucose) to the next carrier in the chain.

Hydrogen iodine. A colourless gas, HI; m.p. -51°C; b.p. -35.38°C. It can be made by direct combination of the elements using a platinum catalyst. It is a strong acid dissociating extensively in solution (**hydroiodic acid or hydriodic acid**). It is also a reducing agent.

Hydrogen molecule ion. The simplest type of molecule, consisting of two hydrogen nuclei and one electron. In the Born-Oppenheimer approximation, in which the nuclei are regarded as being fixed, the Schrodinger equation for the hydrogen molecule ion can be solved exactly. This enables ideas and approximation techniques concerned with chemical bonding to be teasted quantitatively.

Hydrogen-Oxygen Fuel Cell. Fuel cell in which hydrogen is the fuel (reducing agent) and oxygen is the oxidizing agent.

Hydrogensulphate. A salt containing the ion HSO4 or an ester of the type RHSO4, where R is an organic group. It was formerly called hydro-sulphate.

Hydrogensulphite. A salt containing the ion HSO3 or an ester of the type RHSO3, where R is an organic group.

Hydrolysis. The reaction of a substance with water or its ions.

Hydrolysis Constant. An equilibrium constant for a hydrolysis reaction.

Hydrometer. A device used to measure the densities of liquids and solutions.

Hydron. The positive ion H. The name is used when it is not relevant to specify the isotope, as is usually the case in compounds in which the hydrogen is in natural abundance. When the isotope is relevant then proton , deuteron, or triton should be used.

Hydrophilic. Having an affinity for water.

Hydrophilic Colloids. Colloidal particles that repel water molecules.

Hydrophobic. Lacking affinity for water.

Hydrosol. A sol in which the continuous phase is water.

Hydroxide. A metallic compound containing the ion OH (**hydroxide ion**) or containing the group -OH (**hydroxyl group**) bound to a metal atom. Hydroxides of typical metals are basic; those of metalloids are amphoteric.

Hydroxylamine. A colourless solid, NH2OH, m.p. 33°C. It explodes on heating and may be employed as an oxidizing agent or reducing agent. It is made by the reduction of nitrates or nitrites, and is used in making nylon. With aldehydes and ketones it forms oximes.

Hydroxylation. The introduction of a hydroxyl group (-OH) into an organic compound. For example, alkenes can be hydrocylated using potassium permanganate or lead ethanoate to give alcohols In biochemistry, various enzymes can bring about hydroxylation.

Hydroxyl group. The group-OH in a chemical compound.

Hydroscopic. Describing a substance that can take up water from the atmosphere.

Hyperchromic effect. An increase in absorption intensity; if structural modification leads to an increase in the molar extinction coefficient for a particular chromophoric group it is said to have brought about a hyperchromic effect.

Hyperfine structure. The multiplet of peaks you see in the ESR spectrum. The source of this splitting is the magnetic field arising from nuclear magnetic momets within the molecule. Generally, for molecules with a spin of I, you see 2n+1 peaks coming from the splitting. The appearance of the peaks is governed by pascal's triangle, much like the fine structure in NMR.

Hyperpolarizability. The second order polarizability of a molecule. It describes how easily you can push or pull electrons around the molecule. A high hyper polarizability is good if you want to detect second order processes like second harmonic generation.

Hypochromic effect. A decrease in absorption intensity.

Hypsochromic shift. The shift of an absorption to a shorter wavelength due to substitution or solvent effect (blue shift).

Hysteresis. The tendency of a magnetic substance to remain in a certain magnetic condition

Hyugen's principle. Every point on a wave front can be considered as a source of tiny wavelets that spread out in the forward direction at the speed of the wave itself. The new wave front is the envelope of all these wavelets.

I

IAD. Ion-assisted deposition; used to make optical coatings at low temperatures.

Ice. The solid form of water. The transition point 273.ISK between liquid and solid water at one atmosphere pressure is defined as 0° on the Centrigrade scale, also equal to C° Celsius. This freezing temperature is lowered by increasing the pressure. By crystallization of water under greatly increased pressure is possible to obtain forms of solid water which are physically distict from ordinary ice (Ice I). The molecules in ice are held together by hydrogen bonds.

Icosahedral. Having the symmetry of an icosahedron, a solid figure with twelve apices; each face is triangular Icosahedral units are found in many boron derivatives.

Ideal Gas. A hypothetical gas that obeys exactly all postulates of the kinetic-molecular theory.

Ideal Gas Law. The product of pressure and the volume of an ideal gas is directly proportional to the number of moles of the gas and the absolute temperature.

Ideal Solution. A solution that obeys Raoult's Law exactly.

IET. Intramolecular electron transfer.

Ignition temperature. The minimum temperature at which a fuel can self-ignite. The temperature obtained will depend on the technique used as on the air-fuel ratio of the mixture.

Ilmenite. $FeTiO3$. Ablack Ti ore occurring in massive form and in sands. The structure has cp oxygen with Fe and Ti in octahedral co-ordination.

Imazamethabenz-methyl. Herbicide, imidazole derivative.

Imazamox. Herbicide, imidazole derivative.

Imazapyr. Herbicide, imidazole derivative.

Imazaquin. Herbicide, imidazole derivative.

Imazathapyr. Herbicide, imidazolinone derivative.

Imazlil. Fungicide, azole derivative.

Imazosulfuron. Herbicide, Sulphonylurea derivative.

Imibenconazol. Fungicide, azole derivative.

Imidacloprid. Insecticide, imidazolidine derivative.

Immersion lens. A hemispherical lens which is used to decrease the detector size. Essentially, the image is reduced without loss of resolution.

Imines. Compounds containing an >NH group. May be cyclic (e.g. dihydroa-zirine) or linear.

Iminium salts. Salts containing cations in which the charge delocalization includes a nitrogen atom.

Imino. The name given to the group >NH where the nitrogen atom is part of a ring system or is united by both bonds to a single atom. Such compounds as R-CO-NHR are usually regarded as substituted amides and not as imino compounds.

Iminoctadine. Fungicide, guanidine derivative.

IMS. Industrial methylated spirits.

Inabenfid. Plant growth regulator, pyridine derivative.

Incandescence. When materials are self-luminous solely owing to their high temperatures.

Inclusion. When something is incorporated in a crystal, either in a lattice site or interstitial site.

Incongurent melting. Me-lting into its components wi-thout formation of a liquid phase.

Indan. B.p. 176° C. The first reduction product indene. Occurs in coal tar.

Indanthrene dyestuffs. An important series of dyestuffs based on amino derivates of anthraquinone.

Indican. C14H17NO. Also the potassium salt of indoxyl-3-sulphuric acid, the form in which toxic indoxyl is excreted as one of the ethereal sulphates.

Indicator. Any substance which allows the progress of a chemical change to be followed, usually by a change of colour, of fluorescence of a solution, or by the alteration in the nature of a solution, or by the alteration in the nature of a precipitate. E.g. methyl orange, an indicator used in the neutralization of acids with bases, is red as pH less than 3.1 and gradually cha-nges through orange to a full yellow colour as the pH increases to 4.4.

Indigold dyes. Vat dyes and pigments containing indigo-like groupings and giving similar colours. Contain indole of thionaphthene systems.

Induced dipole moment. Distortion of a molecule by an electric field.

Inductive effect. A substituent effect on an organic compound due to the permanent polarity or polarziability of groups is called an inductive effect. It may be visualized as the inducement of charge either towards or away from a group or atom, with a resulting dipole. Accounts for e.g. the increased acidity of trichloroethanoic acid over ethanoic acid.

Industrial methylated spirits (IMS). Ethanol rendered non-potable by mixing 95% alcohol with methanol.

Inelastic neutron scattering. Study of the motion of molecules in liquids from passage of a beam of neutrons through a sample.

Inner Orbital Complex. Valence bond designation for a complex in which the metal ion utilizes d orbitals for one shell inside the outermost occupied shell in its hybridization.

Inertia. The tendency of a body to maintain its state of rest or uniform motion.

Inert atmosphere box. A container for carrying out chemical reactions in which the atmosphere has been purged of water, oxygen and nitrogen by recycling over active absorbants for the particular gases to be removed. Used for hadling very sensitive materials; modifications can be used for handling reactive metals, e.g. Ti at high temperatures.

Inert complex. A complex which participates in reaction, particularly ligand-exchange reactions, either very slowly or sufficiently slowly that the rates of reaction can be readily followed.

Inert gases. Semi-obsolete name for the NOBLE GA-SES.

Inert gas formalism. The OCTET RULE; the effective ATOMIC NUMBER RULE.

Inert s-pair Effect. Characteristic of the post-transition minerals; tendency of the outermost s electrons to remain nonionized or un shared in compounds.

Infrasonic. Sound waves with smaller frequency than we can hear (20 Hz).

Infra-red spectroscopy. Vibrations within molecules show characteristic absorption bands in the infrared region of the spectrum. Infrared spectroscopy provides valuable information about structure, and gives information on groups present and on molecular symmetry. The technique has been highly developed and is widely used as a routine tool in analysis and research.

Infusions. Dilute solutions containing the water soluble components of vegetable drugs prepared by aqueous extraction of the drugs.

Ingrain dyestuffs. Insoluble dyestuffs formed directly on the fibre from soluble components.

Inhibitor. A general term for any compound which will inhibit, i.e. slow down stop, a reaction, generally by preventing propagation of chain reactions or by passivation of surfaces, etc. The term is often used to describe any additive which will prevent a particular tendency during working operations, e.g. antioxidants, anti-corrosion agents, etc.

Inhibitory Catalyst. An inhibitor, a catalyst that decreases the rate of reaction.

Initial boiling point. In a laboratory distillation the th-ermometer reading observed when the first drop of condensate falls from the lower end of the condenser tube.

Inks. Colouring matter dissolved or dispersed in a solvent or carrier; on drying the colouring matter is bonded (by an additive) to the substrate.

Inner sphere mechanism. A mode of redox reaction in which complexes form an intermediate with a shared ligand.

Inorganic chemistry. The chemistry of all the elements other than carbon. Simple carbon compounds, e.g. carbides, carbonates, carbonyis and cyanides are often regarded as inorganic. Organic derivatives of metals and metalloids are considered as ORGANOMETALLIC.

Insecticides. Materials used to control insects by poisoning (chrysanthemic acids, contact poisons, systemic poisons) by use of attractants or repellants.

Insect repellants. Materials that may have a repellant effact on insects.

Insoluble Compound. A very slightly soluble compound.

Instability constant. The reverse of a STABILITY CO-NSTANT; the measure of dissociation.

Insulator. A substance with a very low electrical conductivity. In insulators there is a wide bandgap between completely filled and completely empty electronic energy levels. Most pure solid ionic substances are insulators although impurities or imperfections may introduce SEMI-CONDUCTIVITY.

Insulin. The hormone, secreted by the Islets of Langerhans in the pancreas, which maintains the balance of glucose metabolism. The absence of insulin leads to the disease diabetes mellitus.

Integral tripack material. Colour films and papers in which the three separate emulsions (for violet-blue, green and red) are coated on the same support in layers and, after exposure and COLOUR DEVELOPMENT, give dyes of the complementary colour (yellow, magenta and cyan).

Interatomic distances. The distances between the nuclei of atoms, bonded or non-bonded, in a molecule or crystal as determined by X-ray or electron diffraction, spectroscopic or other ph-ysical methods.

Intercalation. Incorporation of a foreign atom into some crystal lattice (usually in the interstitial spaces).

Intercalation compounds. Derivatives, particularly of graphite, in which molecules are accommodated in holes or between layers in the lattice. The resulting compounds are easily handled and stored (e.g. graphite-SbF5, used as a fluorinating agent; graphite-FeCl3; stable to water).

Integrated Rate Equation. An equation giving the concentration of a reactant remaining after a specified time; has different mathematical form for different orders of reactants.

Interfacial angles, constancy of The angle between any particular pair of faces a crystals is constant and characteristic of the substance of the crystal. It does not depend on the size of the crystal.

Interferons. A group of proteins which prevent viral replication of cells.

Interleukins. Lymphocyte communication factors.

Intermediate. A transient species occurring between reactants and products.

Intermolecular Forces. Forces between individual particles (atoms, molecules, ions) of a substance.

Internal compensation. A type of optical activity in which a molecule contains two asymmetric centres which produce equal and opposite rotation of the plane of polarization, with the result that the substance is optically inactive.

Internal pressure. Variation of internal energy with volume at constant temperature.

Internal property. Property that does not depend on the amount of substance, e.g. temperature, pressure.

Interstitial compounds. Compounds in which the structure may be considered to be derived by inserting small species into the holes of a cp metallic lattice (particularly of transition elements).

Intrinsic semiconductor. A material in which the band gap is small enough to make the material a semiconductor.

Invariant system. A system which, when at equilibrium, possesses no degrees of fr-eedom.

Inversion temperature. Most gases when rapidly expanded experience a cooling effect (the Joule-Thomson effect). Below 193 K hydrogen also shows this effect, but above this temperature it has a negative Joule-Thomson coefficient and is warmed by expansion. This temperature of 193 K is called the inversion temperature Helium shows similar behaviour to hydrogen with an inversion temperature of 40 K.

Invert sugar. The slightly laevorotatory mixture of glucose and fructose obtained by hydrolysing sucrose.

Iodic acids. The acids giving rise to IODATE anions. Only HIO_3 is known in the free form. All are strong oxidizing agents.

Iodimetry. The use of iodine in titrations, generally titrated with thiosulphate and converted to 1 using starch (blue to colourless) as indicator. Used indirectly in estimating oxidizing agents which liberate I_2 from acid KI solution.

Iodoform reaction. A test used to detect the presence of a $C(O)$-CH_3 group (or groups which may be converted to this under the reaction conditions). Iodine in alkali converts the acetyl group into iodoform.

Iodomethane. CH_3I. Colo-urless liquid with characteristic colour; b.p. 42°C. Prepared by heating methanol and iodine with red phosphorous. Used in organic chemistry for methylation and for preparing methyl lithium and methyl Grignard reagents.

Ion. An atom or a group of atoms that carries an electric charge.

Ion exclusion. The medium inside the pores of an ion-exchange resin is subject to the Donnan membrane equilibrium. It therefore contains a lower concentration than does the external solution of any electrolysis that may be present in the latter. This is 'ion exclusion'. On the other hand, non-electrolytes are not subject to the Donnan effect.Hence, a partial separation of electrolytes from non-electrolytes can be obtained; by using a chromatographic technique complete separation can be effected in favourable cases.

Ionic Bonding. Chemical bonding resulting from the transfer of one or more electrons from one atom or a group of atoms to another.

Ionic Compunds. Compounds containing predominantly ionic bonding.

Ionic Geometry. The arrangement of atoms (not lone pairs of electrons) about the central atom of a polyatomic ion.

Ionic liquids. Low melting ionic solids containing large ions that can act as useful, nonpolluting, reaction media. Example: 1-cotyl-3-methylimidazolium hexaf-luoro-phosphate.

Ionic migration. A way of conducting electricity where you have charged particles moving through a matrix of some sort.

Ionic product. The product of the concentration of the ions of a substance in solution. This factor is a constant for weakly ionized substance because the concentration of undissociated material may be taken to be constant if it is present in a large excess.

Ionic radii. The effective radius of ions in crystal lattices.

Ionization. In aqueous solution, the process in which a molecular compound reacts with water and forms ions.

Ionization, heat of The energy required to split one mole of an electrolyte into its constituent ions. For water the heat of ionization is 57.3 kj mol^{-1}.

Ionization chamber. A device for measuring the absolute intensity of a beam of X-rays or ionizing particles.

Ionization Constant. Equilibrium constant for the ionization of a weak electrolyte.

Ionization Isomers. Isomers that result from the interchange of ions inside and outside the coordination sphere.

Ion Product for Water. Equilibrium constant for the ionization of water, $Kw = [H_3O^+][OH^-] = 1.00 \times$ 10-14 at 25 °C.

Ionization Energy. The minimum amount of energy required to remove the most loosely held electron of an isolated gaseous atom or ion.

Ionogenic surface. The stability of a colloid particle is due to the charge it carries. This charge is ionic in nature and if the stabilizing ions on the surface are due to the ionization of the particle wall material, the surface is used to be ionogenic.

Ion selective electrodes. An electrode whih responds specifically to one ion present in solution and develops a potential according to the concentration of that ion. Used for metals and for anions The electrode contains a standard solution or other specific an a membrane or other conductor placed in contact with the solution to be examined. Glass electrodes are widey used as ion-selective electrodes.

Iris diaphragm. Used in fluorimeters to control the amount of radiation from the source; consists of a series of overlapping plates arranged to move so that a roughly circular opening of variable size is produced. This is achieved by maintaining a nearly constant angle between the edges of adjacent plates.

Iron buff. Hydrated iron(III) oxide. Important pigment used for black dyeing of silk and for khaki dyeing of cotton, in paints and enamels.

Iron, complex cyanides. Used as pigments and to prevent caking of salt. Derivatives of cyanoferrates, e.g. pentactanonitrosylferrates, nitroprussides, containing $[Fe(CN)_5NO)^{2-}$, are also known.

Irtran 1. Magnesium fluoride.

Irtran 2. Zinc sulfide.

Isoelectric. Having the samé electronic configurations.

Isenthalpic. A change that occurs without a change in enthalpy.

Isomers. Different substances that have the same formula.

Isomorphous. Refers to crystals having the same atomic arrangement.

Isoprene polymers. Stereoscopic polymerization of isoprene to cis-polyisop-rene, the synthetic analogue of natural rubber, occurs with Ziegler-Natta catalysts or lithium alkyls. used as an ela-stomer and replacement for natural rubber (as polyisoprene) and in copolymers. Trans-polyisoprene is used in golf-ball covers.

Isosbestic point. Points on the spectra, particularly of reacting transition metal complexes, at which extinction coefficients are equal. Used in spectrophotometric studies of complex formation or of kinetics of reactions in solution to investigate processes such as isomenzation.

Isotherm. A curve on a vol. vs. temp. vs. pressure diagram that corresponds to a single temperature.

Isotopes. Two or more forms of atoms of the same element with different masses; atoms containing the same number of protons but different numbers of neutrons.

Isotopomer. Having the same topography.

Isotropic medium. A medium in which the waves travel at equal speed indep-endantly of which direction they travel.

J

Jablonski diagram. A diagram that represents the electronic energy levels (and their relative positions) of a molecule. A Jablonski diagram enables radiative transitions between energy levels in molecules, as well as such phenomena as internal conversion, to be shown. The vertical axis measures energy, with the electronic energy levels in their lowest vibrational states being short horizontal lines. The vibrational energy levels of a particular electronic state are drawn as shaded regions above the horizontal line for that state. In a Jablonski diagram the horizontal location of the electronic state is not related to the internuclear distance between the atoms in these states.

Jade. A hard semiprecious stone consisting either of jadeite or nephrite. Jadeite, the most valued of the two, is a sodium aluminium pyroxene, $NaAlSi_2O_6$. It is prized for its intense translucent green colour but white, green and white, brown, and orange varieties also ocur. The only important source of upper Burma. Nephrite is one of the amphibole group of rock-forming minerals. It occurs in a variety of colours, including green, yellow, white, and black. Sources include the Siberia, Turkistan, New Zealand, Alaska, China, and W USA.

Jahn-Teller effect. If a likely structure of a nonlinear molecule or ion would have degenerate orbitals (i.e. two molecular orbitals with the same energy levels) the actual structure of the molecule or ion is distorted so a to split the energy levels ('raise' the degeneracy). The effect is observed in inorga-nic complexes. For example, the ion $[Cu(H_2O)_6]^{2+}$ is octahedral and the six ligands might be expected to occupy equidistant positions at the corners of a regular octahedron. In fact, the octahedron is distorted, with four ligands in a square and two opposite ligands further away. If the 'original' structure has a centre of symmetry, the distorted structure must also have a centre of symmetry. The effect was predicted theoretically by H.A.Jahn (1907-79) and Edward Teller (1908-2003) in 1937.

Jasper. An impure variety of chalcedony. It is associated with iron ores and as a result contains iron oxide impurities that give the mineral its characteristic red or reddish-brown colour. Jasper is used as a gemstone.

Jet.A variety of coal that can be cut and polished and is used for jewellery, ornaments, etc.

Jeweller's rough. Red powdered haematite, iron (III) oxide, Fe_2O_3. It is a mild abrasive used in metal cleaners and polishes.

J-J coupling. A type of coupling occurring between electrons in atoms and nucleons in nuclei, in which the energies associated with the spin-orbit interactions are much higher that the energies associated with electrostatic repulsion. Multiplets of many-electron atoms having a large atomic number are characterized by J-J coupling. The multiplets of many atoms and nuclei are intermediate between J-J coupling and Russell-Saunders coupling, a state called **intermediate coupling.**

Joliot-Curie,Irene (1897-1956) French physicist, daughter of Marie and Pierre Curie, who was educated by her mother and her scientist associates. In 1921 she began work at the Radium Institute, becoming director in 1946. In 1926 she married Frederic Joliot (1900-58). They shared the 1935 Nobel Prize for chemistry for their discovery of artificial radioactivity the previous year.

JMol. A commonly used molecular viewing program, similar to RasMol. It can be used as an applet in a web page.

Jones reductor. A metal reductor column filled with zinc.

Joule. A unit of energy in the SI system. One joule is 1 kg. m2/s2 which is also 0.2390 calorie.

Joule, James Prescott. (1818-89) British physicist. In 1840 he discovered the relationship between electric current passing through a wire, its resistance, and the amount of heat produced. In 1849 he gave an account of the kinetic theory of gases, and a year later announced his bestknown finding, the mechanical equivalent of heat. Later with William Thomson (Lord Kelvin), he discovered the Joule-Thomson effect.

Joule's law. The internal energy of a given mass of gas is independent of its volume and pressure, being a function of temperature alone. This law, which was formulated by James Prescott Joule-applies only to ideal gases (for which it provides a definition of thermodynamic temperature) as in a real gas intermolecular forces would cause changes in the internal energy should a change of volume occur.

Joule-Thomson effect (Joule-Kelvin effect). The change in temperature that occurs when a gas expands through a porous plug into a region of lower pressure. For most real gases the temperature falls under these circumstances as the gas has to do internal work in overcoming the intermolecular forces to enable the expansion to take place. This is deviation from joule's law. There is usually also a deviation from Boyle's law, which can cause either a rise or a fall in temperature since any increase in the product of pressure and volume is a measure of external work done. At a given pressure, there is a particular temperature, called the **inversion temperature** of the gas, at which the rise in temperature from the Boyle's law deviation is balanced by the fall from the Joule's law deviation. There is then no temperature change. Above the inversion temperature the gas is heated by expansion, below it, it is cooled. The effect was discovered by James Prescott Joule working in collaboration with William Thomson (later Lord Kelvin).

Juvenile hormones. A widely distributed group of compounds which regulate larval development or reproduction of insects. Hormone activity is shown by some simple terpenoids such as the two trans farnesols, their methyl ethers and methyl farnesoate dihydrochloride. Knowledge of such compounds has important implications for insect control.

K

K Capture. Absorption of a K shell (n=1) electron by a proton as it is converted to a $neutro_2$

Kainite. A naturally occurring double salt of magnesium sulphate and potassium chloride, $MgSO_4.KCl.3H_2O$.

Kalinite. A mineral form of aluminium potassium sulphate $(Al_2(SO_4)_3.K_2SO_4.24H_2O$.

Kaolin. A soft white clay that is composed chiefly of the mineral kaolinite. It is formed during the weathering and hydrothermal alteration of other clays or feldspar. Kaolin is mined in the UK, France, the Czech Republic, and USA. Besides its vital importance in the ceramics industry it is also used extensively as a filler in the manufacture of rubber, paper, paint, and textiles and as a constituent of medicines.

Kastle Mayer test. A presumptive test used to indicate blood. Phenolpthalein and hydrogen peroxide are used; reaction with haemoglobin in the blood gives a pink colour.

Katharometer. An instrument for comparing the thermal conductivities of two gases by comparing the rate of loss of heat from two heating coils surrounded by the gases.

The instrument can be used to detect the presence of a small amount of an impurity in air and is also used as a detector in gas chromatography.

Kekule, Friedrich August von Stradonitz. German chemist, who became professor at Ghent (1858) and later at Bonn (1867). He studied the structures of organic molecules and was the first to recognise that carbon atoms form stable chains. Kekule is best remembered for his proposed structure for in 1865, which he correctly interpreted as having a symmetrical ring of six carbon atoms.

Kekule structure. A proposed structure of benzene in which the molecule has a hexagonal ring of carbon atoms linked by alternating double and single bonds. Kekule structures contribute to the resonance hybrid of benzene. The structure was suggested in 1865 by Friedrich August Kekule.

Keratin. Any of a group of fibrous proteins occurring in hair, feathers, hooves, and horns. Keratins have coiled polypeptide chains that combine to form supercoils of several polypetides linked by disulphide bonds between adjacent cysteine amino acids.

Kepler's laws of planetary motion. 1) The path of each planet about the sun is an ellipse with the sun at one focus

2) Each planet moves so that an imaginary line drawn from the sun to the planet sweeps out equal areas in equal periods of time.

3) The ratio of the squares of the periods of any two planets revolving about the sun is equal to the ratio of the cubes of their mean distances to the sun.

Ketals. Organic compounds, similar to *acetals, formed by addition of an alcohol to a ketone. If one molecule of ketone (RR'CO) reacts with one molecule of alcohol R"OH, then a **hemiketal** is formed. The rings of ketose sugars are hemiketals. Further reaction produces a full ketal ($RR'C(OR")_2$).

Ketone. Compound in which a carbonyl group is bound to two alkyl or two aryl groups, or to one alkyl and one aryl group.

Ketoenol tautomerism. A form of tautomerism in which a compound containing a $-CH_2-CO-$group (the keto form of the molecule) is in equilibrium with one containing the -CH=C(OH)-group (the enol). It occures by migration of a hydrogen atom between a carbon atom and the oxygen on a adjacent carbon.

Ketol. An organic compound that has both an alcohol ($-CH_2OH$) and a keto (=CO) group. Ketols are made by a condensation reaction between two ketones or by the oxidation of dihydric alcohols (glycols).

Khat. A plant, Catha edilis, found in East Africa and the Arabian peninsular. The leaves are chewed to give a mildly stimulating and euphoric effect. Its activity co-mes from two alkaloids: Cathine and, in fresh leaves, the more potent cathinone. It is a controlled substance in many countries including the US. In the UK it is not a controlled substance and is used by certain Somalian and Yemeni ethnicgroups.

Kieselguhr. A soft fine-grained deposit consisting of the siliceous skeletal remains of diatoms, formed in lakes and ponds. Kieselguhr is used as an absorbent, filtering material, filler, and insulator.

Kilo. Symbol k. A prefix used in the metric system to denote 1000 times. For example, 1000 volts = 1 kilovolt (kV).

Kilogram. Symbol kg. The SI unit of mass defined as a mass equal to that of the international platinum-iridium prototype kept by the International Bureau of Weights and Measures at Sevres, near Pairs.

Kimberlite. A rare igneous rock that often contains diamonds. It occurs as narrow pipe intrusions but is often altered and fragmented. It consists of ϕliv,ine and fragmented. It consists of olivine and phlogropite mica, usually with calcite, serpentine, and otherminerals. The chief occurrences of kimberlite are in South Africa, especially at Kimberley (after which the rock is named), and in the Yakutia area. of Siberia.

Kinetic effect. A chemical effect that depends on reaction rate rather than on thermodyamics. For example, diamond is thermodynamically less stable than graphite; its apparent stability depends on the vanishingly slow rate at which it is converted. Overpotential in electrolytic cells is another example of a kinetic effect. **Kinetic isotope effects** are changes in reaction rates produced by isotope substitution. For example, if the slow step in a chemical reaction is sthe breaking of a C-H bond, the rate for the deuterated compound would be slightly lower because of the lower vibrational frequency of the C-D bond. Such effects are used in investigatng the mechanisms of chemical reactions.

Kinetics. The branch of physical chemistry conc-erned with measuring and studying the rates of chemical reactions. The main aim of chemical kinetics is to determine the mechanism of reactions by studying the rate under different conditions (temperature, pressure, etc.).

Kinetic Energy. Energy that matter processes by virtue of its motion.

Kinetic-molecular Theory. A theory, that attempts to explain macroscopic observations on gases in microscopic observations on gases in microscopic observations on gases in microscopic or molecular terms.

Kipp's apparatus. A laboratory apparatus for making a gas by the reaction of a solid with a liquid (e.g. the reaction of hydrochloric acid with iron sulphide to give hydrogen sulphide). It consists of three interconnected glass globes arranged vertically, with the solid in the middle globe. The upper and lower globes are connected by a tube and contain the liquid. The middle globe has a tube with a tap for drawing off gas. When the tap is closed, pressure of gas forces the liquid down in the bottom reservoir and up into the top, and reaction does not occur. When the tap is opened, the release in pre-sure allows the liquid to rise into the middle globe, where it reacts with the solid. It is named after Petrus Kipp (1808-64).

Kirchoff's rules. 1) At any junction point, the sum of the currents entering the junction must equal the sum of the currents leaving the junction.

2) The sum of the changes in potential around any closed path of a circuit must be zero.

Kjeldahl method. Oxidize a sample to turn nitrogen gas to ammonium ions; used to determine the amount of nitrogen in a sample.

Klystron. Microwave generator.

Knoop hardness. A static measure of material hardness based on the size of impression made in the material with a pyramidal diamond indenter under specific conditions.

Knot theory. Abranch of mathematics used to classify knots and entanglements. Knot theory has applications to the study of the properties of polymers and the statistical mechanics of certain models of phase transitions.

Kohlrausch's law. If a salt is dissolved in water, the conductivity of the (dilute) solution is the sum of two values-one depending on the positive ions and the other on the negative ions. The law, which depends on the in-depedent migration of ions, was deduced experimentally by Friedrich Kohlrausch.

Koopmans theorem. The principle that the ionization energy of a molecule is equal to the orbital energy of the ejected electron. It is the basis of the interpretation of spectra in photoelectron spectroscopy. Koopmans theorem is an approximation in that it ignores any reorganization of electrons in the ion formed. It is named after the Dutch mathematician and economist Tjalling Charles Koopmans (1910-85).

Kovar. A tradename for an alloy of iron, cobalt, and nickel with an expansivity similar to that of glass. It is therefore used in making glass-to metal seals, especially in circumstances in which a temperature variation can be excepted.

Kronecker delta. When you take the integral over all space of a wavefunction and its complex conjugate, you get this. If it is equal to one, the wavefunctions are the same.

KRS-5. Thallium bromoiodide.

Kupfer nickel. A naturally occurring form of nickel arsenide, NiAs; an important ore of nickel.

L

Labile. Describing a chemical compound in which certain atoms or groups can easily be replaced by other atoms or groups. The term is appiled to coordinaion complexes in which ligands can easily be replaced by other ligands in an equilibrium reaction.

Lactams. Organic compounds containing a ring of atoms in which the group -NH.CO.- forms part of the ring. Lactams can be formed by reaction of an $-NH_2$ group in one part of a molecule with a -COOH group in the other to give cyclic amide. They can exist in an alternative tautomeric form, the lactim form, in which the hydrogen atom in the nitrogen has migrated to the oxygen of the carbonyl to give -N=C(OH). The pyrimidine base uracil is an example of a lactam.

Lactose (milk sugar). A sugar comprising one glucose molecule linked to a galactose molecule. Lactose is manufactured by the mammary gland and occurs only in milk. For example, cow's milk contains about 4.7% lactose. It is less sweet than sucrose (cane sugar).

Ladenburg benzene. An structure for benzene proposed by Albert Ladenburg (1842-1911), in which the six carbon atoms were arran-ged at the corners of a triangular prism and linked by single bonds to each other and to the six hydrogen atoms.

Laevorotatory. Designating a chemical compound that rotates the plane of planepiolarized light to the left (anticlockwise for someone facing the oncoming radiation).

LAH. Lithium aluminium hydride.

Lake. A pigment made by combining an organic dyestuff with an inorganic compound (usually an oxide, hydroxide, or salt). Absorption of the organic compound on the inorganic substrate yields a coloured complex, as in the combination of a dyestuff with a mordant. Lakes are used in paints and printing inks.

Lambertian radiator. When a light emitted from a source or scattered from a surface has a radiance that is independant of viewing angle.

Lamb formula. Used to find the shielding constants for nuclei.

Lamb shift. A small energy difference between two levels ($^2S_{1/2}$ and $^2P_{1/2}$) in the hydrogen spectrum. The shift results from the quantum interaction between the at-omic electrion and the electromagnetic radiation. It was first explained by Willis Eugene Lamb.

Lamellar solids. Solid substances in which the crystal structure has distinct layers (i.e. has a layer lattice). The micas are an example of this type of compoumd. Intercalation compounds are lamellar compounds formed by interposition of atoms, ions, etc., between the layers of an existing element or compou-nd. For example, graphite is a lamellar solid. With strong oxidizing agents (e.g. a mixture of concentrated sulp-huric and nitric acids) it for-ms a nonstoichiometric 'graphitic oxide', which is an intercalation compound having oxygen atoms between the layer of carbon atoms. Substances of this type are called graphite compounds.

Laminar flow. When the neighboring layers of a moving liquid slide by each other smoothly.

Lamp black. A finely divided (microcrystalline) form of carbon made by burning organic compounds in insufficient oxygen. It is used as a black pigment and filler.

Landau levels. The energy levels found by quantum mechanics of free electrons in a uniform magnetic field. These energy levels, named after the Soviet Physicist Lev Davidovich Landau (1908-68), who analysed the problem in 1930, have discrete values, which are integer multiples of heB/m, where h is the Planck constant, e is the charge of the electron, m is the massof the electron, and B is the magnetic flux density. Each Landau level is a highly degenerate level, with each level being filled by 2eB/h, where the factor 2 is due to the spin of the electron.

Lande interval rule. A rule used in interpreting atomic spectra stating that if the spin-orbit coupling is weak in a given multiplet, the energy differences between multiplet, the energy differences between two successive J levels (where J is the total resultant angular momentum of the coupled electrons) are proportional to the larger of the two values of J. The rule was stated by the German-born US physicist Alfred Lande (1888-1975) in 1923. It can be deduced from the quatum theory of angular momentum. In addition to assuming Russell Saunders coupling, the Lande interval rule assumes that the interactions between spin magneti moments can be ignored, an assumption that is not correct for very light atoms, such as helium. Thus the Lande interval rule is best obeyed by atoms with medium atomic numbers.

Langmuir-Blodgett film. Lipid bilayer sorts of films. They can be made of any size and almost any thickness. They are plated on solid surfaces by taking these surfaces and dipping them into a container which has a liquid with the film floating on top.

Langmuir-Hinshelwood mechanism. A possible me-chanism for a bimolecular process catalyzed at a solid surface. It is assumed that two molecules are absorbed on adjacent sites and that a reaction takes place via an activated complex on the surface to yield the products of the reaction. This mechanism was suggested by the US chemist Irving Langmuir (1881-1957) in 1921 and developed by the British chemist Sir Cyril Hinshel-wood (1897-1967) in 1926. Some bimolecular reactions at surfaces are in agreement with the predictions of this model.

Langmuir-Rideal mechanism. A possible mechanism for a bimolecular process catalyzed at a solid surface. It is envisaged that one of the molecules is absorbed and then reacts with a second molecule that is not absorbed. This mechanism was suggested by the US chemist irving Langmuir (1881-1957) in 1921 and developed by the British chemist Sir Eric Rideal in 1939. The Langmuir Rideal mechanism is not common but cerain reactions involving hydrogen atoms probably occur by this mechanism.

Lanolin. An emulsion of purified wool fat in water, containing cholesterol and certain terpene alcohols and esters. it is used in cosmetics.

Lanthanides. Elements 58 to 71 (after lanthanum)

Lanthanide Contraction. A decrease in the radii of the elements following the lanthanides compared to what would be expected if there were no f-transition metals.

Lapis lazuli. A blue rock that is widely used as a semiprecious stone and for ornamental purposes. It is composed chiefly of the deep blue mineral **lazurite** embeded in a matrix of white calcite and usually also contains small specks of pyrite. It occurs in onoly a few places in crystalline limestones as a contact metamorphic mineral. The chief source is Afghanistan; Lapis lazuli also occurs near Lake Baikal in Siberia and in Chile. It was formerly used to make the artists 'pigment ultramarine.

Laporte selection rule. A selecton rule in atomic spectra stating that spectral lines associated eith electric-dipole radiation must arise from transitions between states of opposite parity. The Laporte selection rule was discovered by O, Laporte in 1924 and was explained by the application of group theory to the quantum mechanics of atoms. In the case of magnetic-dipole and quadrupole radiation the selection rule for spectral rule, i.e. transitions are only allowed between states of the same parity in these cases.

Larmour frequency. Precessional angular velocity of an atom. Equal to the product of the magnetogyric ratio and strength of the applied magnetic field.

Laser desorption mass spectrometry (LDMS). When you take a sample and hit it with a laser, you send the particles that come flying off and send them into a mass-spec.

Laser spectroscopy. Spectroscopy that makes use of lasers. The beams of coherent monochromatic radiation produced by lasers have several significant advantages compared with other spectroscopic tecniques, particularly in those that employ the Raman effect.

Lassa igne's test. A method of testing for the presence of a halogen, nitrogen, or sulphur in an organic compound. A sample is heated in a test tube with a pellet of sodium. The hot tube is dropped into pure water and the fragments ground up in a mortar. The presence of a halogen (now in the form of a sodium halide) is detected by precipitation with silver nitrate solution. Nitrogen is revealed by the formation of a precipitation of Prussian blue on heating part of the solution with iron(II) sulphate solution containg hydrochloric acid and a trace of iron(III) ions. Lead ethanoate of sodium nitroprusside gives a precipitate with any sulphur present.

Laser threshold damage level (LDT level). The intensity at which a laser will damage a surface; coated surfaces have a lower LDT level than uncoated surfaces. My dad did a lot of research on stuff like this.

Latex. Natural rubber as it is obtained from a rubber tree or any stable suspension in water of a similar synthetic polymer. Synthetic latexes are used to make articles from rubber or plastics by such techniques as dipping (rubber gloves), spreading (waterproof cloth), and electrodeposition (plastic-coated metal). They are also employed in paints and adhesives.

Lattice. The regular arrangement of atoms, ions, or molecules in a crystalline solid.

Lattice energy. A measure of the stability of a crystal lattice, given by the energy that would be released per mole if atoms, ions, or molecules of the crystal were brought together form infinite distances apart of form the lattice.

Latent heats. The heats of fusion and evaporation.

Lateral magnification. The height of an image divided by the height of the object.

Lattice energy. The energy required to separate completely the ions in an ionic solid.

Law of Combining Volumes (Gay-Lussac's Law). At constant temperature and pressure, the volumes of reacting gases (and any gaseous products) can be expressed as ratios of small whole numbers;

Law of Conservation of Energy. Energy cannot be created or destroyed; it may be changed from one form to another.

Law of Conservation of Matter. There is no detectable change in the quantity of matter during an ordinary chemical reaction.

Law of Conservation of Matter and Energy. The total amount of matter and energy available in the universe is fixed.

Law of Definite Proportions (Law of Constant Composition). Different samples of a pure compound always contain the same elements in the same proportions by mass.

Law of Partial Pressures (Dalton's Law). The total pressure exerted by a mixature of gases is the sum of the partial pressures of the individual gases.

Law of octaves. An attempt at classifying elements made by John Newlands (1837-98) in 1863. He arranged 56 elements in order of increasing atomic mass in groups of eight, pointing out that each element resembled the element eight places from it in the list. He drew scale. **Ne-wlands octaves** were groups of similar elements distinguished in this way: e.g. oxygen and sulphur; nitrogen and phosphorus; and fluorine, chlorine, bromine, and iodine. In some cases it was necessary to put two elements in the same position. The proposal was rejected at the time.

Lawrencium. Symbol Lr. A radioactive metallic transuranic element belonging to the actinoids; a.n. 103; mass number of the first discovered isotope 257 (half-life 8 seconds). A number of very short-lived isotopes have now been synthesized. The element was identified by Albert Ghiorso and associates in 1961. It was named after E.O. Lawrence (1901-58).

Law of universal gravitation. Every particle attracts every other particle with a force that is proportional to the product of the masses and inversely proportional to the square of the distance between them.

Layer lattice. A crystal structure in which the atoms are chemically bonded in plane layers, with relatively weak forces between atoms in adjacent layers. Graphite and micas are examples of substances having layer lattices (i.e. they are lamellar solids).

Leaching. Extraction of so-luble components of a solid mixture by percolating a solvent through it.

Lead Storage Battery. Secondary voltaic cell used in most automobiles.

Lead carbonate. A white solid, $PbCO_3$, insoluble in water, rhombic; r.d. 6.6.It occurs as the mineral cerussite, which is isomorphous with aragonite and may be prepared in the laboratory by the addition of cold ammonium carbonate solution to a cold solution of a lead(II) salt (acetate or nitrate). It decomposes at 315°C to lead (II) oxide and carbon dioxide.

Lead-chamber process. An obsolete method of making sulphuric acid by the catalytic oxidation of sulphur dioxide with air using a potassium nitrate catalyst in water. The process was carried out in lead containers (which was expensive) and only produced dilute acid. It was replaced in 1876 by the contact process.

Lead(IV) ethanoate (lead tetra acetate). A colourless solid, $Pb(CH_3COO)_4$, which decomposes in water and is soluble in pure ethanoic acid; monoclinic: r.d. 2.228: m.p. 175°C. It may be prepared by dissolving dilead(II) lead(IV) oxide in warm ethanoic acid. In solution it behaves essentially as a covalent compound (no measurable conductivity) in contrast to the lead(II) salt, wh-ich is a weak electrolyte.

Lead(II) sulphide. A black crystalline solid PbS, which is insolble in water; r.d. 7.5; m.p. 1114°C. It occurs naturally as the metallic-looking mineral galena (the principal ore of lead). It may be prepared in the laboratory by the reaction of hydrogen sulphide with soluble lead(II) salts. Lead(II) sulphide has been used as an electrical rectifier.

Leakage current. A current that travels along an unintended path.

Leclanche Cell. A common type of dry cell.

Lectin. Any of a group of proteins, derived from plants, that can bind to specific oilgosaccharides on the surface of cells, causing the cells to clump together. Lectins can be used to identify mutant cells in cell cultures and to determine blood groups as they can cause the agglutination of red blood cells. Lectins are found in seeds of legumes and in other tissues, in which they are thought to act as a toxin.

LEED. Low-energy electron diffraction; can be used to investigate surface structures.

Le Chatelier's Principle. States that a system at equilibrium, or striving to attain equilibrium, responds in such a way as to counteract any stress placed upon it.

If a stress (change of conditions) is applied to a system at equilibrium, the system shifts in the direction that reduces stress.

Length contraction. The idea that the length of an object is measured to be shorter when it is moving than when it is at rest. A consequence of relativity.

Lenz's law. An induced emf always gives rise to a current whose magnetic field opposes the original change in magnetic flux.

Leucomalachite green test. A presumptive test for blood. The reagent is the dye leucomalachite green dissolved in water along with sodium perborate ($NaBO_3$). A blue green colour indicates a positive result.

Leveling Effect. Effect by which all acids stronger than the acid that is characteristic of the solvent react with solvent to produce that acid; similar statement applies to bases. The strongest acid (base) that can exist in a given solvent is the acid (base) characteristic of the solvent.

Levorotatory. Refers to an optically active substance that rotates the plane of plane polarized light counterclockwise; also called levo.

Lewis, Gilbert Newton (1875-1946) US physical chemist who spent most of his career at Berkeley, California. His ideas on chemical bonding were extremely influential, and he introdu-ced the idea of a stable octet of electrons and of a covalent bond being a shared pair of electrons. He also introduced the concept of lewis acids and bases.

Lewis Acid. Any species that can accept a share in an electron pair.

Lewis Base. Any species that can make available a share in an electron pair.

Lewis Dot Formula (Electron Dot Formula). Representation of a molecule, ion or formula unit by showing atomic symbols and only outer shell electrons.

LDOS. Local density of states.

Liebermann's reaction. A method of testing for phe-nols. A small sample of the test substance and a crystal of sodium nitrite are dissolved inwarm sulphuric acid. The solution is then poured into excess aqueous alkali, when the formation of a bluegreen colour indicates the presence of a phenol.

Liebermann test. A presumptive test sometimes used for cocaine and morphine. The **Liebermann reagent** is a solution of potassium nitrite (KNO_2) in sulphuric acid. With morphine a black colour is produced cocaine gives a yellow colour.

Liebig, Justus von (1803-73) German organic chemist who worked at Gessen in Frankfurt. Liebig was the first to recognise that two different chemical compo-unds can have the same formula. He also developed a method of analysing organic compounds by burning then and weighing the carbon dioxide and water produced. With his students, he analy-sed many compounds and was extremely influential in the development of organic chemistry.

Liebig condenser. A laboratory condenser having a straigjt glass tube surrounded by a coaxial glass jacket th-rough which cooling water is passed. The device is named after the German organic chemist Justus von Liebig (1803-73).

Ligand. A Lewis base in a coordination compound.

Ligase. Any of a class of enzymes that catalyse the formation of covalent bonds using the energy released by the cleavage of ATP. Ligases are important in the synthesis and repair of many biological molecules, including DNA, and are used in genetic engineering to insert foreign DNA into cloning vectors.

Lignin. A complex organic polymer that is deposited within the cellulose of plant cell walls during secondary thickening, Lignification makes the walls woody and therefore rigid.

Limestone. A sedimentary rock that is composed lar-gely of carbonate minerals, especially carbonates of calcium and magnesium. Calcite and aragonite are the ch-ief minerals; dolomite is also present in the dolomitic limestones. There are many varieties of limestones but most are deposited in shallow water. **Organic limestones** (e.g. chalk) are fo-rmed of organisms; **precipitated limestones** include ooliths-spherical bodies formed by the precipitation of carbonate around a nucleus; and **clastic limestones** are derived from fragments of pre-existing calcareous rocks.

Limiting Reactant. Substance that stoichiometrically limits the amount of product(s) that can be formed.

Limonite. A generic term for a group of hydrous iron oxides, mostly amorphous. Goethite and haematite are important constituents, together with colloidal silica, clays, and manganese oxides. Limonite is formed by direct precipitation from marine or fresh water in shallow seas, lagoons, and bogs (thus it is often called **bog iron ore**) and by oxidation of iron-rich minerals. It is used as an ore of iron and as a pigment.

Linear Accelerator. A device used for accelerating charged particles along a straight line path.

Linear molecule. A molecule in which the atoms are in straight line, as in carbon dioxide, O=C=O. Linear molecules have only two rottional degrees of freedom.

Linear polarizer. Changes unpolarized light to polarized light.

Line notation. A notation system for writing the structures of a chemical compound as a string of letters, numbers, and symbols. Examples of line notation are *Wiswesser line notation (WLN), *SMILES, SYBYL line notation (SLN), *ROSDAL, and *InChl.

Line Spectrum. An atomic emission or absorption spectrum.

Linkage Isomers. Isomers in which a particular ligand bonds to a metal ion through different donor atoms.

Light pipe. A hollow cone with highly reflecting walls which collects light at one end and channels it through successive reflections to the other end. When the walls are changed to a highly absorptive material, it can be used as a light collector.

Linseed oil. A pale yellow oil pressed from fax seed. It contains a mixture of glycerides of fatty acids, including linoleic acid and linolenic acid. It is a drying oil, used in oil paints, varnishes, linoleum, etc.

Lipase. An enzyme secreted by the pancreas and the glands of the small intestine of vertebrates that catalyses the breakdown of fats into fatty acids and glycerol.

Lipid bilayer. The arrangement of lipid molecules in biological membranes, which takes the form of a do-uble sheet. Each lipid molecule comprises a hydrophilic 'head' (having a high af-finity for water) and a hydrophobic 'tail' (having a low affinity for water). In the lipid bilayer the molecules are aligned so that their hydrophilic heads face outwards, forming the outer and inner surface of the membrane, while the hydrophobic tails face inwards, away from the external aqueous environment.

Lipoic acid. A vitamin of the vitamin B complex. It is one of the coenzymes involved in the decarboxylation of pyruvate by the enzyme pyruvate dehydrogenase. Good sour-ces of lipoic acid include liver and yeast.

Lipolysis. The breakdown of storage lipids in living organisms. Most longterm energy reserves are in the form of triglycerides in fats and oils. When these are needed, e.g. during starvation., lipase enzymes convert the triglycerides into glycerol and the component fatty acids. These are then transported to tissues and oxidized to provide energy.

Lipowitz alloy. A low melting (70-74°C) alloy of bismuth (50%), lead (27%),tin (13%), and cadmium (10%).

Liquation. The separation of mixtures of solids by heating to a temperature at which lower-melting components liquefy.

Liquid. A phase of matter between that of crystalline solid and a gas. In a liquid, the large-scale three dimensional atomic (or ionic or molecular) regularity of the solid is absent but, on the other hand, so is the total disorganization of the gas. Although liquids have been studied for many years there is still no comprehensive theory of the liquid state. It is clear, however, from diff-raction studies that there is a short-range structural regularity extending over several molecular diameters. These bundles of ordered atoms, molecules, or ions move about in relation to each other, enabling liquids to have almost fixed volumes, which adopt the shape of their containers.

Liquid Aerosol. Colloidal suspension of liquid in gas.

liquid crystal: a substance that has liquid-like long range disorder but some crystal-like aspects of short range order.

liquid crystal polymer. A polymer with a liquid-crystal structure, this being the most thermodynamically stable. Liquid-crystal polymers contain long rigid chains and combine strength with lightness. They are, however, difficult to produce commercially.

Lithium hydride. A white solid, LiH; cubic; r.d. 0.82; m.p. 680°C; decomposes at about 850°C. It is produced by direct combination of the elements at temperatures above 500°C. The bonding in lithium hydride is believed to be largely ionic; i.e. $Li^{+}H^{-}$ as supported by the fact that hydrogen is released from the anode on electrolysis of the molten salt. The compound reacts violently and exothermically with water to yield hydrogen and lithium hydrooxide. It is used as a reducing agent to prepare other hydrides and the ^{2}H isotopic compound, **lithium deuteride**, is particularly valuable for deuterating a range of organic compounds. Lithium hydride has also been used as a shielding material for thermal neutrons.

Lithium hydrogencarbonate. A compound, $LiHCO_3$, formed by the reaction of carbon dioxide with aqueous lithium carbonate and known only in solution. It has found medicinal uses similar to those of lithium carbonate and is sometimes included in proprietary mineral waters.

Lithium hydroxide. A white crystalline solid, LiOH, soluble in water, slig-htly soluble in ethanol and insoluble in ether. It is known as the monohydrate (monoclinic; r.d. 1.51) and in the anhydrous form (tetrago-nal, r.d.1.46; m.p. 450°C; decomposes at 924°C). The compound is made by reacting lime with lithium salts or lithium ores. Lithium hydro-xide is basic but has a closer resemblance to group 2 hydroxides than to the other group 1 hydroxides (an example of the first member of a periodic group having atypical properties).

Lithium oxide. A white crystalline compound, Li_2O; cubic; r.d. 2.01; m.p. 1700°C. It can be obtained from a number of lithium ores; the main uses are in lubricating greases, ceramics, glass and refractories, and as a flux in brazing and welding,

Lithium tetrahydroaluminate (III). A white or light grey powder, $LiAlH_4$; r.d. 0.917; decomposes at

125°C. It is prepared by the reaction of excess lithium hydride with aluminium ch-loride. The compound is soluble in ethoxyethane, reacts violenty with water to release hydrogen, and is widely used as a powerful reducing agent in organic chemistry. It should always be treated as a serious fire risk in storage.

Litmus. A water-soluble dye extracted from certain lichens. It turns red under acid conditions and blue under alkaline conditions, the colour change occurring over the pH range 4.5-8.3 (at 25°C). It is not suitable for titrations because of the wide range over which the colour cha-nges, but is used as a rough *indicator of acidity or alkalinity, both in solution and as litmus paper (absorbent paper soaked in litmus solution).

Litre. Symbol l. A unit of volume in the metric system regarded as a special name for the cubic decimetre. It was formerly defined as the volume of 1 kilogram of pure water at 4°C at standard pressure, which is equivalent to 1.000 028 dm^3.

Littrow prism. Used in laser cavities to select oscillation at a particular frequency. For a particular wavelength the refracted ray on entering the prism travels normally to the exit face. The exit face is reflectively coated so that this beam travels back along the original path.

Lixiviation. The separation of mixtures by dissolving soluble constituents in water.

Localization. The confinement of electrons to a particular atom in a molecule or to a particular chemical bond.

Localized bond. A chemical bond in which the electrons forming the bond remain between (or colse to) the linked atoms.

Lock-and-key mechanism. A mechanism proposed in 1890 by Emil Fischer (1852-1919) to explain binding between the active site of an enzyme and a substrate molecule. The active site was thought to have a fixed structure (the lock), which exactly matched the structure of a specific substrate (the key). Thus the enzyme and substrate interact to form an enzyme-substrate complex. The substrate is converted to products that no longer fit the active site and are therefore released., liberating the enzymes. Recent observations made by X-ray diffraction Studïes have shown that the active than the enzyme is more flexible than the lock-and-key theory would suggest.

London Forces. Very weak and very short-range attractive forces between short-lived temporary (induced) dipoles; also called dispersion Forces.

Lone pair. A pair of electrons having opposite spin in an orbital of an atom. For instance, in ammonia the nitrogen atom has five electrons, three of which are used in forming single bonds with hydrogen atoms. The other two occupy a filled atomic orbital and constitute a lone pair. The orbital containing these electrons is equivalent to a single bond (sigma orbital) in spatial orientation, accounting for the pyramidal shape of the molecule. In the water molecule, there are two lone pairs on the oxygen atom. In considering the shapes of molecules, repulsions between bonds and lone pairs can be taken into account.

Longitudinal relaxation time (T1). The time it takes after a pulse in NMR for the nuclei to get the same spin up/spin down ratio they had before the pulse. Also called spin-lattice relaxation.

Longitudinal wave. When the vibration of the particles in the medium move in the same direction as the motion of the wave, for example, a sound wave in air.

Long-range coupling. An NMR term, this describes the fact that sometimes you get spin-spin coupling between protons over distances longer than three bond lengths. This usually happens in highly conjugated systems, and the coupling constants are generally less than 3Hz.

Lone Pair. Pair of electrons residing on one atom and not shared by other atoms; unshared pair.

Lowering of vapour pressure. A reduction in the saturated vapour pressure of a pure liquid when a solute is introduced.If the solute is a solid of low vapour pressure of the liquid is proportional to the concentration of particles of solute; i.e.to the number of dissolved molecules or ions per unit volume. To a first approximation, it does not depend on the nature of the particles.

Lowest unoccupied molecular orbital. The orbital in a molecule that has the lo-west unoccupied energy level at the absolute zero of temperature. The lowest unoccupied molecular orbital and the highest occupied molecular orbital (HOMO) are the two frontier orbitals of the molecule.

Low Spin Complex. Crystal field designation for an inner orbital complex; contains electrons paired t2g orbitals before e.g. orbitals are occupied in octahedral complexes.

Lumen. Symbol lm. The Si unit of luminous flux equal to the flux emitted by a uniform point source of 1 candela in a solid angle of 1 steradian.

Luminol test. A presumptive test for blood. The reagent is a mixture of 3-aminopthalhydrazide, sodium carbonite, and sodium perbo-rate. When sprayed with the reagent, traces of blood (even old blood) emit a faint chemoluminescence.

Lux. Symbol lx. The Si unit of illuminance equal to the illumination produced by a luminous flux of 1 lumen distributed uniformly over a area of 1 square metre.

Lyophilic. Having an affinity for a solvent ('solvent-loving'; if the solvent is water the term **hydrophilic** is used).

Lyophobic. Lacking any affinity for a solvent ('solvent-hating'; if the solvent is water the term **hydrophobic** is used).

M

Macrolides. Compounds with atibiotic activity made by Streptomyces spp. and characterized by having a macrocyclic ring and often containing sugars. The macrolides, which include ERYTHROMYCIN, are most active against gram-positive bacteria.

Macromolecule. Molec-ules of high molecular weight (usually greater than 10000). Examples are proteins and some polymers. The term macromolecular is also used to describe structures such as that of diamond, which may be regarded as being one large molecule.

Magic agle spinning (MAS). Nuclear magnetic resonance technique for solids.

Magnesia. Magnesium oxide.

Magnesite, $MgCo_3$. A mineral form of magnesium carbonate used as a source of magnesium compounds and in the manufacture of refractories.

Magnesium alloys. Used on account of their light weight (e.g. aircraft industry) and for casting, forging, extrusion, etc.

Magnesium halides. Magnesium fluoride, MgF_2, is precipitated from aqueous solution. It has the rutile structure. Perovskites, e.g. $KMgF_3$, are known. The other halides are similar to the CHLORIDE although complexes are not known. They have layer lattices. Used in ceramics and glass.

Magnesium nitrate, $Mg(NO_3)_2$. Stable salt, Forms 9,6 and 2 hydrates. Hydrates dehydrate to basic salts but $Mg(NO_3)_2$ can be obtained by heating hydrates in nitric acid vapour.

Magnesium nitride, MG_3N_2. Formed from elements above 300°C (used to remove N_2). Hydrolysed to NH_3 and $Mg(OH)_2$. The amide is used as a polymerization catalyst.

Magnesium oxide. MgO. Occurs naturally as periclase. Prepared (m.p. 2640°C) by combustion of Mg in O_2 or ignition of $Mg(OH)_2$, $MgCO_3$ or $Mg(NO_3)_2$. Has NaCl structure. Hydrated (rate depends on whether previously ignited) to $Mg(OH)_2$. Used as a refractory, for heat insulation and as an antacid. Forms a peroxide which can give H_2O_2.

Magnesium perchlorate. $Mg(ClO_4)_2$. $6H_2O$. Formed from solution. The anhydrous material (anhydrone) is used for drying gases.

Magnesium silicates. Many silicates contain Mg^{2+}. Used medicinally to reduce stomach acidity and (after hydrolysis to active Sio_2) to remove toxins.

Magnet. Body possessing magnetism, either temporary or permanent.

Magnetic equivalence. When a group of nuclei are chemically equivalent and have identical spin-spin interactions.

Magnetic polarization of light. When a beam of plane polarized light is passed through a transparent medium which is placed in a magnetic field, the plane of polarization is rotated. This phenomenon is known as magnetic rotation, magnetic optical rotatory dispersion, the Faraday effect. The beam must be travelling in the same direction as the magnetic lines of force. Magnetic rotation is not connected with normal optical activity. The effect is shown by transparent substances whether or not they possess a centre of asymmetry.

Magnetic Quantum Number (mc). Quantum mechanical solution to a wave equation that designates the particular orbital within a given set (s, p, d, f) in which a electron resides.

Magnetogyric ratio. Tthis is an empirical factor with which you can find the magnetic moment of a nucleus with a non-zero magnetic moment. It cannot be calculated because there is not enough knowledge about how the nucleus works.

Magnetic separation. Separation techniques involving magnetic properties. Materials, e.g. minerals, can be separated into ferromagnetic, magnetic diamagnetic and non magnetic fractions. Separation is generally carried out on crushed material small particle size.

Magnetic tape. Used for recording information (sound, video, computer output, instrumental output). Consists of magnetic particles. Informatin is imprinted via electrical signals converted to magnetic fields, which in turn affect the magnetization of the tape particles.

Magnetite, Fe_3O_4. The mineral form of black Fe_3O_4 with the spinel structure. Used as an iron ore, a flux, a pigment for glazes and occasionally as a refractory material for lining furnaces for producing iron.

Magnetogyric ratio (Y). The proportionality factor between orbital angular momentum and magnetic moment.

Magneton. The fundamental quantum of magnetic moment.

Mahogany acids. The sulphonic acids remaining in the oil phase following the refining of lubricating oil by oleum or sulphuric acid.

Malachite. $Cu_2(OH)_2CO_3$. A native green hydrated carbonate of copper used as a decorative stone as it takes a high polish. Produced artificially (green verditer) from Na_2CO_3 and a solution of $CuSO_4$ and used as an artist's colour.

Malathion. Insecticide, acaricide, organophosphate derivative.

Malleability. The property which enables a body-particularly a metal-to be extended in all directions by hammering or rolling. The degree of malleability is gauged by the thinness of leaf orfoil which is possible to produce.

Malonic acid. $C_3H_4O_4$, $CH_2(C(O)OH)_2$. Colourless crystals; m.p. 136°C. Occurs in the mixed calcium salts obtained during the processing of sugar beet. Prepared from sodium cyanoethanoate with NaOH. Decomposes above 140°C to give ethanoic acid.

Malt. Cereal grains which have been allowed to sprout and then are heated. The sproting activates the enzyme systems, Barley, wheat, rye, oats, sorghum, corn and rice are converted to malt. Malt is used in brewing, in food additives and as animal feed.

Maltase. The enzyme found in malt that is specific in spliting maltose into two mo-lecles of glucose. Also found in the digestive systems of animals and in yeast.

Mancopper. Fungicide; thio-carbamate of Mn and Cu.

Mancozeb. Fungicide; dithiocarbamate of Mn and Zn.

Manganese alums. Derivatives of manganese (III) sulphate prepared by electrolytic oxidation of Mn(II).

Manganese borates. Rather indefinite materials precipitated from

Mn^{2+} solutions by borates and used as driers for inseed oil (catalysts for oxidation of the oil).

Manganese bromide, $MnBr_2$. Forms hydrates (anhydrous by heating hydrates in stream of HBr gas). Very soluble in water.

Manganese carbonate. $MnCO_3$. Occurs naturally as the mineral rhodochrosite, precipitated from Mn^{2+} solutions by used of $NaHCO_3$ solution saturated with CO_2. Normally precipitated as basic carbonates. Rapidly oxidized in air. Pigment..

Manganic salts. Generally manganese (III) salts.

Manganites. Generally applied to MANGANATES (IV).

Manganous salts. Maganese(II) derivatives.

Mannans. Polysaccharides made up a chain of mannos units. Occur in some cell walls.

Manometer. A two-armed barometer.

Manufactured gas. A general term for fuel gas obtained by a conversion process from solid or liquid hydrocarbons.

Marble. $CaCO_3$. A dense form of CALCIUM CARBONATE often used decoratively.

Margarine. Manufactured food product used as spread. Produced from vegetable oils; contains some polyunsaturated fats. About 20% is in aqueous phase (milk or water) together with food additives, vitamins and colour.

Marsh's test for arsenic. The arsenic containing specimen is converted to volatile AsH_3 which is decomposed to a brown stain on heating. Estimation is by comparison of stains. Sb reacts similarly but the Sb stain is not soluble in NaOCl.

Martensitic transformation. Transformations involving lattice shear and no diffuson.

Maser. A device which involves the laser principle but produces microwave radiation.

Masking. An analytical technique involving addition of a masking agent which stops interfering species participating in a reaction. Dem-asking is the reverse process, e.g. breakdown of a cyanide complex with acid.

Masking agent. A chemical added to a mixture which will block any impurity from affecting the chemical analysis; this is very handy if you have a transition metal ion which may interfere with the analysis of another transition metal ion.

Mass. A measure of the amount of matter in an object. Mass is usually measured in grams or kilograms.

Mass Action Expression. For a reversible reaction, aA + bB cC + dD the product of the concentrations of the products (species on the right), each raised to the power that corresponds to its coefficient in the balanced chemical equation, divided by the product of the concentrations of reactants (species on the left), each raised to the power that corresponds to its coefficient in the balanced chemical equation. At equilibrium the mass action expression is equal to K; at other times it is Q.[C]c[D]d [A]a[B]b = Q, or at equilibrium K

Mass Deficiency. The amount of matter that would be converted into energy if an atom were formed from constituent particles.

Mass Number. The sum of the numbers of protons and neutrons in an atom; an integer.

Mass Spectrometer. An instrument that measures the charge-to-mass ratio of charged particles.

For further information see Mass Spectrometry.

Mass Spectrum. The results obtained from a mass spectrometer are called mass spectra. They consist of ions of varying intensity at different (m/e) ratios and are recorded graphically or as computer output. For elements the individual lines correspond to different isotopes. For compounds individual lines may be due to the presence of isotopic species, fragmentation of the molecule or ionization of the parent species in the mass spectrometer.

Match. Practical method of producing flame. The usual method of flame production is a friction-initiated reaction between potassium chlorate and red phosphorous. The active materials are in a glue matrix and a glass powder is often used in the striker. The match may be wood or cardboard.

Matte. The indefinite mixture of artificial sulphides produced by a smelting operation.

Matter. Anything that has mass and occupies space.

Maxsorb. A form of high surface area activated carbon manufactured by Kansai Coke and Chemicals, Japan.

MCT. Mercury-cadmium-telluride detector. Used in doing IR spectroscopy.

Mean free path. The average distance traveled by a gas molecule between collisions.

Mechanical waves. Waves that travel in a material medium, such as water waves.

Mechanism. The sequence of steps by which reactants are converted into products.

Melting Point. The temperature at which liquid and solid coexist in equilibrium; also the freezing point.

Membrane. Porous materials which allow passage of solvent but impede passage of solids and larger molecles. Generally made of polymers. Used for purification cells, osmosis and separation.

Membrane cell. An electrolytic cell for the production of NaOH and Cl_2 from brine in which the anode and cathode are separated buy a membrane.

Membrane separation. Chemical separation through a membrane.

Menaquirines, menadione. Part of the vitamin A series.

Meniscus. The shape assumed by the surface of a liquid in a cylindrical container.

Mer isomer. The isomer of octahedral Ma_3b_3 in which the 3a ligands occupy one edge of the octahedron. In the fac isomer the 3a ligands occupy one face.

Mercarbam. Insecticide, acaricide, orgaophosphate derivative.

Mercaptals, $RR'C(SR'')_2$. Sulphur analogues of acetals. Oily liquids with upleasant odours. Formed by treating mercaptants with aldehydes or ketones. They are frequently employed in synthetic organic chemistry as PROTECTING GROUPS for the carbonyl group.

Mercury arc. An IR source that operates from 1-100 atmospheres. Good for producing IR radiation from 50-1400 microns.

Mercury diffusion pump. In this sort of device, mercury is boiled to produce a very high vacuum. The principle working here is that the heated mercury vapor is dragging the molecules of gas in the system, and getting them out of the place you are trying to maintain a high-vacuum.

Mercury Sulphide, HgS. Occurs naturally as red cinnabar but a metastable black form (zinc blende structure) may be formed by precipitation or by grinding Hg plusS. Dissolves in alkali suphide solutions to give thiomercurates. Used as a red pigment.

Merocyanine dyes. Polymethine dyestuffs comprising a nitrogen-containing heterocyclic system linked thr-ough a conjugated chain to an acidic ketomethylene heterocycle. Used as dyestuffs and as spectral sensitizers in photography.

Meso compounds. Compounds which contain tetrahedral atoms with four different groups but for which the whole molecule is achiral.

Meso ionic. A compound is defined as mesoionic if it is a heterocycle which cannot be represented satisfactority by any one covalent or polar structure, and possesses a sextet of electrons in association with all the atoms comprising the ring, e.g. SYDNONES and NITRON.

Mesophase. A phase intermediate between liquid and solid. May also be a smectic phase.

Metal. An element below and to the left of the stepwise division (metalloids) in the upper right corner of the periodic table; about 80% of the known elements are metals.

Metallic Bonding. Bonding within metals due to the electrical attraction of positively charges metal ions for mobile electrons that belong to the crystal as a whole.

Metallic Conduction. Conduction of electrical current through a metal or along a metallic surface.

Metalloids. Elements with properties intermediate between metals and nonmetals: B, Al, Si, Ge, As, Sb, Te, Po, and At.

Metallurgy. Refers to the overall processes by which metals are extracted from ores.

Metallofullerenes. Fullerenes which contain metal atoms or ions in them. Commonly, many fullerenes are produced with metal impurities because the metal acts as a catalyst for their formation; this is especially true for nanotubes.

Metal reductor column. A metal-filled column which is used to reduce metals in solution that are passed through it.

Metathesis Reactions. Reactions in which two compounds react to form two new compounds, with no changes in oxidation number. Reactions in which the ions of two compounds exchange partners.

Method of Initial Rates. Method of determining the rate-law expression by carrying out a reaction with different initial concentrations and analyzing the resultant changes in initial rates.

Mica. Potassium aluminosilicate.

Micelle. A term used to describe the colloidal particles in aggregation colloids, e.g. soaps and dyes. A micelle is a submicroscopic aggregate of molecules or polyelectrolyte particles with non-polar groups on the inside and hydrophillic groups on the outside.Micelles form only above the critical micelle concentration CMC.

Michaelis constant. An experimentally determined parameter inversely indicative of the affinity of an enzyme for its substrate. For a constant enzyme concentration, the Michaelis constant is that substrate concentration at which the rate of reaction is half its maximum rate. In general, the Michaelis constant is equivalent to the dissociation constant of the enzyme-substrate complex.

Michael reaction. Originally applied in a restricted sense to the base catalysed addition of active methylene compounds (e.g. malonic ester) to activated unsaturated systems, now used in a broader sense to define the conjugate of nucleophiles across double bonds.

Microgravimetry. When you go about trying to figure out the mass of something that doesn't change much in weight. Usually you need very sensitive equipment that costs a lot.

Microporous carbon. A form of carbon in which you see many small pores in the surface. Generally, the micropore walls consist of graphitic crystallites, causing them to have a hydrophobic nature.

Microscope. Magnifying instrument using visible light with relatively low magnification. Used chemically for identification, particularly of minerals (often by study of crystal form) and explosives. For higher magnification an electron microscope is used.

Microwaves. Electromagnetic radiation of frequency 10^{10} to 10^{12} Hz-frequencies 300 to 3 GHz. Absorption produces rotation in molecules and MICROWAVE SPECTRA are used to det-ermie precise molecular dimensions. Physical effects-heating used for food-polymerization and reaction can be induced by microwaves.

Microwaves spectroscopy. Electromagnetic frequencies 300-3 GHz. Spectra are obtained by passing a microwave beam, produced by a Klystron master or magnetron. The resolution of such a microwave spectrometer is vastly superior to the best infra-red instruments and wavelengths are measured to seven figures. The spectra correspond to transitions between rotational levels. Microwave spectroscopy is used for the identification of interstellar molecules

Mie scattering. Similar to Rayleigh scattering, except that it is dependant on the shape of the particles.

Milk. Obtained from mammals but particularly cows. Constitution: fat 4%, solids 12%, protein 3%, lactose 4.5%, vitamins, essential fatty acids, calcium, phosphate, iron.

Miller indices. The labels applied to planes in a crystal lattice. The reciprocal of the intercept on the axes.

Millipore filter. A water purification filter which has changeable filter cartridges. Depending on how pure the water needs to be, the filter sensitivity can be changed.

Mineral colours. Inorganic pigments (prussian blue, chrome yellow, iron buff, etc.), Once used extensively when precipitated within fibres, now mainly used for colouring paints, papers, plastics.

Mineral dressing (ore dressing). Concentration of the valuable constituents of a mineral by application of purely physical processes. Techniques in use include dense media separation, froth flotation, electrostatic and magnetic separation, and jigging.

Mirex. Former insecticide, carcinogenic, nolonger used.

Miscibility. The ability of one liquid to mix with (dissolve in) another liquid.

Mispickel. FeAsS. A whitish common mineral. A principal source of As.

Mixed conductor. A conductor in which both ionic migration and electrons or positive holes in the materials is responsible for current flow.

Mixed crystals. Crystals deposited together from a solution containing two substances (which are normally isomorphous). Also termed solid solutions.

Mixed indicator. The use of a mixture of two or more INDICATORS in order to sharpen the colour change or to restrict the pH range (etc.) over which the colour change occurs.

Mixed metal oxides. Compounds which are formally derived from oxides but contain two or more metal species often in an arbitrary ratio. generally formed by he-ating mixtures of the appropriate oxy-salts. The structures are determined Largely by close packing of the oxide ions and the metal atoms occupy octahedral or tetrahedral holes between the oxygen atoms. Very few mixed metal oxides contain discrete oxyanions.

Mixture. A sample of matter composed of two or more substances, each of which retains its identity and properties.

MLAR. Multi-layer antireflection coating.

Moderator. A substance such as hydrogen, deuterium, oxygen or paraffin capable of slowing fast nuetrons upon collision.

Modulus. A constant which expresses a force.

Molality. Concentration expressed as number of moles of solute per kilogram of solvent.

Molarity. Number of moles of solute per litre of solution.

Molar Solubility. Number of moles of a solute that dissolve to produce a litre of saturated solution.

Molecular Equation. Equation for a chemical reaction in which all formulas are written as if all substances existed as molecules; only complete formulas are used.

Molecular Formula. Formula that indicates the actual number of atoms present in a molecule of a molecular substance.

Molecular Geometry. The arrangement of atoms (not lone pairs of electrons) around a central atom of a molecule or polyatomic ion.

Molecular Orbital. An orbit resulting from overlap and mixing of atomic orbitals on different atoms. An MO belongs to the molecule as a whole.

Molecular Orbital Theory. A theory of chemical bonding based upon the postulated existence of molecular orbitals.

Molecular Weight. The mass of one molecule of a nonionic substance in atomic mass units.

Molecule. The smallest particle of an element or compound capable of a stable, independent existence.

Mole Fraction. The number of moles of a component of a mixture divided by the total number of moles in the mixture.

Monochromator. Light goes in, hits a dispersing element (such as a diffraction grating or prism) and some portion of light is allowed out the other side.

Monodisperse. When a polymer has only one molecular mass. They are typically generated by natural processes.

Monte Carlo method. A semi-empirical method for determining molecular dynamics of a system. What you do is to move the particles via a random method. Whether or not this new configuration is accepted depends on 1) If the PE is not greater than before the change, it is accepted. 2) If it is accepted, it is accepted in proportion to how much the potential change is for all the particles in the system.

Monoprotic Acid. Acid that can form only one hydronium ion per molecule; may be strong or weak.

Acid that contains one ionizable hydrogen atom per formula unit.

MOST. Korean Ministry of Science and Technology

Mother Nuclide. Nuclide that undergoes nuclear decay.

Moulding. The making of shaped objects in metals, plastics or other materials. Moulding can involve use of liquid material or may involve fashioning under pressure.

MTBE. Methyl t-butyl ether. Used as a gasoline additive but use is being curtailed.

Mucilages. Polysacchari-des, generally containing galacturonic acid, xylose and arabinose residues which swell in water.

Mucins. Glycoproteins fo-und in saliva, intestinal juices, etc.

Mucopeptides. Glyco-proteins, structural components of the cell walls of bacteria. They are insoluble polymers of N-acetyl-glucosamine and N-acetylmuramic acid.

Muffle furnaces. A furnace designed so that the charge does not come into contact with the hot combustion gases. This is effected by putting the charge in a retort or 'box' and heating the outside walls.

Mull. A finely ground powder dispersed in an oil for IR spectroscopy.

Mulliken symbols. The designators, arising from group theory, of electronic states of an ion often in a crystal field..A and B are singly degenerate, E doubly degenerate, T triply degenerate states. The D state of a free ion shows E and T states in a octahedral field.

Mullite. $Al_6Si_2O_{13}$. The stablest aluminium silicate, formed by heating other aluminosilicates, used in refractories and glasses.

Multicentre bond. A bond formed by a bonding molecular orbital between three or more atoms containing a single pair of electrons, Such bonds occur in, e.g. the boron hydrides.

Multimeter. A device that can measure voltage, current and resistance; may also be called a voltohm-meter (VOM).

Multiple bonding. Bonding between atoms in which there is overlap of orbitals in more than one region in space. The electrons may come equally from each atom or be derived from only one of the atoms (co-ordnate bond, back bonding).

Multiple-effect evaporator. In a simple evaporator, containing only one evaporator unit or effect, approximately 1 kg of steam is required to evaporate 1 kg of water. A multiple-effect evaporator contains several evaporator units in series, and the steam generated in one effect is fed to the calandria of the next, where it acts as a heating medium and prodces further evaporator. Thus 1 kg of steam is able to evaporate, very approximately, N kg of water, where N is the number of effects.

Multiple proportions, law of. Originally proposed by Dalton is 1804, the law states that when two elementrs A and B combine to form more than one compound, the weights of B which combine with a fixed weight of A are in the proporiton of small whole numbers. E.g. in dinitrogen oxide, nitrogen oxide and dinitrogen tetroxide the amounts of oxygen which combine with one part of nitrogen are in the proportion 1:2:4. This law is of very limited value as very any examples of non-stoichiometric compounds are known.

Multiplicity. Equal to 2S+1 b: A computer program that allows people to generate accurate structures for biomolecules.

Muriatic acid. An old name for hydrochloric acid, still occasionally used in industry. Potassium chloride is sometimes called 'muriate of potash'.

Muscone. $C_{16}H_{30}O$.A yellow liquid; b.p. 330°C. The perfume base obtained from the scent glands of the Tibetan musk deer; also available by synthesis.

Musk, artificial. Fixatives for perfumes Musk itself is used but many other species, e.g. nitroaromatics, teral-ones, are also used.

Mustard gas. $C_4H_8Cl_2S$, $(CH_2ClCH_2)_2S$. Colourless oily liquid with a faint garlic-like odour; m.p. 13-14°C, b.p. 215-217°C. Manufactured by treating S_2Cl_2 with ethene at 30-35°C. Decomposed violently by bleaching powder. It is a powerful violently by bleaching powder . It is powerful vesicant and poison, and causes conjunctivitis and temporary blindness. Agent in chemical walfare. Bistering agent.

Mutagens. Chemical substances or physical agents which raise the frequency of mutation greatly above the normal level. Many chemical mutagens are carcinogens.

Mutarotation. The change of optical activity of an optically active substance when it is dissolved in water, or some other solvent, and undergoes chemical charge.

Mycobutanil. Fungicide, triazole derivatives.

Myoglobin. The oxygen-carrying protein of vertebrate muscle. Myoglobin is used by muscle as a rapidly available source of oxygen.

N

Nanoparticles. Small ordered particles formed by self-assembly.

Nanoscale materials. Materials of physical size of a few nanometres. Have exceptional and potentially useful properties, e.g. films of CaF_2 and BaF_2 of less than 20 nm have ionic conductivities up to 1000 times greater than in bulk.

Nanotube. A long cylindrical structure related to the fullerenes. The structure of these rods appears to be a stacked graphite ring structure on the outside, and a randomized graphitic crystal structure on the inside. Generally, these tubes form best at temperatures above 1200C, and not at all under 200C.

Napalm. The aluminium soap of NAPHTHENIC and PALMITIC acids used to get gasoline. The thickened gas-oline has been used for military flame throwers and incendiary bombs.

Naptha. A term used to describe SPECIAL BOILING POINT spirits but also used as a description of light distillate feedstock for gas or petrochemical manufacture. The boiling range is generally about 40-150°C. Used as solvent.

Naphthenes. Cyclo-alkanes; saturated hydrocarbons containing at least one closed ring of carbon atoms, e.g. cyclohexane. Also naphthalene.

Naphthenic acids. Carboxylic acids obtained from crude petroleum via the water-soluble sodium salts. Many are derivatives of cyclopentane. The sodium salts are important detergents and emulsifying agents, while many other salts have importance.

Naphthoic acids. Naphthalene carboxylic acids. Prepared by oxidization of methyl naphthalenes or from bromo derivatives via Grignard regents.

Naproanilide. Herbicide, alkanamide derivative.

Napropamide. Herbicde, alkanoate deriative.

Nascent. Beginning to develop, immature.

Nascent hydrogen. A term formerly used for hydrogen produced by electrolysis or chemical reaction and used in situ for reduction. The powerful reducing action is due to reaction at surfaces or to the formation of hydride species.

Native State. Refers to the occurrence of an element in an uncombined or free state in nature.

Natural gas. Gas obtained from underground accumulations which may or may not be directly associated with crude oil. Such gas would normally contain at least 90% methane and other low-boiling hydrocarbons, the remainder being nitrogen and carbon dioxide. When natural gas is associated with crude oil it frequently contains appreciable amounts of higher hydrocarbons, pentanes, hexanes, etc., and is referred to as wet gas. used as a fuel and raw material.

Natural Radioactivity. Spontaneous decomposition of an atom.

Nd:YAG laser. A laser with a Nd/ Yttrium aluminum garnet rod.

Near infrared. Region of the electromagnetic spectrum corresponding to electronic and vibrational transitions.

Nebulizer. A way of producing an aerosol for AAS.

Neburon. Herbicide, urea derivative.

Neel point. The temperature above which magnetic susceptibility becomes normal.

Neel temperature. Where antiferromagnetic transitions occur.

Negative adsorption. When adsorption at a surface occurs from a solution the concentration of some components may be higher at the surface than in the bulk, whist with other components the concentration will necessarily be less at the surface than in the bulk. These latter components are said to undergo negative adsorption. According to the Gibb's adsorption isotherm any solute which increases the interfacial tension of the system will be negatively adsorbed, e.g. the negative adsorption of sodium chloride at the air/water interface, which has been confirmed experiment-ally.

Neighbouring group effect. Effect or reactivity or spectra attributed to neighbouring groups; either steric or electronic.

Nematocide. A substance for reducing numbers of worm-like species.

Nephelometry. A method of quantitative analysis which involves the spectrophot-ometic estimation of the scattering of the light by coloidal suspension of a precipitate.

Nernst Equation. Corrects standard electrode potentials for nonstandard conditions.

Nernst glower. Produces IR light to 15 microns. A hollow rod about three centimeters long and one millimeter diameter made from ZrO2 and Y2O3 mixed with CeO2 or ThO2. Operated at temperatures from 1500-2000K.

Nernst heat theorem. Entropy change of a transformation approaches zero as the temperature approaches zero.

Nessler's reagent. An alkaline solution of HgI_2 in KI used for detecting and estimating amonia (brown colour or precipitate formed).

Nessler tubes. Cylinders of thin glass, generally gradu-ated, used for comparing tubidities and colours of solutions.

Net Ionic Equation. Equation that results from canceling spectator ions and eliminating brackets from a total ionic equation.

Neutralization. The reaction of an acid with a base to form a salt and water. Usually, the reaction of hydrogen ions with hydrogen ions to form water molecules.

Neutral spirits. Distillate from ethanolic solutions containing >95% ethanol (>190 proof), used for blending.

Neutrino. A particle with no charge or mass that is given off during beta decay.

Neutron. A neutral subatomic particle having a mass of 1.0087 amu.

Neutron activation analysis (NAA). Method for determination of trace concentrations by neutron capture followed by study of induced radioactivity.

Neutron diffraction. Met-hod of structure analysis using a beam of neutrons.

Neutron scattering. Determination of structure using a beam of neutrons.

Newton. Kg m/second squared; unit of force.

Newton's rings. When a curved glass surface is placed in contact with a flat glass surface, a series of concentric rings is observed when illuminated from above with monochromatic light. This is caused by the reflection of light from the surfaces, giving constructive and destructive interference. This phenomena can be used to test whether or not a lens is properly ground.

Neville-Winther acid. The trivial name given to 4-hydroxy-1-naphthalene sulpho-nic acid.

Nicin. Small peptide used as a food preservative. Also has anti-microbial properties. Vitamin cofactor.

Nickel alloys. Have corrosion and scaling resistance but are expensive and so are confined to specialized applications. Examples are monel, hastelloy, nichrome, inconel, nimonics, perma-lloy, invar, nilo.

Nickel arsenide. NiAs. An importance structural type, the As is hcp with the Ni in octahedral holes and the As in trigonal prismatic co-ordination. This structure is ad-opted by, e.g: CoTe, CrSb, FeS, NbS.

Nickel carbonyl. $Ni(CO)_4$. M.p.- 25°C , b.p. 43°C. Toxic material prepared Ni plus CO at less than 100°C. Decomposes to pure Ni at higher temperature (Mond process for purifying Ni). Forms extensive ranges of sustituted derivtives including some cluster-carbonyl derivatives. used in synthesis and coatings.

Nickel-cadmium cell (Nicad battery). A dry cell in which the anode is Cd, the cathode is NiO2, and the electrolyte is basic.

Nickel chloride. $NiCl_2$. Forms hydrates with octahedral nickel. Complex chlorides, e.g. blue $[NiCl_4)^{2-}$ (fo-rmed in ethanol), are known.

Nickel dimethylglyoxime. $C_8H_{14}N_4NiO_4$. The normal form in which nickel is we-ighed in analysis. There is metal-metal bonding in the solid. The red complex is precipitated from alkaline solution.

Nickel hydroxide. Apple-green $Ni(OH)_2$ is formed by precipitation from aqueous slutions of Ni(II) salts. It is not amphoteric. Black Nio-OH ($Ni(NO_3)_2$ solution plus Br_2 in aqueous KOH) and related compounds are useful oxidizing agents.

Nickel oxides. Nickel(II) oxide, NiO, has the NaCl structure (heat on oxyacid salt or $Ni(OH)_2$). Dissolves in acids. Higher nickel oxides are not known although indefinite oxidehydroxides are formed.

Nicol prism. A calcite crystal, cut in such a way that only one of the refracted rays emerges. The emerging beam is plane polarized.

Nicotinamide adenine dinucleotide phosphate (NADP). An important coenzyme of the pyridine nucleotide class. The structure is that of NAD except that the adenosine has an additional phosphate group at the 2'-position. Involved in oxidization-reduction reactions.

Nicotines. $C_{10}H_{14}N_2$. Pure nicotine is a colourless liquid, b.p. 247°C, but darkness on exposure to air and light. Crude nicotine contains small amounts of other alkaloids, but (-)-nicotine is the princi pal component. Insecticide, usually manufactured from tobacco.

NIST. National Institute of Standards and Technology.

Nitrating acid. Generally a mixture of nitric and sulphuric acids used for commerical nitration, e.g. in the production of nitro compounds and NITROGLYCERIN.

Nitriding. A method of surface hardening steel by treating it in an atmosphere of NH_3 which gives a surface layer of nitride. The steel must contain specific alloying elements,e.g. Al, Cr, Mo.

Nitrile rubber. A copolymer of butadiene (55-80%) with propenenitrile, acrylonitrile. Polymerized in an emulsion. An oil-and solvent-resistant rubber used in sealing rings, gaskets, hoses, etc.

Nitrilotriacetic acid. $N(CH_2COOH)_3$. An important complexing (sequestering) agent. Forms particularly stable chelates with Zn^{2+}. Used in detergents, may be carcinogenic.

Nitrites. Salts containing the $[NO_2]^-$ ion. Salts of NITROUS ACID. Organic O-bonded derivative RONO. Metal complexes O- or N-bonded. Alkali nitrites are used as preservatives.

Nitroamines. Aromatic organic compounds containing both nitro and amino groups, usually prepared by partial reduction of polynitro compounds. They have importance as dyestuffs intermediates.

Nitrogenase. A complex of metal-containing proteins present in nitrogen-fixing bacteria and blue-green algae.

Nitrogenases. A class of enzymes found in bacteria within root nodules in some plants, which catalyze reactions by which N2 molecules from the air are converted to ammonia.

Nitrogen Cycle. The complex series of reactions by which nitrogen is slowly but continually recycled in the atmosphere, lithosphere and hydrosphere.

Nitrogen chlorides. Nitrogen trichloride, NCl_3, explosive oily liquid formed from Cl_2 and NH_4Cl solution. $NHCl_2$ and NH_2Cl (mono and dichloroamine) are also formed ClNO, NITROSYL chloride, NF_2Cl and $NFCl_2$ are also known.

Nitrogen-donors. Trip-osotive nitrogen compo-unds, particularly ammonia and its derivatives, form extensive series of complexes. Nitrosyl complexes are N-bonded $(NO_2)^-$ can be O-or N-bonded but the latter is more stable. Nitrates are O-bonded.

Nitrogen fixation. The use of atmospheric nitrogen in the manufacture of commercially important nitrogen compound, nitric acid, ammonia and ammonium salts, mainly used as fertilizers. Conversion to ammonia is effected by the Haber process, and nitric acid is obta-ined by oxidation of ammonia. Bacteria present in the roots of certain plants fix atmospheric nitrogen; so do Azotobacter, free-living soil micro-organisms. Some metal complexes interact with N_2 to give N_2 complexes which may be reduced to NH_3. The return of the fixed nitrogen to the atmosphere is DENITRIFICATION which involves nitrogen oxides.

Nitroso dyes. Dyestuffs containing nitroso-, NO, groups, generally quinone oximes prepared from nitrous acid and phenols or hydroxylamine on quinones. Acid dyes.

Nitrosonium tetrafluo-roborate. $NOBF_4$. White solid; NOF plus BF_3. It is very hydroscopic; reaction with water gives oxides of nitrogen, but reactions with alcohols give nitrito esters. Aromatic primary amine hydrogen chlorides give diazonium tetrafluoroborates wh-ich may be pyrolysed to give aromatic fluoro derivatives. Secondary aliphatic amines react with if to give nitrosoamines.

Nitrourea, $NH_2CONHNO_2$. Colourless crystalline solid; m.p. 158°C. Prepared by adding urea nitrate to concentrated sulphuric acid at 0°C and pouring the mixture on to ice. It is a strong acid, and forms salts. Not readily oxidized but can be detonated. Used in the preparation of semicarbazide.

Nitroxides. Compounds containing an R^1R^2NO group, Paramagnetic and widely used to study free radicals or the effect of spin-labelled species.

Noble Gases (Rare Gases). Elements of the periodic Group 0; also called rare gases; formerly called inert gases, He,Ne,Ar, Kr, Xe, Rn.

Nodal Plane. A region in which the probability of finding an electron is zero.

Nodes. Points of destructive interference between two waves.

Non-aqueous solution. A solution in which the solvent is not water but also may be organic (e.g. Et_2O) or inorganic (e.g. NH_3), protonic (e.g. EtOH) or non-protonic (e.g. BrF_3). Nonaqueous solvents may be self-ionized.

Non-aqueous titrations. Analytical procedures carried out in organic and other nonaqueous media because of insolubility of the reactants in water, or because some acids and bases cannot be titrated in water, Thus H_2S_4 and $HClO_4$ can be titrated as a mixture in methyl isobutyl ketone whilst amines can be titrated in 3-methylsulpholane.

Nonbonding Orbital. A molecular orbital derived only from an atomic orbital of one atom; lends neither stability nor instability to a molecule or ion when populated with electrons.

Nonconservative field. Describes the electric field produced by a changing magnetic field.

Nonelectrolyte. A substance whose aqueous solutions do not conduct electricity.

Nonpolar Bond. Covalent bond in which electron density is symmetrically distributed.

Non-stoiciometric compounds. Compounds in which the ratios of the numbers of atoms present do not follow simple integers. Many transition metal oxides, silicates, etc. are non-stoiciometric and the phenomenon is common. Non-stoichiometry has great effect on phy-sical properties, e.g. conductivity, catalysis.

Nonylphenol. $C_{15}H_{20}O$. Made phenol plus nonylenes (propene trimer), contains branched chains. Used to form phenolic resins (with aldehydes) and reaction with ethylene oxide to give surfactants.

Normal liqid. A liquid in which the molecules have no tendency to associate. The simpler liquid hydrocarbons approximate to this type, while water, ethanoic acid and alcohol are partially associated.

Normal solution. A solution which contains 1 g equivalent of the substances in 1 litre of solution. A normal solution must have the equivalent referred to a specific reaction but this is often not done. A normal solution may be indicated by the letter N, thus, N hydrochloric acid signifies a normal solution of hydrogen chloride (for titration with base). Use of molarity is preferred.

N-type semiconductor. Donor band that is full donates to another empty band, giving rise to conductivity.

Nuclear Binding Energy. Energy equivalent of the mass deficiency; energy released in the formation of an atom from the subatomic particles.

Nuclear Fission. The process in which a heavy nucleus splits into nuclei of intermediate masses and one or more protons are emitted.

Nuclear quadrupole coupling constant. A molecular parameter which provides a sensitive probe of electronic and surrounding molecular structure near some quadrupolar nucleus of interest.

Nuclear Reaction. Involves a change in the composition of a nucleus and can evolve or absorb an extraordinarily large amount of energy

Nuclear Reactor. A system in which controlled nuclear fisson reactions generate heat energy on a large scale, which is subsequently converted into electrical energy.

Nuclear quadrupole moment. The electric quadrupole moment of the nucleus. Affected by chemical environment and can be used to investigate structure (NQR spectroscopy).

Nuclear spin. The nucleus has a property with the characteristics of spin. The angular momentum of nuclear particles is expressed in units of.

Nucleons. Particles comprising the nucleus; protons and neutrons.

Nucleation. When a small particle or molecule spurs the condensation of a vapor or solid. Can occur with solid or liquid particles, or even ions.

Nucleus. The very small, very dense, positively charged center of an atom containing protons and neutrons, as well as other subatomic particles.

Nuclides. Refers to different atomic forms of all elements in contrast to ?isotopes?, which refer only to different atomic forms of a single element.

Nuclide Symbol. Symbol for an atom A/Z E, in which E is the symbol of an element, Z is its atomic number, and A is its mass number.

Nucleus, atomic. The nucleus of an atom is the small but massive internal core of the atom in which is concentrated the weight and positive charge. The weight, magnetic resonance and radioactive properties of the atom are associated with the nucl-eus, whereas chemical properties and u.v. and visible spectra are associated with the outer electrons. The nucleus is built up from sub-atomic particles.

Nujol. A high-boiling petroleum oil often used as a solvent for IR spectroscopy because it is relatively free of IR absorption bands.

O

Observable. A physically-measurable property of a system.

Occlusion. When a impurity is "surrounded" by the material of interest, but not actually incorporated into the crystal lattice.

Octahedral. A term used to describe molecules and polyatomic ions that have one atom in the center and six atoms at the corners of a octahedron.

Octane Number. Motor or aviation gasolines are designated for

KNOCK RATING by the arbitrary scale octane number. Iso-octane (2,2,4 trimethylpentane) is given a value of 100 and n-heptane a value of 0. The octane number of the gasoline is the percentage of iso-octane in a blend with n-hepthane which has the same anticlock performance as the gasoline under standard test conditions.

Octant rule. Empirical rule which relates the sign and the amplitude of COTTON EFFECT curves with the geometry and substitution of cyclohexanone derivatives and has been applied especially to steroids. It may also be extended to steroids. It may also be extended to other cyclic letones.

Octaves, law of Newlands found that when the elements were arranged in order of increasing atomic weights, the first known element was similar to the eighth knonw, the second to the ninth, the third to the tenth and so on. He termed this relationship the 'law of octaves.'

Octet Rule. Many representative elements attain at least a share of eight electrons in their valence shells when they form molecular or ionic compounds; there are some limitations.

Odd b: if g(-x)=-g(x), then g is an odd function.

Off-axis chromatic aberration. When chromatic aberration results in a difference in image size.

Ohm's law: V=I/R (voltage equals current/resistance).

Oil. Liquid triester of glycerol and unsaturated fatty acids.

Oil of cinnamon. Volatile oil from the bark of Cinnam-omum zeylanicum. The chief constituent of this oil is cinamic aldehyde, C_6H_s-CH:CH-CHO (50%). In the U.S. the rectified oil of cassia is known as oil of cinnamon. Used in flacouring, perfumery.

Oil of citronella. From Flowers of Cymbopogum (Andropogan) nardus. 67% geraniol. Used as perfume, insect repellant.

Oil of cloves. The volatile oil distilled from cloves consisting largely of eugenol. Used in confectionery and toothpaste.

Oil of capaiba. Contains caryophyilene and cadinene. Used in perfumery.

Oil of geranium. From pelargonium geranium. Contains geraniol esters. Used in perfumery, ointments, manufacture of rhodinol.

Oil of juniper. From berries of juniper. Contains pinene, cadinene,. Used in foodstuffs and perfumery.

Oil of lemon. From lemon peel. Contains limonene, terpinene, phellandrene, pinene. Used in flavouring and perfumery.

Oil of mustard-expressed. Expressed from mustard seeds. Contains glycerides. Used in manufacture of margarine. soap, and as a lubricant.

Oil of orange. From orange peel and flowers. Contains D-limonene. Used in flavouring and perfumery.

Oil of papper. From unripe fruit of black pepper. Contain L-phellandrene. Used as condiment.

Oil of pappermint. The oil distilled from the fresh flowering tops of Mentha pip-erita, containing about 50% of menthol together with menthyl esters and the ketone. MENTHONE. Mulled aromatic carminative. Used in flavouring.

Oil of sweet almond. Expressed from kernels of various species of prunus. Mainly glyceryl oleate. Used in perfumery, soaps, lubricants.

Oil of turpentine. From va-rious pines. Contains terp-enes. Used as a solvent for oils, resins, varnishes, paints.

Open Sextet. Refers to species that have only six electrons in the highest energy level of the central element (many Lewis acids).

Operator. A rule that transforms a given function into another function.

Opperman source. An IR source that consists of a ceramic tube with an internal noble metal heater. It requires no preheating.

Opiods. Natural or synthetic drugs exerting analgesic effects.

Opium. Dried latex which exudes from the unripe capsules of Papaver samniferum. It contains a large number of alkaloids, chief among which are MORPHINE, CODEINE and papaverine.

Oppenauer oxidation. The oxidation of secondary alcohols to ketones using aluminium tert-butoxide propanone. Reverse of the Meerwein-Ponndrof-Varley reduction.

Optical Activity. The rotation of plane polarized light by one of a pair of optical isomers.

Optic axis. Tthe direction in a birefringent crystal along which no splitting of the beam occurs.

Optical electrons. In general, only the outermost electrons in an atom are concerned in producing the emission or absorption of visible light. Such electrons are termed optical electrons.

Optical exaltation. An abnormal increase in the refractivity of an organic compound, over and above the additive amount to be expected from the bonds present, due to the presence of a system of conjugated dou-ble bonds.

Optical Isomers. Stereoisomers that differ only by being non-superimposable mirror images of each other, like right and left hands, also called enantiomers.

Orbital. Loosely used to describe the geometrical figure which describes the most probable location of an electron. More accurately an allowed energy level for electrons.

Orbital angular momentum. The total angular momentum of a set of electrons in an atom or ion. For filled and empty shells, L is zero.

Orbital eletron capture. Electron capture by the nucleus in which a proton forms a newtron and the atomic number decreases by one.

Orbital magnetic moment. The component of the magnetic moment of an atom or ion resulting from the motion of the electron aro-und the nucleus.

Orbital splitting. The raising of the degeneracy of a series of orbitals of equivalent energy. e.g. by placing in a CRYSTAL FIELD.

Ordinary ray. The beam that does not deviate upon being split by a birefringent crystal.

Order of reaction. The total power to which the concentration terms are raised in the mathematical equation which describes the variation of the rate of a reaction with concentration of reactants at a given temperature. For example, if in the reaction of two substances A and B the rate of reaction is proportional of the concentrations of each reactant, the reaction is said to be first order in A and in B and second order overall. The order may be other than unity and in some cases may be non-integral. It is an experimentally determined quantity which does not necessarily have any relationship to the actual number of molecules involved in the reaction since many reactions proceed in a series of steps. The order refers only to the slowest step.

Ore. A natural deposit containing a mineral of an element to be extracted.

Organic Chemistry. The chemistry of substances that contain carbon-hydrogen bonds.

Organochlorine insecticides. Highly active insecticides, formerly widely used. They field their way into the bodies of animals and insects and are stored, principally in the fat. The application of organochlorine insecticides is now widely restricted. Organochlorine compounds are produced by some lilies as antifungal compounds.

Organoelement compounds. Compounds of an element containing organic residues bonded directly to the element.

Organometalloids. Compounds containing a direct bond between one or more carbon atoms and one or more metalloid atoms.

Organosol. A collodial dispersion in which an organic dispersion medium in used. Specific names such as alcosol, benzosol may be used to indicate that the dispersion medium is alcohol or benzene. Name used for, e.g. cellulose nitrate, collodions, rubber solutions in toluene or naphtha.

Orgel diagrams. Simple graphs showing the relation between the energies of various electronic states and the crystal field splitting.

Orthorhombic system. The CRYSTAL SYSTEM with a 2-fold axis at the intersection of two planes of symmetry or perpendicular to two other 2-fold axes. A unit cell has three unequal axes at right angles.

Osazones. Organic compounds containing two (C=N-NHAr) groups on adjacent carbons. Formed by treating a-diketones, a-hydroxyaldehydes, hydroxyketones, aminoaldehydes or aminoketones with aryl-hydrazines. Sugars can be identified by their osazones, which have characteristic melting-points, formation times or crystal appearance.

Osmic acid. The name given to osmium tetraoxide and its solution in water. This solution contains free OsO_4. In alkaline solution $[OsO_4(OH)_2]^{2-}$ ions are pres-ent.

Osmiridium. Native or synthetic alloys of osmium (15-40%) and iridium (50-80%). It is used for special purposes in which a very hard and incorrodible material is required, such as the tips of fountain pen nibs and sparking points.

Osmium chemistry. The chemistry is similar to that of Ru but there is greater stability of the higher oxidations states (halides and oxides); oxidations states from +8 to 0 are known. $Os(CO)_s$ and some polymeric carbonyls are formed and the organometallic chemistry is similar to that of Fe. Os(III) and Os(II) (predominantly octahedral) form extensive series of complexes with N, P- and As- ligands. Osmium nitrosyls are very stable, as are nitrido derivatives.

Osmosis. The process by which solvent molecules pass through a semipermable membrane from a dilute solution into a more concentrated solution.

Osmotic Pressure. The hydrostatic pressure produced on the surface of a semip-ermable membrane by osmosis.

Ostwald dilution law. Variation of molar conductivity with concentration.

Ostwald Process. A process for the industrial production of nitrogen oxide and nitric acid from ammonia and oxygen.

Ostwald ripening. Coarsening in crystal structures; it is an inherent property of crystals at a solid-liquid interface. The coarsening and enarging of crystals at surfaces is driven by a thermodynamic driving force to reduce the surface to volume ratio; this in turn lowers the interfacial or line energy.

Ounce (oz). Non-S.I. unitof weight. Used chemically for platinum metals. 1 az=$3.1110*10^{-2}$ kg.

Outer Orbital Complex. Valence bond designation for a complex in which the metal ion utilizes d orbitals in the outermost (occupied) shell in hybridization.

Outer sphere complexes. Weak complexes in which there is minimal disturbance of the inner coordinated ligands. Postulated as the mechanism in many electron transfer reactions.

Ovalbumin (egg albumin). The chief polypeptide consitituent of white of egg. Used as foodstuff.

Overlap. The interaction of orbitals on different atoms in the same region of space.

Overtones. Weak vibrational absorption corresponding to multiples or adducts of fundamental frequencies.

Over-voltage. The excess potential, over and above that of the reversible electrode, that must be applied to an electrode for electrolysis to proceed at a measurable rate. E.g. at a platinized platinum electrode the evolution of hydrogen will occur at practically the reversible electrode potential. However, at a mercury electrode no hydrogen is envolved unit an over-voltage of approximately 1 volt is reached. Of great practical importance in process such as electroplating, electroanalysis, electro-reduction, polarography, etc. Overvoltage occurs because of irreversible processess at the electrode or depletion of the electrolyte close to the electrode.

Oxidase. Enzymes that participate in oxidation reactions.

Oxidation. An algebraic increase in the oxidation number; may correspond to a loss of electrons.

Oxidation Numbers. Arbitrary numbers that can be used as mechanical aids in writing formulas and balancing equations; for single-atom ions they correspond to the charge on the ion; more electronegative atoms are assigned negative oxidation numbers (also called Oxidation states).

Oxidation-reduction Reactions. Reactions in which oxidation and reduction occur; also called redox reactions.

Oxidative addition. Reaction in which there is direct addition to an element or multiple bond with increase in oxidation state. E.g. addition of Cl_2 to PCl_3 gives PCl_5.

Oxidative phosphorylation. The process occurring along the respiratory or ELECTRON TRANSPORT CHAIN by which ATP is generated through a series of coupled reactions from reduced coenzymes, such as NADH.

Oxide. A binary compound of oxygen.

Oxidized rubber. Produced by oxidation rubber with air in the presence of a catalyst. Can be vulcanized and chlorinated. Used for impregnation, electrical insulation and as an adhesive.

Oxidizing Agent. The substance that oxidizes another substance and is reduced.

Oximes. Organic compo-unds containing the group= N-OH united directly to a carbon atom.

Oxine. 8-hydroxyquinoline. Oxine copper fungicide.

Oxonium. A positive ion containing a central oxygen atom. The hydroxonium ion, H_3O^+, exists in aqueous sol-utions of acid, and solid salts containing this ion may be prepared. The trimethyloxonium, Me_3O^+, and triphenyloxonium, Ph_3O^+, ions and their derivatives are also known. Trialkyloxonium salts are strong alkylating agents for organic and inorganic nucleophiles.

Oxyazo dyes. Azo dyestuffs containing a hydroxyl group.

Oxycarboxin. Fungicide, amide derivative.

Oxygen carrier. A molecule which can react directly with molecular oxygen (to form a peroxide or susperoxide derivatives, a complex) and can subsequently use the oxygen in an oxidation reaction-generally of an organic substrate, e.g. hemoglobin.

Oxygen cathode. A platinum or gold electrode used in amperometry for measuring oxgen content by measuring the rate of cathodic reduction of O_2. The cathode is used with a reference electrode. Can use enzymes immobilized on the electrode to measure O_2 uptake. A Clark electrode is a typical oxygen electrode.

Oxygen-free high-conductivity copper (OFHC). A form of copper used frequently for instrument applications because of high purity, good conductivity and resistance to hydrogen embrittlement.

Oxymercuration. Addition of OH and HgO(O)CR to a multiple bond.

Oxytetratyclin. Widely used antibiotic.

Oxythallation. Thallium (III) salts oxidize a wide variety of organic substrates under mild conditions in alcohol, dilute acid or diglyme solution, Unstable organoth-allium derivatives are produced as intermediates.

Oxytocin. A polypeptide hormone secreted by the posterior lobe of the pitutary gland.

Ozokerite. A naturally occurring mineral wax which on refining yields a hard white wax known as CERESIN.

Ozone,O_3 Allotrope of oxygen, m.p.-193°C, b.p.-112°C, blue in colour. Pr-esent in upper atmosphere and absrobs u.v. radiation and hence protects earth's surface from excess u.v. radiation. Holes can be caused in the ozone layers because of the reaction of zone with species formed by, e.g. CFCs. Ozone is formed at ground level by interaction of nitrogen oxides. NO_x, with hydrocarbons. It is a respiratory irritant and can cause crop damage. Prepared by action of electric discharge on O_2 and can be separated from O_2 by fractionation. Hasbent molecule. Used for oxidation, sterilization and purification.

Ozonides. Products of the action of ozone on various classes unsaturated organic compounds. Prepared by passing ozonized air or oxygen into the unsaturated compound dissolved in a su-itable solvent. Thick oils with an unpleasant choking smell. Readily decompose, some by water or ethanoic acid and formerly used to establish the position of the double bond in the original unsaturatred compound. Inorganic ozonides, such as potassium ozonide, KO_3, also exist. These contain the O_3^- ion.

P

PAGE (Polyacrylamide gel electrophoresis). A type of electrophoresis used to determine the size and composition of proteins. Proteins are placed on a matrix of polyacrylamide gel and an electric field is applied. The protein molecules migrate towards the positive pole, the smaller molecules moving at a faster rate through the pores of the gel. The proteins are then detected by applying a stain.

PAH. Polyaromatic hydrocarbon.

Pairing. A favourable interaction of two electrons with opposite m , values in the same orbital.

Pairing Energy. Energy required to pair two electrons in the same orbital.

Palmitate. A salt or ester of palmitic acid.

Papain. A proteindigesting enzyme occurring in the fruit of the West indian papaya tree. It is used as a digestant and in the manufacture of meat tenderizers.

Para-1. Prefix designing a benzene compound in which two substituents are in the 1,4 positions, i.e. directly opposite each other, on the benzene ring. The abbreviation p- is used; for example, pxylene is 1,4 dimethylbenzene.

2. Prefix denoting the form of diatomic molecules in which the nuclei have opposite spins, e.g. parahydrogen.

Parallel spins. Neighbo-uring spining electrons in which the spins, and hence the magnetic moments, of the electrons are aligned in the same direction.

Paramagnetic. A paramagnetic material has unpaired electrons; when such a material which has molecules with permanent dipole moments is placed in an external field, they orient themselves. When there is no field, the molecules are randomly oriented.

Paramagnetism. Attraction toward a magnetic field, stronger than diamagnetism, but still weak compared to ferromagnetism.

Paraquat. Tradename for an organic herbicide used to control broad-leaved weeds and grasses. It is poisonous to humans, having toxic effects on the liver, lungs, and kidneys if ingested. Paraquat is not easily broken down and can persist in the environment absorbed to soil particles.

Parity operator. Replaces each cartesian coordinate with its negative.

Parrafins. Normal alkanes with no functionality and no branching.

Partially permeable membrane. A membrane that is permeable to the small molecules of water and certain solutes but does not allow the passage of large solute molecules. This term is preferred to semipermeable me-mbrane when describing biological membranes.

Partial Pressure. The pressure exerted by one gas in a mixture of gases.

Particulate matter (PM). Matter present as small particles. Particulate matter, also known as particulates, is produced as an airborne pollutant in many processes. It may be inorganic, e.g. silicate or caron, or organic, e.g. polyaromatic hydrcarbons (PAHs).

Particulate Matter. Fine divided solid particles suspended in polluted air.

Pascal. Newton/sq. meter.

Pascal. The *SI unit of pressure equal to one newton per square metre. It is named after the French mathematician Blaise Pascal.

Pascal's triangle. The diagram that gives the peak intensity ratios for NMR and ESR. It does have the appearance of a triangle, and each row has numbers which correspond to the sum of the numbers on top of it.

Passband. The primary wavelength interval of transmission of a gas filter.

Passive. Describing a solid that has reacted with another substance to from a protective layer, so that further reaction stops. The solid is said to have been rendered passive'. For example, aluminium reacts spontaneously with oxygen in air to form a thin layerof aluminium oxide, which prevents further oxidation. Similarly, pure iron forms a protective oxide layer with concentrated nitric acid and is not dissolved further.

Pauli, Wolfgang Ernst. (1900-58) Austrian-born Swiss physicist. After studying with Niels *Bohr and Max *Born, he taught at Heidelberg and, finally Zurich. His formulation in 1924 of the Pauli exclusion principle explained the electronic make-up of atoms. For, this work he was awarded the 1945 Nobel Prize for physics. In 1931 he predicted the existence of the neutrino.

Pauli Exclusion Principle. No two electrons in the same atom may have identical sets of four quantum numbers.

Pellicles. Beam-splitting mirrors made of high-tensile-strength polymer stretched over a flat metal surface.

Pencil angle. A half angle which describes the rays emanating from a point at the edge of an object.

Pentahydrate. A crystalline hydrate that has five moles of water per mole of compound.

Pentose. A sugar that has five carbon atoms per molecule.

Penta prisms. Deviate a ray of light by 90 degrees without inversion or reversion. Called penta prisms because they are pentagonal solids.

PES. Potential energy surface.

Pepsin. An enzyme that catalyses the breakdown of proteins to polypeptides in the vertebrate stomach. It is secreted as an inactive precursor, **pepsinogen.**

Peptide mapping. The techniqe of forming two-dimensional patterns of peptides (on paper or gel) by partial hydrolysis of a protein followed by electrophoresis and chromatography. The pe-ptide pattern produced is characteristic for a partiular protein and the technique can be used to separate a mixture of peptides.

Peptidoglycan. A macromolecule that is a component of the cell wall of bacteria; it is not found in eukaryotes. Consistingof chains of amino sugars (N-acetylgucosamine and N-acetylmuramic acid) linked to a tripeptide (of alanine, glutamic acid, and lysine or diaminopimelic acid), it confers strength and shape to the cell wall.

Per. Prefix indicating that a chemical compound contains an excess of an element, e.g. a peroxide.

Percentage Ionization. The percentage of the weak electrolyte that ionizes in a solution of given concentration.

Percent by Mass. 100% times the actual yield divided by theoretical yield.

Percent Composition. The mass percent of each element in a compound.

Percent Purity. The percent of a specified compound or element in an impure sample.

Pericyclic reaction. A type of concerted chemical reaction that proceeds through a cyclic conjugated transition state. Pericyclic reactions include *cheletropic reactions, some*cycloadditions, *sigmatropic reactions, and *electrocyclic reactions. They can be understood using frontier orbital theory or the *Woodward Hoffmann rules.

Period. The elements in a horizontal row of the periodic table.

Periodicity. Regular periodic variations of properties of elements with atomic number (and position in the periodic table).

Periodic Law. The properties of the elements are periodic functions of their atomic numbers.

Periodic Table. An arrangement of elements in order of increasing atomic numbers that also emphasizes periodicity.

Permalloys. A group of alloys of high magnetic permeability consisting of iron and nickel (usually 40-80%) often with small amounts of other elements (e.g. 3-5% molybdenum, copper, chromium, or tungsten) They are used in thin foils in electronic transforms, for magnetic shielding, and in computer memories.

Permanent gas. A gas, such as oxygen or nitrogen, that was formerly thought to be impossible to liquefy. A permanent gas is now regarded as one that cannot be liquefied by pressure alone at normal temperatures (i.e. a gas that has a critical temperature below room temperature).

Permutit. Tradename for a zeolite used for water softening.

Peroxide. A compound containing oxygen in the -1 oxidation state. Metal peroxides contain the peroxide ion, O_{22}^{-}

Persistent. Describing a pesticide or other pollutant that is not readily broke down and can persist for long periods, causing damage in the environment. For example, the herbicides *Paraquat and *DDT can persist in the soil for many years after their application.

Perspex. Tradename for a form of *polymethylmethacrylate.

Peta. Symbol P. A prefix used in the metric system to denote one thousand million million times.

Petrochemicals. Organic chemicals obtained from petroleum or natural gas.

Petroleum ether. A colourless volatile flammable mixture of hydrocarbons, mainly pentane and hexane. It oils in the range 30-70°C and is used as a solvent.

Petroleum jelly. A semi-solid mixture of hydrocarbons extracted from petroleum. It is used in skincare products and cosmetics, and as a lubricant. Petroleum is widely available under the tradename Vaseline.

Pewter. An alloy of lead and tin. It usually contains 63% tin; pewter tankards and food containers should have less than 35% of lead so that the lead remains in solid solution with the tin in the presence of weak acids in the food and drink. Copper is sometimes added to increase ductility and antimony is added if a hardalloy is required.

pH. Negative logarithm of the concentration (mol/L) of the $H_3O^+[H^+]$ ion; scale is commonly used over a range 0 to 14.

Phase. A homogenous part of a hetergenous system that is separated from other parts by a distinguishable boundary. A mixtureof ice and water is a two-phase system. A solution of salt in water is a single phase system.

Phase Diagram. Diagram that shows equilibrium temperature-pressure relationships for different phases of a substance.

Phase rule. For any system at equilibrium, the relationship P+F=C+2 holds, where P is the number of distinct phases, C the number of co-mponents, and F the number of degrees of freedom of the system. The relationship derived by Josiah Willard *Gibbs in 1876, is often called the **Gibbs phase rule.**

Phase velocity. The velocity at which the crests of a wave move.

Phenol. Hydrocarbon derivative containing an [OH] group bound to an aromatic raing.

Phenol-formaldehyde resin. A class of resins prod-uced by polymerizing phenols with formaldehyde using acid or basic octalysts. They are generally cross-linked thermosetting materials. Bakelite is the original example.

Phenolic resins. Synthetic resins made by copolymerizing phenols with aldehydes. *Phenol-formaldehyde resins are the commonest type.

Phenolphthalein. A dye used as an acid-base indicator. It is colourless below pH 8 and red above pH 9.6. It is used in titrations involving weak acids and strong bases. It is also used as a laxative.

Phenoxy resins. Thermoplastic materials made by condensation of phenols, used mainly for packaging.

Philips process. A process for making high-density polyethene by polymerizing ethene at high pressure and 150°C. The catalyst is chromium(III) oxide supported on silica and alumina.

Phonon. A lattice vibration.

Phonochemistry. The use of highfrequency sound (ultrasound, with a frequency greater than about 20 kHz) to induce or accelerate certain types of chemical reaction.

Phosphagen. A compound found in animal tissues that provides a reserve of chemical energy in the form of high-energy phosphate bonds. The most common phosphagens are creatine phosphate, occurring in vertebrate muscle and nerves, and arginine phosphate, found in most invertebrates. During tissue activity (e.g. muscle contraction) phos-phages give up their phosphate groups. thereby generating *ATP from ADP. The phosphagens are then re-formed when ATP is available.

Phosphodiester bond. The covalent bond that links a phosphate group and a sugar group, by means of a oxygen bridge, in the sugar-phosphate backbone of a nucleic acid molecule.

Phosphor bronze. An alloy of copper containing 4% to 10% of tin and 0.05% to 1% of phosphorous as a deoxidizing agent. It is used particularly for marine purposes and where it is exposed to heavy wear, as in gear wheels.

Phosphorescence. Spontaneous emission persists for a long time after the exciting radiation ceases. This long-lived relaxation arises from the fact that the transition being made here is a forbidden intersystem crossing.

Photoacoustic spectroscopy. A spectroscopic technique in which spectra of opaque materials, such as powders, are obtained by exposing the material to light that is modulated at acoustic frequencies. This produces a photoacoustic signal, the magnitude of which can be related to the ultraviolet of infrared absorption coefficient of the material.

Photoconductive detector. A change in number of incident photons causes a fluctuation in the number of free charge carriers in a semiconductor. Electrical conductivity is inversely proportional to the number of incident photons.

Photochemical Oxidants. Photochemically produced oxidizing agents capable of causing damage to plants and animals.

Photochemical reaction. A chemical reaction caused by light or ultraviolet radiation. The incident photons are absorbed by reactant molecules to give excited molecules or free radicals, which undergo further reaction.

Photochemical Smog. A brownish smog occurring in urban areas receiving large amounts of sunlight; caused by photochemical (light-induced) reactions among nitrogen oxides, hydrocarbons and other components of polluted air that produce photochemical oxidants.

Photochemistry. The bra-nch of chemistry concerned with photochemical reactions.

Photochromism. A change of colour occurring in certain substances when exposed to light. Photochromic materials are used in sunglasses that darken in bright sunlight.

Photoelastic effect: Sensitivity of the optical dielectric response to changes in density.

Photoelectric Effect. Emission of an electron from the surface of a metal caused by impinging electromagnetic radiation of certain minimum energy; current increases with increasing intensity of radiation.

Photoelectron. An electron emitted from a substance by irradiation as a result of the photoelectric effect or photoionization.

Photoelectron spectro-microscopy (PESM). A technique for investigating the composition of surfaces, based on ionization of atoms at the surfaces. Ionizing radiation is used to eject electrons from atoms in the surface. The ejected electrons are then focused, thus enabling an image of the surface to be constructed.

Photoelectron spectroscopy (PES). Measures the ionization energies of molecules when electrons are ejected from different orbitals; it uses these to infer the orbital energies. UV photoelectron spectroscopy is for hitting more energetic molecules, and X-Ray photoelectron spectroscopy is handy for pulling off the core electrons.

Photoemission. The process in which electrons are emitted by a substance as a result of irradiation.

Photoionization. The *ionization of an atom or molecule as a result of irradiation by electromagnetic radiaton. For a photoionization to occur the incident photon of the radiation must have an energy in excess of the *ionization potential of the species being irradiated. The ejected photoelectron will have an energy, E, givern by E=hf-I, where h is the Planck constant, f is the frequency of the incidet radiation, and I is the ionization potential of the irradiated species.

Photolysis. A chemical reaction produced by exposure to light or ultraviolet radiation. Photolytic reactions often involve free radicals, the first step being homolytic fission of a chemical bond. The photolysis of water, using energy from sunlight absorbed by chlorophyll, produces gaseous a oxygen, electrons, and hydrogen ions and is a key reaction in photosynthesis.

Photomultiplier tube (PMT). When light comes in, it hits an anode surface that releases many electrons. When nine of these are placed in series, there is a huge increase in the original signal. The anode surfaces are called dynodes.

Photon. A particle with zero rest mass consisting of a quantum of electromagnetic radiation. The photon may also be regarded as a unit of energy equal to hf, where h is the *Planck constant and is the frequency of the radiation in hertz. Photons travel at the speed of light. They are required to explain the photoelectric effect and other phenomena that require light to have particle character.

Photosensitive substance. 1. Any substance that when exposed to electromagnetic radiation produces a photoconductive, photoelectric, or photovoltaic effect. **2.** Any substance, such as the emulsion of a photographic film, in which electromagnetic radiation produces a chemical change.

Photosensitized reaction. When the reagent is not actually what absorbs light; instead, a photosensitizer picks up light and transfers the energy to the reagents.

Photosynthetic pigments. The plant pigments responsible for the capture of light energy during the light-dependent reactions of photosynthesis. The green pigment chlorophyll is the principal ligt receptor, absorbing blue and red light.

Photovoltaic detector. A change in the number of photons incident of a p-n junction causes fluctuations in the voltage generated by the junction.

Phthalic ester. An ester of phthalic acid. Phthalic esters are made by reacting phthalic anhydride with an alcohol in the presence of sulphuric acid. They are high boiling-point-liquids used as plasticizers and in the manufacture of polymers and alkyd resins. The dimethyl ester is us-ed as an insect repellent.

Physical Change. A change in which a substance changes from one physical state to another but no substances with different composition are formed. Example Gas to Liquid - Solid.

Physical chemistry. The branch of chemistry conce-rned with the effect of ch-emical structure on physical properties. It includes chemical thermodynamics and electrochemistry.

Physical vapor deposition (PVD). Get a source material into the vapor phase and then allow the molecules to condense on the surface of a thin film.

Piezoelectric effect. The phenomenon in which a crystal under the action of a mechanical stress becomes electrically charged, with opposite charges at the two ends of the crystal. Does not occur in centrosymmetric crystals, except for those in the cubic 432 group.

Pig iron . The impure form of iron produced by a blast furnace, which is cast into pigs for converting ast a later date into cast iron, steel, etc. The composition depends on the ores used, the smelting procedure, and the use to which the pigs will later be put.

Pipette. A graduated tube used for transferring measured volumes of liquid or, sometimes, gases.

Pitch. A black or dark-brown residue resulting from the distillation of coal tar, wood tar, or petroleum (bitumen). The term is also sometimes used for the naturally occurring petroleum residue. Pitch is used as a binding agent (e.g. in road tars), for waterproofing (e.g. in roofing fe-lts), and as a fuel.

Plasma. A physical state of matter which exists at extremely high temperatures in which all molecules are dissociated and most atoms are ionized.

Plasticizer. A substance ad-ded to a synthetic resin to make it flexible.

Plastic deformation. The strain at which a solid can no longer regain its original shape.

Plastocyanin. A blue copper containing protein that is found in chloroplasts and acts as an electron carrier molecule in the light-dependent reactions of *photosynthesis. Plastocyanin consists of amino acid groups in association with a copper molecule which gives this compound a blue colour.

Plastoquinone. A quinone, found in chloroplasts, that functions as one of the carrier molecules of the electron transport chain in the light-dependent reactions of photosynthesis.

Platinum black. Black finely divided platinum metal produced by vacuum evaporation and used as an absorbent and a catalyst.

Pleochroic. Denoting a crystal that appears to be of different colours, depending on the direction from which it is viewed. It is caused by polarization of light as it passes through an anisotropic medium.

Plumbane. An extremely unstable gas, PbH_4, said to be formed by the action of acids on magnesium-lead alloys. It was first reported in 1924. although doubts have since been expressed about the existence of the compound. It demonstrates the declining stability of the hydrides in group 14. More st-able organic derivatives are known; e.g. trimethyl plu-mbane, $(CH_3)_3PbH$.

Plumbic compounds. Compounds of lead in its higher (+4) oxidation state; e.g. plumbic oxide is lead (IV) oxide, PbO_2.

Plumbous compounds. Compounds of lead in its lower (+2) oxidation state; e.g. plumbous oxide is lead (II) oxide, PbO.

Pockel's cell. An optical phase modulator.

Point group. A group of symmetry elements that leave a point unchanged, used in classifying molecules.

Poise. The cgs unit of viscosity; equal to dyne*sec/centimeters squared.

Poison. **1.** Any substance that is injurious to the health of a living organism. **2.** A substance that prevents the activity of a catalyst. **3.** A substance that absorbs neutrons in a nuclear reactor and th-erefore slows down the reaction. It may be added intentionally for this purpose or may be formed as a fission product and need to be periodically removed.

Polar Bond. Covalent bond in which there is an unsymmetrical distribution of electron density.

Polar compound. A compound that is either ionic (e.g. sodium chloride) or that has molecules with a large permanent dipole moment (e.g. water).

Polarimeter. A device used to measure optical activity.

Polariscope. A device used to study optically active substances. The simplest type of instrument consists of a light source, collimator, polarizer, and analyser. The specimen is placed between polarizer and analyser, so that any rotation of the plane of polarization of the light can be assessed by turning the analyser.

Polarization. The buildup of a product of oxidation or a reduction of an electrode, preventing further reaction.

Polar molecule. A molecule that has a dipole moment; i.e. one in which there is some separation of charge in the *chemical bonds, so that one part of the molecule has a positive charge and the other a negative charge.

Polaroid. A doubly refracting material that planepolarizes unpolarized light passed through it. It consists of a plastic sheet strained in a manner that makes it birefringent by aligning its molecules. Sunglasses incorporating a Polaroid material absorb light that is vibrating horizontally-produced by reflection from horizontal surfaces-and thus reduce glare.

Pollutant. Any substance, produced and released into the environment as a result of human activities, that has damaging effects on living organisms. Pollutants may be toxic substances (e.g. *pesticides) or natural constituents of the atmosphere (e.g. carbon dioxide) that are present in excessive amounts.

Poly. Prefix indicating a polymer, e.g. polyethene. Sometimes brackets are used in polymer names to indicate the repeated unit, e.g. poly(ethene).

Polyamide. A type of condensation polymer produced by the interaction of an amino group of one molecule and a carboxylic acid group of another molecule to give a protein like structure. The polyamide chains are linked together by hydrogen bonding.

Polyampholyte. When a macromolecule has mixed anion and cation character.

Polydentate. Refers to ligands with more than one donor atom.

Polydisperse. When a polymer exists over a wide range of molecular masses; characteristic of man-made polymeric materials.

Polyene. A compound that contains more than one double bond per molecule.

Polymerization. The combination of many small molecules to form large molecules.

Polymer. A large molecule consisting of chains or rings of linked monomer units, usually characterized by high melting and boiling points.

Polymorphous. Refers to substances that crystallize in more than one crystalline arrangement.

Poynting vector. The energy an EM wave transports per unit time per unit area. Denoted as the vector S.

Polyprotic Acid. An Acid that can form two or more hydronium ions per molecule; often a least one step of ionization is weak.

Positron. A Nuclear particle with the mass of an electron but opposite charge.

Potential Energy. Energy that matter possesses by virtue of its position, condition or composition.

Precipitate. An insoluble solid formed by mixing in solution the constituent ions of a slightly soluble solution.

Primary Standard. A substance of a known high degree of purity that undergoes one invariable reaction with the other reactant of interest.

Primary Voltaic Cells. Voltaic cells that cannot be recharged; no further chemical reaction is possible once the reactants are consumed.

Pressure amplitude. Represents the maximum and minimum amounts by which the pressure varies from normal ambient pressure. Usually used in describing shock waves or sound waves.

Primary creep. When you put strain on a substance, this is the movement that is still recoverable.

Proton. A subatomic particle having a mass of 1.0073 amu and a charge of +1, found in thew nuclei of atoms.

Proton decoupling. When you are doing C-NMR, you have the possibility that the spins of the carbon and that of the protons will couple, and the spectrum would then be very hard to understand. In this method, you get rid of any coupling by following the initial pulse with a pulse that randomizes the spins of the protons; in this way, the signal averaging gets rid of any spin coupling between them. It does make it easier to see how many carbons there are, although it makes it impossible to integrate peak heights to figure out the abundances of each equivalent carbon.

PseudobinaryIonic Compounds. Compounds that contain more than two elements but are named like binary compounds.

Pseudo order. An order of a chemical reaction that appears to be less than the true order because of the experimental conditions used. Pseudo orders occur when one reactants is present in large excess. For example, reaction of substance A undergoing hydrolysis may appear to be proportional only to (A) because the amount of water present is so large.

Psilocybin. A hallucinogen, similar in effect to psi *mescaline, found in certain species of mushroom. It is accompained by a related, more active, compound **psilocin**. Both are classified as class A drugs in the UK. They can be detected by the Marquis test or the Froehde test.

Ptyalin. An enzyme that digest carbohydrates. It is present in mammalian saliva and is responsible for the initial stags of starch digestion.

P-type semiconductor. Low-lying acceptor band gives rise to conductivity.

Pulsed gradient spin echo (PSGE). An NMR technique which is used to study the speed of liquid motion.

Pullulan. A water-soluble polysaccharide composed of glucose units that are polymerized in such a way as to make it viscous and impermeable to oxygen. Pullulan is used in adhesives, food packaging, and moulded articles. it is derived from the fungus Aureobasidium pullulans.

Pumice. A porous volcanic rock that is light and full of cavities due to expanding gases that were liberated from solution in the lava while it solidified. Pumice is often light enough to float on water. It is usually acid composition, and is used as an abrasive and for polishing.

Pyranose. A six-membered ring sugar molecule.

Pyroelectricity. The property of certain crystals, such as tourmaline, of acquiring opposite electrical charges on opposite faces when heated. In tourmaline a rise in temperature of 1 K at atom temperature produces a polarization of some 10^{-5} Cm^{-2}.

Pyrolysis. Chemical decomposition occurring as a result of high temperature.

Pyrolytic. Breaking apart through heat.

Pyrrole. An organic nitrogen containing compound that forms part of the structure of *porphyrins.

Pyromagnetic. When you can change magnetic properties of a compound through heating.

Q

Quadrupole. A "double dipole"; a molecule with a quadrupole will have no dipole moment because the two dipoles present in the molecule cancel each other out. A good example is carbon dioxide.

Quadrupole mass filter. Used in mass spec, this tool has four voltage-carrying rods which serve to give ions which travel between them oscillations. Only ions with the right mass/charge ratio (m/z) can undergo these oscillations without hitting one of these rods.

Quantitative structure-activity relationship (QSAR). A statistical algorithm that quantitatively defines the relationship between the chemical structure of a drug and its effect on an organism. QSAR studies are often used to predict the activity or toxicity of new drugs. Similar methods can be used to predict the metabolism of new drugs (quantitative structure-metabolism relationshps).

Quantum. The minimum amount by which certain properties, such as energy or angular momentum, of a system can change. Such properties do not, therefore., vary continuously, but in integral multiples of the relevant quantum, and are described as quantized. This concept forms the basis of the quantum theory. In waves and fields the quantum can be regarded as an excitation, giving a particle-like interpretation to the wave or field. Thus, the quantum of the electromagnetic field is the photon and the graviton is the quantum of the gravitational field.

Quantum chaos. The quantum mechanics of systems for which the corresponding classical system can exhibit chaos. This subject was initiated by Einstein in 1917, who showed that the qnantization conditions associated with the *Bohr theory need to be modified for systems that show chaos in classical mechanics. The subject of quantum chaos is an active field of research in which many basic issues still require clarification. It appears that systems exhibiting chaos in classical mechanicsdo not necessarily exhibit choas in quantum mechanics.

Quantum chemistry. The application of quantum mechanics to chemistry. Quantum chemistry mostly used empirical methods at first but as computing power has developed it has been increasingly based on the first principles of quantum mechanics.

Quantum entanglement. A phenomenon in quantum mechanics in which a particle or system does not have a definite or system does not have a definite state but exists as an intermediate form of two 'entangled' states.One of the these states is realized when a 'measurement' is made.

Quantum jump. A change in a system from one quantum state to another.

Quantum Mechanics. Mathematical method of treating particles on the basis of quantum theory, which assumes that energy (of small particles) is not infinitely divisible.

Quantum Numbers. Numbers that describe the energies of electrons in atoms; derived from quantum mechanical treatment.

Quantum simulation. The mathematical modelling of systems of large numbers of atoms or molecules by computer studies of relatively small clusters. It is possible to obtain information about solids and liquids in ths way and to study surface properties and reactions.

Quantum state. The state of a quantized system as described by its quantum numbers. For instance, the state of a hydrogen *atom is described by the four quantum numbers n.l, m, m_s. In the ground state they have values 1,0,0, and 1/2 respectively.

Quantum yield. In a photochemical reaction, the number of events occurring per photo absorbed. It is given by the number of moles of product formed (or reactant consumed) divided by the number of moles of photons absorbed.

Quarter wave plate. Used to change linearly polarized light to circularly polarized light.

Quartz. The most abundant and common mineral, consisting of crystalline silica (silicon dioxide, SiO_2), crystallizing in the trigonal system. It has a hardness of 7 on the Mohs' scale. Well-formed crystals of quartz are six-sided prisms terminating in six-sided pyramids. Quartz is ordinarily colourless and transparent, in which form it is known as **rock crystal.** Coloured varieties, a number of which are used as gemstones, include *amethyst, citrine qu-artz (yellow), rose quartz (pink), milk quartz (white), smoky quartz (grey-brown), *chalcedony, *algate, and *jasper. Quartz occurs in ma-ny rocks, especially igneous rocks such as granite and quartzite (of which it is the chief constituent), metamorphic rocks a such as gneisses and schists, and sedimentary rocks such as sandstone and limestone. The mineral is piezoelectric and is used in oscillators. It is also used in optical instruments and in glass, glaze, and abrasives.

Quenching. 1. The rapid cooling of a metal by immersing it in a bath of liquid in order to improve its properties. Steels are quenched to make them harder but some nonferrous metals are que-nched for other reasons (copper, for example, is made softer by quenching). 2. The process of inhibiting a continuous discharge in a *Geiger counter so that the incidence of further ionizing radiation can cause a new discharge. This is achieved by introducing a quenching vapour, such as methane mixed with argon or with neon, into the tube.

Quinalphos. Insecticide, acaricide, organophosphate derivative.

Quinhydrone electrode. An electrode used in pH measurement relying on the redox reaction, hydroquinone quinone. Can be used in non-aqueous solvents.

Q-value. The total energy released by the radioactive disintegration of a nucleus.

QWOT. Quarter-wave optical thickness.

R

Racah parameters. The parameters used to express quantitatively the interelectronic repulsion between the various energy levels of an atom. Generally expressed as B and C. The ratios between B in a compound and B in the free ion give a measure if the NEPHELAUXETIC EFFECT.

Racemate. An equimolecular compound or mixture of the dextro and laevoratatory optically active forms of given compound.

Racemization. The process in which an achiral stereoisomer is converted into a racemate. EPIMERIZATION is a special case of racemization. Heat and the action of acids or bases can encourage recemization.

Radiant power. Total amount of energy emitted by a light source per second.

Radiation. High energy particles or rays emitted during the nuclear decay processes.

Radiative decay process. Loss of excitation energy as a photon. Transfers energy as heat.

Radical. An atom or group of atoms that contains one or more unpaired electrons (usually very reactive species)

Radioactive Dating. Method of dating ancient objects by determining the ratio of amounts of mother and daughter nuclides present in an object and relating the ratio to the object?s age via half-life calculations.

Radioactive decay series. The series of isotopes into which a radioactive nucleus is successively transformed.

Radioactive Tracer. A small amount of radioisotope replacing a nonradioactive isotope of the element in a compound whose path (for example, in the body) or whose decomposition products are to be monitored by detection of radioactivity; also called a radioactive label.

Radioactivity. The spontaneous disintegration of atomic nuclei.

Radiocarbon dating. Carbon in living things contains a uniform proportion of radioactive ^{14}C, which is produced constantly in the atmosphere by the action of cosmic radiation. Once the host dies, the exchange of nonradioactive carbon with the atmospheric ^{14}C ceases. Thus from the amount of ^{14}C in the dead sample the age of it may be determined ^{14}C has a half-life of 5570 years and the method is useful for samples having ages up to 30000 years.

Radium compounds. Radium is an alkaline earth of Group 2. Its compounds are very similar to the corresponding barium derivatives although they are generally less soluble. Radium halides RaF_2, $RaCl_2$ and $RaBr_2$ are known. The carbonate, fluoroberyllate and iodate are insoluble in water.

Raffinose. $C_{18}H_{32}O_{16}$. Large prisms as the pentahydrate; m.p. 80°C or m.p. 118-119°C when anhydrous. The best-known trisaccharide, it is composed of galactose, glucose and fructose. It is found in sugar beet, but the best source is cotton-seed meal, which contains 8%. It has no reducing power.

Ramoplanin. Potent antibiotic, macrocyclic decapeptide.

Raney nickel. A form of nickel prepared by treating an Al-Ni alloy with NaOH solutions. The nickel is the left in a spongy mass which is pyrophoric when dry. This form of nickel is a strong catalyst, especially for hydrogenations.

Raoult's Law. The vapor pressure of a solvent in an ideal solution decreases as its mole fraction decreases.

Rare earths. Strictly the oxides of the lanthanide elements but often applied to the elemeents themselves. World demand rare earth oxides 1997 66 000 tonnes. Used in magnets, Ni-H batteries, catalysis, phosphors and electrical components.

Rast's method. A virtually obsolete method of determining molecular masses by measuring the depression of freezing point of a solvent by a known weight of the solute whose molecular weight is required. Camphor is commonly used as the solvent because of its high molecular depression constant. Has use for determining molecular masses of polymers.

Rate-determining Step. The slowest step in a mechanism; the step that determines the overall rate of reaction.

Rate-law Expression. Equation relating the rate of a reaction to the concentrations of the reactants and the specific rate of the constant.

Rate of Reaction. Change in the concentration of a reactant or product per unit time.

Rationality of intercepts, law of. The intercepts of the faces of a crystal upon the axes of the crystal bear a si-mple ration to each other.

Rayleigh scattering. When light is scattered by particles much smaller than the wavelength. The shorter the wavelength, the more intense the scattering.

Rayon. Artificial fibres made of regenerated cellulose formerly known as viscose, artificial silk, fibre silk, etc.

RC circuit. A circuit that uses both resistors and capacitors.

Reactants. Substances consumed in a chemical reaction.

Reaction mechanism. A step-by-step description of the sequence of processes that together make up a full description of the mechanism.

Reaction Quotient. The mass action expression under any set of conditions (not necessarily equlibrium); its magnitude relative to K determines the direction in which the reaction must occur to establish equilibrium.

Reaction Ratio. The relative amounts of reactants and products involved in a reaction; maybe the ratio of moles. millimoles, or masses.

Reaction Stoichiometry. Description of the quantitative relationships among substances as they participate in chemical reactions.

Reaction velocity. The rate of a chemical reaction expressed either as the rate of disappearance of reactant molecules or the rate of formation of product molecules.

Reactive dyes. Dyes which contain a functional group (chloro-substituted heterocycle, acrylamide sulphonic acid derivative) capable of reacting directly with the fibre.

Reactive plasma deposition (RPD). Similar to CVD, except that an rf plasma helps the decomposition/recombination process of the reactants.

Rectifier. A device that turns ac power into dc power.

Rector. Large-scale chemical processes are carried out in various environments, usually in tanks, tubes, towers of FLUIDIZED BEDS. These are usually referred to as chemical reactors and form the heart of the overall chemical process. Reactor design involving scale-up from laboratory reactions is an important aspect of chemical technology or chemical engineering. The term reactor is also usedfor a nuclear reactor.

Realgar. The mineral form of As_4S_4, formerly used as an ornage-red pigment. Formed antificially be distilling sulphur and excess of arsenic.

Rearrangement. A reaction that takes place, apparently completely internally, to give a new compound, e.g. a cis-to trans-rearrangement.

Recoil atom. When an atomic nucleus disintegrates the fragments receive equal momentum. In the case of a heavy nucleus emitting a light fragment, the heavy remnant, termed a recoil atom, will recoil with a comparatively low velocity. The recoil atom has a sufficiently high energy to rupture bonds which it may form or have with other atoms. The resulting group may not recombine and it may thus be possible to separate chemically disintegration. The 'hot atom' may reocombine with its original partner or may combine with another group to form a new chemical compound.

Recrystallization. The process of repeated crystallization carried out with the object of removing impurities or of obtaining more satisfactory crystals of a substance which is already pure.

Rectified spirit. A solution of ethanol in water which contains 90% v/v ethyl alcohol. Rectified spirit is 57.8% over proof (oP).

Recuperators. Heatex-changes used in furnace operations where combustion air or lean fuel gas may be preheated.

Red mercury. A colloid from an amalgam of Hg and $Hg_2Sb_2O_7$. If used to dissolve a neutron emitter such as ^{252}Cf can induce nuclear fission.

Redox. An abbreviation for oxidation-reduction, e.g. redox potential; reduction-oxidation potential.

Redox catalyst. A combination of a free-radical catalyst with a reducing ion or salt which increases the rate of free-radical production.

Used in polymerization reactions. A catalyst which increases the rate of a free-radical reaction often polymerization.

Redox indicator. A substance which undergoes a visible colour change during its reversible oxidation or reduction. The substance has a definite, and preferably narrow, potential range over which the colour change occurs. E.g. methylene blue is colourless when reduced, blue when oxidized.

Reducing Agent. Ahe substance that reduces another substance and is oxidized.

Reducing sugar. A sugar that shows reducing properties-contains hemiacetal or hemi-ketal groups.

Reductones. Enediols stabilized by conjugation to a carbonyl or similar group.

Reduced mass: =m1m2(m1+m2).

Reference state. The most stable at a particular temperature and 1 bar (except for phosphorous where white P is designated the standard state).

Refining. The removal of impurities from metals or alloys in metallurgy using, e.g. oxidation, electrolysis, chemical separation, distillation, zone refining.

Refining, petroleum. The general process of converting crude oil into a wide range of petroleum products including fuels, lubricants, bitumens, waxes, etc. Specific refining operations include physical separation techniques such as DISTILLATION, solvent extraction, ABSORPTION, etc. Chemical refining operations involve many treatments including sulphuric acid treatment, SWEETENING, DESSULPHURIZATION, etc.

Reflux. Liquid from partial condensation of vapour which is returned to the top of a fractionating column and allowed to flow down the column counter-current to the ascending vapour.

Reforming. The process of subjecting straightrun gasoline from primary distillation to a thermal or catalytic treatment. Straight-chain alkanes are converted to isomers while cycloalkanes are dehydrogenated to form aromatics. Thermal reforming is similar to THERMAL CRACKING but higher temperature and pressures are used. The process results in gasoline of higher OCTANE NUMBER and wider boiling range. The reforming process is usually carried out in the presence of a catalyst as lower temperatures and pressures may be used and higher yields of particular gasoline are obtained.

Refractory metals. Include tungsten, tantalum and molybdenum; used for electrode materials because they have a low, uniform surface potential, do not oxidize, and are bakeable.

Relativity principle. The basic laws of physics are the same in all inertial reference frames.

Relaxation times. Consist of T1 (longitudinal relaxation time) and T2 (transverse relaxation time). Basically, the relaxation times correspond to the time it takes after the pulse in NMR or other spectroscopic tecniques for the molecules to go back to their Boltzmann distribution of states.

REMPI. Resonance enhanced multi-photon ionization.

Resistance thermometer. Uses the dependance of electrical resistance on temperature to measure the temperature.

Resolution (of a lens). The ability of a lens to produce distinct images of two point objects very close together

Resonance. The concept in which two or more equivalent dot formulas for the same arrangement of atoms (resonance structures) are necessary to describe the bonding in a molecule or ion.

Resonant two-photon ionization (R2PI). A process in which two photons strike a sample and ionize the molecules. One good thing about this process is that the product ions generally have known structure.

Rest mass. The mass of an object as measured in a reference frame where it is at rest.

Reststrahlen filter. Utilizes the phenomena that reflections of white light from crystal surfaces will contain only one region of the spectrum.

Resultant. The sum of two or more vectors.

Reversion. Right-to-left reversion of an image.

Reverse Osmosis. Forcing solvent molecules to flow through a semipermable membrane from a concentated solution into a dilute solution by the application of greater hydrostatic pressure on concentrated side than the osmotic pressure opposing it.

Reversible Reaction. Reactions that do not go to completion and occur in both the forward and reverse direction.

Reynold's number. Characterizes the onset of turbulence in a tube. Re = 2vr(rho)/n, where n=viscosity, r=radius of tube, rho=density of the fluid, v=velocity of the fluid; If Re<2000, there is laminar flow; if Re>2000, there is turbulent flow.

Rheopexy. The rheological phenomenon whereby the gelation of some thixotropic sols is accelerated by gentle mechanical agitation. An example is gypsum-water paste which, of allowed to stand, solidifies in about 10 minutes, but when gently agitated solidifies in seconds.

RHME. Rotating hanging meniscus electrode.

Rhodanine. Prepared sodium chloroethanoate on ammonium dithiocarbamate. Used in synthesis of pheny-lalanine. Rhodanine 6G used in dyelasers.

Rhodopsin. A major photosensitive pigment of the eye, composed of the protein opsin and retinol.

Rhombohedral system. An alternative representation of the TRIGONAL or HEXAGONAL crystal systems.

Rhomboid prism. Used for lateral deviation of a light ray.

Riboflavin. $C_{17}H_{20}N_4O_6$. Crystallizes in orange needles; m.p. 271°C. Soluble in water. Riboflavin is part of the original vitamin B_2 complex. It occurs widely in nature, particularly in liver, milk and white of egg. It is the precursor of FLAVOPROTEINS.

Ribonucleic acid. Single standed nucleic acid containing ribose and uracil. Involved in protein synthesis.

Ribosomes. The protein synthesizing material in living cells can act as ribozymes. Ribosomes 'translate' the code in a messenger RNA molecule to form a polypeptide chain.

Ribozymes. RNA species whch act as catalysts. The protein synthesizing material in living cells can act as rib-ozymes.

Ricin. A poisonous protein of the lectin class from the seeds of the castor bean.

Rietveld analysis. method of analysis of neutron diffraction and X-ray powder data and derivation of structure.

Rifampicin. Important anti-tuberculosis drug. Semi-synthetic.

Rinmann's green. $ZnCo_2O_4$. A spinel formed when cobalt nitrate solution is placed on zinc oxide and the mixture heated to redness. The green colour forms a delicate test for Zn.

Rolling friction. The friction from when one body rolls across a surface; generally much smaller than the sliding friction.

Rontgen. The quantity of io-nizing radiation. A lethal whole-body single dose of radiationis about 500 nitrogen for man. Rarely used-expressed as coulombs per kg.

Rosin. A solid resin which occurs in the coil from pine trees and is also obtained from TALL OIL. Mainly composed of monocarboxylic acids related to abietic acids. used in the preparation of various compounds (including esters) and in lacquers, plasticizers flotation agents, adhensives, paper size.

Root-mean-square speed (rms). The square root of the average of the squared speeds of gas molecules in a sample.

Roots blower. A type of vacuum pump capable of pressures down to .01 torr.

Rotamers. Isomers formed by restricted rotation.

Rotating disk electrode (RDE). Method to determine kinetics of electrodes. If you have the electrode be a rotating disk, the current of the sample can be related to the speed of rotation.

Rowland ghosts. Spurious intensity maximum spurred from periodic errors in the spacing of the ruled grooves in a diffraction grating.

RPM. Radical pair mechanism.

Ruby. Aluminum oxide, Al2O3.

S

Sabatier-Senderens process. A method of organic synthesis employing hydrogenation and a heated nickel catalyst. It is employed commercially for hydrogenating unsaturated vegetable oils to make margarine. It is named after Paul Sabatier and Jean-Baptiste Senderens.

Sacrificial protection. The protection of iron or steel against corrosion by using a more reactive metal. A common form is galvanizing, in which the iron surface is coated with a layerof zinc. Even if the zinc layer is is scratched, the iron does not rust because in preference to iron ions. Pieces of magnesium alloy are similarly used in protecting pipelines, etc.

Salinometer. An instrument for measuring the salinity of a solution. There are two main types; one is a type of hydrometer to measure density; the other is a apparatus for measuring the electrical conductivity of the solution.

Salt Bridge. A U-shaped tube containing electrolyte, which connects two half-cells of a voltaic cell.

SAM. Self-assembled monolayer.

Sand. Particles of rock with diameters in the range 0.06-2.00 mm. Most sands are composed chiefly of particles of quartz, which are derived from the weathering of quartzbearing rocks.

Saponification. Hydrolysis of esters in the presence of strong soluable bases.

Saponin. A type of toxic glycoside that forms a frothy colloidal solution on shaking with water. Saponins occur in many plants. They break down red blood cells and have been used for poisoning fish. On hydrolysis they yield a variety of sugars.

sapphire. Any of the gem varieties of corundum except ruby, especially the blue variety, but other colours of sapphire include yellow, brown, green, pink, orange, and purple. Saphires are obtained from igneous and metamorphic rocks and from alluvial deposits, The chief sources are Sri Lanka, Kashmir, Burma, Thailand, East Africa, the USA. and Australia, Sapphires are used as gemstones and in recors-player styluses and some types of laser. They are synthesized by the Verneuil flame-fusion process.

SATP. Standard ambient temperature and pressure; corresponds to 25 C, 1 bar.

Saturated Hydrocarbons. Hydrocarbons that contain only single bonds. They are also called alkanes or paraffin hydrocarbons.

Saturated Solution. Solution in which no more solute will dissolve.

Sawhorse projection. A type of projection in which a three dimensional view is drawn.

Scalar. A quantity that is specified completely by giving a number.

Scavenger. A reagent that removes a trace component from a system or that removes a reactive intermediate from a reaction.

SCE. Standard calomel electrode.

Scheelite. A mineral form of calcium tungstate, $CaWo_4$, used as an ore of tungsten. It occurs in contact mentamorphosed deposits and vein deposits as colourless or white tetragonal crystals.

Schiff's reagent. A reagent, devised by Hugo Schiff, used for testing for aldehy-des and ketones; it consists of a solution of fuchsin dye that has been decolorized by sulphur dioxide. Aliphatic aldehydes restore the pink immediately, where as aromatic ketones have no effect on the reagent. Aromatic aldehydes and aliphatic ketones restore the colour slowly.

Schott IRG 11. Calcium aluminate; transmits light between .3-5.5 microns.

Schott IRG 2. Germanate; transmits light between .3-4.6 microns.

Schott IRG N6. Calcium aluminosilicate; transmits light between .3-4.75 microns.

SCRF. Self-consistent reaction field method. A method for calculating the energies of molecules in a reaction.

Schweizer's reagent. A solution made by dissolving copper(II) hydroxide in concentrated ammonia solution. It has a deep blue colour and is used as a solvent for cellulose in the cuprammonium process for making rayon. When the cellulose solution is forced through spinnarets into an acid bath, fibres of cellulose are reformed.

Seaborgium. Symbol Sg. A radioactive *transactinide element; a.n. 106. It was first detected in 1974 by Albert Ghiorso and a team in California. It can be produced by bombarding californium-249 nuclei with oxygen-18 nuclei. It is named after the US physicist Glenn Seaborg (1912-99).

Second Law of Thermodynamics. The universe tends toward a state of greater diorder in spontaneous processes.

Seeback effect. When a metal has a temperature gradient, it has a voltage. The difference in thermally induced voltages of two metals will cause a net voltage in a junction.

Secondary cell. A *voltaic cell in which the chemical reaction producing the e.m.f. is reversible and the cell can therefore be changed by passing a current through it.

Secondary emission. The emission of electrons from a surfaces as a result of the impact of other charged particles, especially as a result of bombardment with electron. As the number of secondary electrons can exceed the number of primary electrons, the process is important in photomultipliers.

Secondary Standard. a solution that has been titrated against a primary standard. A standard solution is a secondary standard.

Secondary Voltaic Cells. Voltaic cells that can be recharged; original reactanats can be regenerated be reversing the direction of the current flow.

Seger cones. A series of cones used to indicate the temperature inside a furnace or kiln. The cones are made from different mixtures of clay, limestone, feldspars, etc., and each one softens at a different temperatures. The droping of the vertex is an indication that the known softening temperature has been reached and thus the furnce temperature can be estimated.

Selenides. Binary compounds of seleium which other more electropositive elements. Selenides of nonmetals are covalent. Most metal selenides can be prepared by direct combination of the elements. Some are well-defined ionic compou-nds, while others are non-stoichiometric interstitial compounds (e.g. Pd_4Se, $PdSe_2$).

Seliwanoff's test. A biochemical test to identify the presence of ketonic sugars, such as fructose, in solution. It was devised by the Russian chemist F.F. Seliwanoff. A few drops of the reagent, consisting of resorcinol crystals, dissolved in equal amounts of water and hydrochloric acid, are he-ated with the test solution and the formation of a red precipitate indicates a positive result.

Semiconductor. A substance that does not conduct electricity at low temperatures but does so at higher temperatures.

Semipermable Membrane. A thin partition between two solutions through which certain molecules can pass but others cannot.

SERR spectroscopy. Surface-enhanced resonance Raman spectroscopy; a Raman method used because it has excellent selectivity to the microscopic environment and orientation of things adsorbed on surfaces.

SERS. Surface-enhanced Raman scattering.

Shale. A form of clay that occurs in thin layers. Shales are very common sedimentary rocks.

SHE. Standard hydrogen electrode; defined as having 0V.

Shellac. A hard resin produced as a secretion by a plant parasite, the south-east Asian lac insect Lacifer laçca. It is used in sealing wax, varnish (French polish), and electrical insulators.

Sheradizing. The process of coating iron or steel with a zinc corrosion-resistant layer by heating it in contact with zinc dust to a temperature slightly below the melting point of zinc. At a temperature of about 371°C the two metals amalgamate to form internal layers of zinc-iron alloys and an external layer of pure zinc. The process was invented by Sherard Cowper-Coles (d.1935).

Shear modulus. The modulus of rigidity; concerned with the elastic deformation of a body in which an applied force results in the shape of a body.

SHG. Second harmonic generation.

Shielded. When the sigma value in NMR is greater than zero. Deshielding is when the value is less than zero.

Shielding Effect. Electrons in filled sets of s , p orbitals between the nucleus and outer shell electrons shield the outer shell electrons somewhat from the effect of protons in the nucleus; also called screening effect.

Shock wave. A very narrow region of high pressure and temperature formed in a fluid when the fluid flows supersonically over a stationary object or a projectile flying supersonically passes th-rough a stationary fluid. A shock wave may also be generated by violent disturbances in a fluid, such as a lightning stock or a bomb blast. Shock waves are generated experimetally to excite molecules for spectroscopic investigation.

Sial. The rocks that form the earth's continental crust. These are granite rock types rich in silica (SiO_2) and aluminium (Al), hence the name.

Side reaction. A chemical reaction that occurs at the same time as a main reaction but to a lesser extent, thus leading to other products mixed with the main products.

Sievert. The SI unit of dose equivalent. It is named after the Swedish physicist Rolf Sievert (1896-1966).

Sigma electron. An electron in a sigma orbital.

Sigmatropic reaction. A type of rearrangement in which a sigma bond is formed between two on linked atoms at the sametime as an existing bond is broken. Sigmatropic rearrangements are a type of *pericyclic reaction. An example is the *Cope rearrangement.

Sigma Bonds. Bonds resulting from the head-on overlap of atomic orbitals, in which the region of electron sharing is along and (cylindrically) symmetrical to the imaginary line connecting the bonded atoms.

Sigma Orbital. Molecular orbital resulting from head-on overlap of two atomic orbitals.

Silica gel. A rigid gel made by coagulating a sol of sodium silicate and heating to drive off water. It is used as a support for catalysts and also as a drying agent because it readily absorbs moisture from the air. The gel itself is colourless but, when used in desiccators, etc., a blue cobalt salt is added. As moisture is taken up, the salt turns pink, indicating that the gel needs to be regenerated (by heatng).

Silicones. Polymeric organosilicon compounds; contain individual or cross-linked Si-O chains or rings in which some oxygens of SiO4 tetrahedra are replaced by other groups.

Silicon controlled rectifier. A switching device; in the on state it has low resistance and in the off state it has very high resistance.

Sima. The rocks that form the earh's oceanic crust and underline the upper crust. These are basaltic rock types rich in silica (SiO_2)) and magnesium (Mg), hence the name. The sima is denser and more plastic than the sial that forms the continental crust.

Single Bond. Covalent bond resulting from the sharing of two electrons (one pair) between two atoms.

Size exclusion chromatography (SEC). Where you separate mixtures based on the sizes of the molecules.

SL units. Systeme International d 'Unites: the international system of units now recommended for all scientific purposes. A coherent and rationalized system of units derived from the *m.k.s. units, SI units have now replaced *c.g.s units and *Imperial units. The system has seven base units and two dimensionless units, all other units being derived from these nine units. There are 18 derived units with special names. Each unit has an agreed symbol (a capital leter or an initial capital letter if it is named after a scientist, otherwise the symbol consists of one or two lower-case letters). Decimal multiples of the units are indicated by a set of prefixes whenever possible a prefix representing 10 raised to a power that is a multiple of three should be used.

Slag. Material produced during the smelting or refining of metals by reaction of the flux with impurities (e.g. calcium silicate formed by reaction of calcium oxide flux with silicon dioxide impurities). The liquid slag can be separated from the liquid metal because it floats on the surface.

SLAR. Single layer antireflection coating.

SLUMO. Second-Lowest unoccupied molecular orbital.

Smectic. A smectic phase is when the molecules align themselves into a pseudo-crystalline lattice. Liquid crystals are one example.

Smelting. The process of separating a metal from its ore by heating the ore to a high temperature in a suitable furnace in the presence of a reducing agent, such as carbon, and a fluxing agent, such as limestone. Iron ore is smelted in this way so that the metal melts and, being denser than the molten *slag, sinks below the slag, enabling it to be removed from the furnae separately.

Snell's law. n1sin(theta1)= n2sin(theta2); describes refraction.

Softening point. The point at which a glass can be molded or worked.

Sol. A stable dispersion of either solids in liquids or solids in solids.

Solenoid. A long coil of wire consisting of may loops; when current flows through it, the magnetic field resembles that of a bar magnet.

Solubility Product Constant. Equilibrium constant that applies to the dissolution of a slightly soluble compound.

Solubility Product Principle. The solubility product constant expression for a slightly soluble compound is the product of the concentrations of the constituent ions, each raised to the power that corresponds to the number of ions in one formula unit.

Solute. The dispersed (dissolved) phase of a solution.

Solution. Homogeneous mixture of two or more substances.

Solvation. The process by which solvent molecules surround and interact with solute ions or molecules.

Solvent. The dispersing medium of a solution.

Solvolysis. The reaction of a substance with the solvent in which it is dissolved.

S Orbital. A spherically symmetrical atomic orbital; one per energy level.

Space-charge effect. Used to describe particle beam aberrations, it arises from the natural repulsion of particles of like charge; a focused beam will disperse, giving a diffuse image.

Spatial coherence. How much the waves are in step as they leave a laser cavity.

Special theory of relativity. 1) The basic laws of physics are the same in all inertial reference frames. 2) Light propagates through empty space with a definite speed c independant of the speed of the source or observer.

Specific Gravity. The ratio of the density of a substance to the density of water.

Specific Heat. The amount of heat required to raise the temperature of one gram of substance one degree Celsius.

Specific Rate Constant. An experimentally determined (proportionality) constant, which is different for different reactions and which changes only with temperature; k in the rate-law expression: Rate = k [A] x [B]v.

Spectator Ions. Ions in a solution that do not participate in a chemical reaction.

Spectral Line. Any of a number of lines corresponding to definite wavelengths of an atomic emission or absorption spectrum; represents the energy difference between two energy levels.

Spectrochemical Series. Arrangement of ligands in order of increasing ligand field strength.

Spectrum. Display of component wavelengths (colours) of electromagnetic radiation.

Speed of sound. Equal to the square root of the bulk modulus/density of the medium. As temperature rises, so does the speed of sound.

Sphere. Radius=4pi(r squared), volume=4/3pi(r cubed).

Spherical aberration. The variation of focus with aperture in which a ray through the edge of the lens intersects the axis at a point other than the paraxial focus.

Spinel. Magnesium aluminate, MgAl2O4.

Spin-spin coupling constant (J). Defines how much of an interaction you have between nuclei in a molecule. Gives rise to the fine structure in NMR.

SPT: sputtering; allow a material into the vapor phase to condense into a thin film.

Square Planar. A term used to describe molecules and polyatomic ions that have one atom in the center and four atoms at the corners of a square.

Square Planar Complex. Complex in which the metal is in the center of a square plane, with ligand donor atoms at each of the four corners

Standard Electrodes. Half-cells in which the oxidized and reduced forms of a species are present at unit activity; 1.0M solutions of dissolved ions, 1.0atm partial pressure of gases, and pure solids and liquids.

Standard Electrode Potential. By convention , potential, Eo, of a half-reaction as a reduction relative to the standard hydrogen electrode when all species are present at unit activity.

Standard Entropy. The absolute entropy of a substance in its standard state at 298 K.

Standard Molar Enthalphy of Formation. The amount of heat absorbed in the formation of one mole of a substance in a specified state from its elements in their standard states.

Standard Molar Volume. The volume occupied by one mole of an ideal gas under standard conditions; 22.4liters.

Standard Reaction. A reaction in which the numbers of moles of reactants shown in the balanced equation, all in their standard states, are completely converted to the numbers of moles of products shown in the balanced equation, also sall at their standard state.

Standard state. The pure form of a substance at 1 bar pressure for any given temperature.

Stereoisomers. Isomers that differ only in the way that atoms are oriented in space; consist of geometrical and optical isomers.

Stoichiometry. Description of the quantitative relationships among elements and compounds as they undergo chemical changes.

Stopband. The primary region of reflection or absorption of a rejection filter.

STP. Standard temperature and pressure; corresponds to 0C, 1 atm.

Streamline. The path taken by any particle in a steady, laminar flow.

Strong Electrolyte. A substance that conducts electricity well in a dilute aqueous solution.

Strong Field Ligand. Ligand that exerts a strong crystal or ligand electrical field and generally forms low spin complexes with metal ions when possible.

Structural Isomers. Compounds that contain the same number of the same kinds of atoms in different geometric arrangements.

Sublimation. The direct vaporization of a sold by heating without passing through the liquid state.

Substance. Any kind of matter all specimens of which have the same chemical composition and physical properties.

Sugar. Any of a group of water-soluble carbohydrates of relatively low molecular weight and typically having a sweet taste. The simple sugars are called monosaccharides. More complex sugars comprise between two and ten monosaccharides linked together: *disaccharides co-ntain two, trisaccharides thr-ee, and so on. The name is often used to refer specificaly to sucrose (table sugar).

Substitution Reaction. A reaction in which an atom or a group of atoms is replaced by another atom or group of atoms.

Superconductor. A material which has no resistance to electricity. When passing current through a superconductor, there is no loss of electrical power due to these materials.

Supercooled Liquids. Liquids that, when cooled, apparently solidify but actually continue to flow very slowly under the influence of gravity.

Supercritical liquid. A liquid which exists at temperatures above the normal boiling point; this is brought about through high pressure. Reactivity of solutes in these liquids can be changed drastically with minor changes in temperature and pressure.

Supercritical Fluid. A substance at temperature above its critical temperature.

Supersaturated Solution. A solution that contains a higher than saturation concentration of solute; slight disturbance or seeding causes crystallization of excess solute.

Superhigh surface area carbon. Any carbon which has a specific surface area greater than 2630 square meters per gram.

Surfactant. A substance, such as a detergent, added to a liquid to increase its spreading or wetting properties by reducing its surface tension.

Suspension. A heterogeneous mixture in which solute-like particles settle out of solvent-like phase some time after their introduction.

Superionic materials. Materials which exist largely in the ion phase. These are extremely useful in making conductors which work via ionic migration.

Supersaturated vapor. A vapor which will spontaneously begin to condense in the presence of nucleation centers.

Surface tension. (gamma); the force F per unit length L that acts across any line in a surface, tending to pull the surface closed.

Surfactant. A species that is active between two phases. It accumulates at the interface and changes the surface tension.

Symmetry. The property of a object that enables it to undergo certain manipulations, called symmetry operations, such that is new state is indistinguishable from its original state, Examples include inversion through a point, reflection through a lane, and rotation about an axis. The geometrical feature of the object with respect to which the symmetry operation is carried out is termed a symmetry element. In the above examples, a point through which inversion can be performed, a plane of reflection. and an axis of rotation are the symmetry elements.

Syneresis. The spontaneous separation of the solid and liquid components of a gel on standing.

Syngas. A mixture of gases (largely carbon monoxide and hydrogen) that results from heating coal in the presence of steam. Can be used as a fuel.

Synthesis. The formation of chemical compounds from more simple compounds.

Synthetic. Describing a substance that has been made artificially; i.e. one that does not come from a natural source.

Synthon. A fragment obtained by disconnection in *retrosynthetic analysis. By analogy, units building up structures by self-assembly in *supramolecular chemistry are sometime known as supramolecular synthons.

T

Tactosol. A colloidal sol containing nonspherical particles capable of orientating themselves. An example of a tactosol is given by an aged vanadium pentoxide sol, in which the particles are rod-shaped. When a tactosol is placed in a magnetic field its particles arrange themselves along the lines of force of the field.

Tannic acid. A yellowish complex organic compound present in certain plants. It is used in dyeing as a mordant.

Tanniin. One of a group of complex organic chemicals commonly found in leaves, unripe fruits, and the bark of trees. Their function is uncertain though the unpleasant taste may discourage grazing animals. Some tannins have commercial uses, notably in the production of leather and ink.

Tar. Any of various black semisolid mixtures of hydrocarbons and free carbon. produced by destructive distillation of coal or by petroleum refining.

Tartrazine. A food additive that gives foods a yellow colour. Tartrazine can cause a toxic response in the immune system and is banned in some countries.

Tautomerism. A type of isomers in which the two isomers are in equilibrium.

TDFS. Time-dependent fluorescence shifts.

Tele-substitution. A type of substitution reaction in which the entering group takes a position on an atom that is more than one atom away from the atom to which the leaving group is attached.

TEM. Transmission electron microscopy. What you do is take the sample, grind it up, then place an aqueous suspension of it on a grid where the electron microscope can get at it.

Temperature. A measure of the intensity of heat, i.e. the hotness or coldness of a sample. or object.

Temperature-independent paramagnetism (TIP). Orbital paramagnetism that is independent of temperature. In some substances TIP can make the molecules paramagnetic; although all the electrons in the ground state are paired, if there are low-lying excited states to which ele-ctrons can readily move.

Temporal coherence. How much waves stay in step along a beam path

Ternary Acid. A ternary compound containing H, O, and another element, often a nonmetal.

Ternary Compound. A compound consisting of three elements; may be ionic or covalent.

Tetrahedral. A term used to describe molecules and polyatomic ions that have one atom in center and four atoms at the corners of a tetrahedron.

Tetrahedral angle. The angle between the bonds in a tetrahedral compound (approximately 109° for a regular tetrahedron).

Tetrahedral compound. A compound in which four atoms or groups situated at the corners of a tetrahedron are linked to a atom at the centre of the tetrahedron.

Tetrahedron. A polyhedron with four triangular faces. In a regular tetrahedron all four triangles are congruent equilateral triangles. It constitutes a regular triangular pyramid.

Tetrahydrate. A crystalline hydrate containing four moles of water per mole of compound.

Texaphyrin. A synthetic molecule similar to a porphyrin but containing five central nitrogen atoms rather than four, thus increasing the size of the central 'hole' and enabling larger cations, such as cadmium, to be bound stably.

Theoretical plates. Represents how many times you do a separation in purification; can be used to describe column chromatography, GC, or HPLC.

Theoretical Yield. Maximum amount of a specified product that could be obtained from specified amounts of reactants, assuming complete consumption of limiting reactant according to only one reaction and complete recovery of product. (Compare with Actual Yield)

Thermal Cracking. Decomposition by heating a substance in the presence of a catalyst and in the absence of air.

Thermal motion. Chaotic, random motion of molecules due to the temperature.

Thermal neutrons. Neutrons that have not been slowed down and have reached equilibrium with matter at room temperature.

Thermistor. A substance which changes its resistance with temperature. Those developed as infrared detectors are known as bolometers.

Thermionic emission. You can get a current to flow from a heated filament to a positive electrode in a vacuum; this emission is simply electrons flowing from the filament to the positive electrode.

Thermochemistry. The branch of physical chemistry concerned with heats of chemical reaction, heats of formation of chemical compounds, etc.

Thermocouple. Two metals are put together side by side when heated, one metal expands more than another due to differences in the coefficients of thermal exansion, and the strip bends. This can be used as a switch, as in a thermostat.

Thermodynamics. The study of the energy transfers accompanying physical and chemical processes.

Thermolysis. The chemical decomposition of a substance by heat. It is an important process in chemical ma-nufacture, such as the thermal cracking of hydrocarbons in the petroleum industry.

Thermogravimetric analysis (TGA). When you heat a sample to observe weight changes; used when studying the loss of waters of hydration or CO2.

Thermonuclear Energy. Energy from nuclear fusion reactions.

Thermoplastics. Plastics that can be softened by heating and return to their original state on cooling.

Thermopneumatic detector. When the radiation incident on a gas in a closed chamber increases the temperature and pressure of a gas, a mirror on the cell wall moves. This movement is measured optically, and can be used to determine the amount of radiation incident on the cell.

Thermostat. A device that controls the heating or cooling of a substance in order to maintain it at a constant temperature. It consists of a temperature-sensing instrument connected to a switching device. When the temperature reaches a predetermined level the sensor switches the heating or cooling source on or off according to a predetermined program.The sensing thermometer is often a bimetallic strip that triggers a bimetallic strip that triggers a simple electrical switch. Thermostats are used for space-heating controls, in water heaters and refrigerators, and to maintain the environment of a scientific experiment at a constant temperature.

thermovoltaic detector: an IR detector where temperature changes of a junction of dissimilar metals because of changes in the level of incident radiation causes a change in voltage.

Thin layer chromatography. A tecnique for the analysis of liquid mixtures using *chromatography. The stationary phase is a thin layer of an absorbing solid (e.g. alumina) prepared by spreading a slurry of the solid on a plate (usually glass) and drying it in an oven. A spot of the mixture to be analysed is pl-aced near one edge and the plate is stood upright in a solvent. The solvent rises through the layer by capillary action carrying the components up the plate at different rates (depending on the extent to which they are absorbed by the solid). After a given time, the plate is dried and the location of spots noted. It is possible to identify constituents of the mixture by the distance moved in a given time. The technique needs careful control of the thickness of the layer and of the temperature.

Third Law of Thermodynamics. The entropy of a hypothetical pure, perfect, crystalline sustance at absolute zero temperature is zero.

Tie line. A horizontal line in a liquid-vapour phase diagram that is perpendicular to an isopleth. The starting point is the first point at which the liquid can coexist with its vapour as the pressure is reduced; the end point is the point beyond which only vapour is present.

Time dilation. The idea that time travels slower for somebody in a moving reference frame; consequence of relativity.

Time-of-flight (TOF). When you apply the same translational energy to all particles; the lighter particles will travel a shorter distance over a charged plate because there is less momentum to carry them forward.

Titration. A Procedure in which one solution is added to another solution until the chemical reaction between the two solutes is complete; the concentration of one solution is known and that of the other is unknown.

Tollens reagent. A reagent used in testing for aldehydes. It is made by adding sodium hydroxide to silver nitrate to give silver(I) oxide, which is dissolved in aqueous ammonia) giving the complex ion $[Ag(NH_3)_2]^+$). The sample is warmed with the reagent in a test tube. Aldehydes reduce the complex Ag^+ ion to metallic silver, forming a bright silver mirror on the inside of the tube (hence the name silver-mirror test). Ketones give a negative result. It is naed after Bernhard Tollens (1841-1918).

Topaz. A variably coloured aluminium silicate mineral, $Al_2(SiO_4)(OHF)_2$, that forms orthorhombic crystals. It occurs chiefly in acid igneous rocks, such as granites and pegmatites. Topaz is valued as a gemstone because of its transparency, variety of colours (the wineyellow variety being most highly prized), and great hardness (8 on the Mohs scale). When heated, yellow or brownish topaz often becomes a rose-pink colour. The main sources of topaz are Brazil, Russia, and the USA.

Torr. A unit of pressure, used in high-vacuum technology, defined as 3 mmHg. 1 torr is equal to 133.322 pascals. The unit is named after Evan-gelista Torricelli (1609-47).

Total binding energy. Energy required to break a nucleus into its component protons and neutrons.

Total internal reflection second harmonic generation (TIR SHG). This is what happens when you shine the exitation beam and probe beam on a liquid-liquid surface. What you are counting on happening is that the beams will reflect off of the bottom liquid and give the second harmonic signal you're looking for.

Total Ionic Equation. Equation for a chemical reaction written to show the predominant form of all species in aqueous solution or in contact with water.

Town gas. Any manufactured gas supplied as a fuel gas to domestic and industrial users. Examples include coal gas, substitute natural gas (SNG), and natural gas itself. Most town gases are based on hydrgen or methane, although coal gas also contains up to 8% carbon monoxide.

Transamination. A bi-ocemical reaction in amino acid metabolism in which an amine group is transferred from a amino acid to a keto acid to form a new amino acid and keto acid. The coenzyme required for this reaction is pyridoxal phosphate.

Transducer. A device that turns one kind of energy to another (like a loudspeaker turns electrical energy to sound); a device that converts a light signal into an electrical signal.

Transfer coefficient. Symbol a. A quanitity used in the analysis of processes in electrochemistry, it is the fraction of the potential difference at the surface of an ele-ctrode that assists charge differene in one direction but discourages it in the other direction. Its values lies between 0 and 1, frequently being about 1/2. It is related to the slope of a graph of the logarithm of the current ag-ainst the potential.

Transformation. The conversion of a compound into a particular product, irrespective of the reagents or mechanism involved.

Transient grating techniques. What you do in one of these studies is to get several beams coming into a sample that have different circular polarity. Their interference sets up a diffraction grating which can be used to run experiments.

Transient species. A short-lived intermediate in a chemical reaction.

Transistor. A device used to give current and power amplification.

Transition. A charge of a system from one quantum state to another.

Transition point. 1. The temperature at which one crystalline form of a substance changes to another form. 2. The temperature at which a substance changes phase. 3. The temperature at which a substance becomes superconducting. 4. The temperature at which some other change, such as a change of magnetic properties, takes place.

Transition State Theory. Theory of reaction rates that states that reactants pass through high-energy transition states before forming products.

Transmutation. The transformation of one element into another by bombardment of nuclei with particles. For example, plutonium is obtained by the neutron bombardment of uranium.

Transverse relaxation time (T2). The time it takes after a pulse in NMR for the spins to get out of phase with one another. This is also called the spin-spin relaxation time.

Transverse wave. When a wave has the property that the particles of the wave move perpindicular to the motion of the wave itself, such as a water wave.

TREPR. Time-resolved electron paramagnetic resonance; a way of identifying transient radicals

Trichroism. Exhibits different colors in 3 different directions when viewed by transmitted light.

Tungsten filament. An IR light source where the emitter is a tungsten filament; the IR output range is limited by the window material, although the window material may actually heat up enough to serve as a blackbody emitter.

Tunneling. The penetration of a particle into a classically-forbidden region.

Turbulent flow. When a moving liquid exhibits erratic, whirlpool-like currents.

Tungsten carbide. A black powder, WC, made by heating powdered tungsten metal with lamp back at 1600°C. It is extremely hard (9.5 on Mohs' scale) and is used in dies and cutting tools. A ditungsten carbide, W_2C, also exists.

Tunnel effect. An effect in which electrons are able to tunnel through a narrow potential barrier that would constitute a forbidden region if the electrons were treated as classical particles. That there is a fnite probability of an electron tunnelling from one classically allowed region to another arises as a consequence of quantum mechanics. The effect is made use of in the tunnel diode.

Turpentine. An oily liquid extrated from pine resin. It contains pinene, $C_{10}H_{16}$, and other terpenes and is mainly used as a solvent.

Turing pattern. Patterns that arise from oscillatory coupled cells. AI.

Twinning. The growth of crystals in such a way that two distinct crystals form sharing a common plane of atoms.

Two-dimensional NMR: A method in which you can take NMR peaks that are stuck on top of each other and separate them. The plot has one axis as the normal NMR axis, and the other corresponds to the spectrum when you hit the sample with 90 degree radiation.

Tyndall Effect. The scattering of light by colloidal particles.

U

Ubiquinones (coenzymes Q). Play an important role in the ELECTRON TRANSPORT CHAIN. Electron-transporting coenzymes.

UHV. Ultrahigh vacuum.

Ullman reaction. The synthesis of diaryls by coupling aromatic halides with the-mselves or other aromatic halides, with the concomitant removal of halogens by a metal, e.g. copper powder, thus bromobeazene gives diphenyl. Also used to prepare diaryl ethers and diaryl thioethers by coupling a metal phenolate with an aryl halide.

Ultimate analysis. A determination of the proportion of every element is a compound without regard to its molecular structure.

Ultracentrifuge. A device used to bring about the sedimentation of colloidal sols by subjecting them to large centrifuge forces. An ultracentrifuge may be used to determine the molecular weights and size distribution of solparticles.

Ultrafiltration. A method of pressure-driven filtration in which particles of colloidal dimensions are separated from molecular and ionic substances by drawing the sol liquid through fine membranes.

The mechanism of ultrafiltration is not simply a sieve effect, but depends also upon the electrical conditions of both the membrane and the colloid.

Ultramarine. An aluminosilicate with an (Al,Si)O_2 framework containing sulphur, some of which is present as S_2 groups. It has a blue colour and is manufactured as a pigment from china clay, sulphur, Na_2CO_3, SiO_2 and some minor constituents. Used in laundry blue and some printing processes.

Ultrasonics. The study and use of pressure waves that have a frequency in excess of 20000 Hz and are therefore inaudible to the human ear. Ultrasonics are used in medical diagnosis, particularly in conditions such as pregnancy, in which X-rays could have a harmful effect. Ultrasonic tecniques are also used industrially to test for flaws in metals, to clean surfaces, to test the thickness of parts, and to form colloids.

Ultravolet absorbers. Compounds which absorb u.v. light and dissipate energy barmlessly. Used to protect polymers against photolytic degradation and also in suntan lotions. Most light stabilizers are aromatic compounds with the aromatic ring conjugated with a C=O or N system.

Ultraviolet light (**u.v.**) Radiation beyond the visible light in the spectrum at wavelength less than about 420nm is termed ultraviolet light.

Radiation of yet shorter wavelength are the vacuum u.v. and X-rays. Ultraviolet, light possesses much greater energy than visible radiation, and is generally much more effective in inducing photochemical reactions, but possesses much less penetrating power. Ordinary glass is opaque to light of wavelength less than about 360nm. Quartz is transparent down to about 180nm, and is therefore used for making prisms and lenses in ultraviolet optical apparatus.

Ungerade. The subscript indicating uneven parity of an orbital. There is no centre of symmetry for inversion for the orbital. Grade-g-(even parity) orbitals have a centre of inversion.

Uniaxial. Crystals which have one principal axis, the other two axes being equivalent. Hexagonal, tetragonal and rhombohedral crystals are uniaxial.

Unimolecular films. When certain insoluble oils and fats (e.g. stearates) are dispersed on the surface of water it is possible to prepare these as unimolecular monolayers. In these unimolecular films the hydrophobic group is orientated away from the water; the hydrophilic group is orientated towards it. In some cases the molecules form close-packed arrays, whilst in other cases the molecules are well separated, thus forming different types of two-dimensional solids, liquids or gases. Monolayes fibres can be transferred to solid surfaces for study.

Unimolecular reaction. Chemical reactions in which the mechanism involves only single species of the reactant. Although many reactions obey first-order kinetics, relatively few true uni-molecular reactions are known. The radioactive decay process is an example, as is the thermal decomposition of certain alkyl halides.

Unit. A specified measures of a physical quantity, such as length, mass, time, etc., specified multiples of which are used to express magnitudes of that physical quantity. For scientific purposes previous systems of units have now been replaced by *SI units.

Unit cell. The characteri-stric portion of the crystal which, if repeated indefinitely in the directions of the crystal axes, reproduces the crystal. The pattern of the crystal is contained within a parallelopiped called the unit cell, whose sides are parallel to the crystal axes.

Universal indicator. A mixture of acid-base *indicators that changes colour (e.g. red-yellow-orange-green-blue) over a range of pH.

Uniphase: A wavefront is uniphase if it has the same phase at all points.

Unsaturated. (of a compound) Having double or triple bonds in its molecules. Unsaturated compounds can undergo addition reactions as well as substitution.

Unsaturated Hydrocarbons. Hydrocarbons that contain double or triple carbon-carbon bonds.

Unsaturated polyesters. Low mol.wt. polymers containing carboxylic ester groupings and double bonds derived from unsaturated soils and saturated acids. Used as copolymers with styrene and other vinyl monomers in free-radical polyme-rization to give very strong cross-linked structures.

UPS. Ultraviolet photo-electro spectroscopy.

UPVC. Unplasticized PVC: a tough hardwearing form of PVC used for window frames and similar applications.

Uracil. A *pyrimidine derivative and one of the major component bases of *nucleotides and the nucleic acid *RNA.

Uraninite. A mineral form of uranium(IV) oxide, containing minute amounts of radium, thorium, polonium, lead, and helium. When uraninite occurs in a massive form with a pitchy lustre it is known as **pitchblende**, the chief ore of uranium. Uraninite occurs in Saxony, Romania, Norway, the UK, E Africa, USA, and Canada.

Urea adduction. The basis of processes for the separation of normal alkanes, especially those from petroleum distillates in the C_{25}-C_{30} range. In the presence of n-alkanes urea crystalizes in a form which allows only the normal alkanes to be clathrated. The clathrate formed is decomposed into two phases y heating with water at 80°C.

Urea cycle. The cycle sequrnce of reactions occurring in the liver, which results in the excretion of excess nitrogen as urea via carbamyl phosphate.

Urea-formaldehyde resins. Typical AMINORESINS used in adhesives foams and moulding.

Urease. Nickel-dependent enzyme which catalyses the hydrolysis of urea to ammonia and Co_2. It is present in many plants but not in vertebrates.

Ureides. Compounds for-med between urea and organic acids by either or both nitrogens. Dicarboxylic acids ir a-hydroxy acids give cyclic ureides, e.g. barbituric acid, hydantoin. Colourless crystalline solids, sparingly soluble in water, soluble in ethanol, decmposed by alkalis, form salts.

Urethane (ethyl carbonate). $NH_2COOC_2H_5$. Colourless prisms; m.p, 49-50°C, b.p. 184°C.

Prepared by the action of ammonia on ethyll chloroformate. Good solv-ent, used in synthesis.

Urethanes. Esters of carbonic acid, NH_2COOH. Colourless crystalline solids which distil without decomposition. They are prepared by the action ammonia on carbonic or chlorocarbonic esters, or by treating alco-hols with urea nitrate or isocyanates. When heated with ammonia they form urea and an alcohol. Phenyl-and a-naphthylurethanes were used for characterizing alcohols and phenols. The term is also used for polyurethanes, major plastics used in foams (85%) and elastomers. World market 2000 8.2 megatonnes.

Uric acid. $C_5H_4N_4O_3$. A colourless microcrystalline powder, odourless and tasteless, which decomposes on heating above 250°C. It is dibasic and forms two series of salts. It occurs in small quantities in human urine as the end product of nucleic acid metabolism and in the excrement of birds and reptiles. It is prepared commercially from guano by extracting with alkali and repreci-pitating with acid. It can he synthesized by fusing glycine with urea, and by other processes.

Uricase. Enzyme which cleaves the purine skeleton.

Uronic acids. Formed by oxidation of the primary alcohol groups of sugars, and named after the sugar from which they are formed , thus glucuronic, D-mannuronic and D-galacturonic acids are important. Polyuronides are constituents of the gums and mucilages;alganic acid is a polymer of mannuronic acid and pectic acid of galacturonic acid.

Ursolic acid. Polycyclic acid from cranberries. Emulsifying agent.

V

Vacuum. A space in which there is a low pressure of gas, i.e. relatively few atoms or molecules. A **prefect vaccum** would contain no atoms or molecules, but this is unobtainable as all the materials that surround such a space have a finite *vapour pressure. In a **soft** (or **low**) **vacuum** the pressure is reduced to about 10^{-2} pascal, whereas a **hard** (or **high**) vacuum has a pressure of 10^{-2}-10^{-7} pascal. Below 10^{-7} pascal is known as an **ultrahigh** vacuum.

Vacuum distillation. Distillation under reduced pressure. The depression in the boiling point of the substance distilled means that the temperature is lower, which may prevent the substance from decomposing.

Vacuum pump. A pump used to reduce the gas pressure in a container. The normal laboratory rotary oil-seal pump can maintain a pressure of 10^{-1} Pa. For pressures down to 10^{-7} Pa a *diffusion pump is required. *Ion pumps can achieve a pressure of 10^{-9} Pa and a *cryogenic pump combined with a diffusion pump can reach 10^{-13} Pa.

Vacuum ultraviolet (VUV). UV radiation of high enough frequency that air will absorb it. UHV is ultrahigh vacuum-UV, which is of higher frequency still.

Valence Bond Theory. Assumes that covalent bonds are formed when atomic orbitals on different atoms overlap and the electrons are shared.

Valence Electrons. Outermost electrons of atoms; usually those involved in bonding.

Valence Shell Electron Pair Repulsion Theory. Assumes that electron pairs are arranged around the central element of a molecule or polyatomic ion so that there is maximum separation (and minimum repulsion) among regions of high electron density.

Valency. The combining power of an atom or radical, equal to the number of hydrogen atoms that the atom could combine with or displace in a chemical compound. It is equal to the ionic charge in ionic compounds; for example, in Na_2S, sodium has a valency of 1 (Na^+) and sulphur a valency of 2 (S^{2-}). In covalent compounds it is equal to the number of bonds formed; in CO_2 oxygen has a valency of 2 and carbon has a valency of 4.

vanadium(V) oxide (vanadium pertoxide). A crystalline compound, V_2O_5, used extensively as a catalyst in industrial gas-phase oxidation processes.

van der Waals' Equation. An equation of state that extends the ideal gas law to real gases by inclusion of two empirically determined parameters, which are different for different gases.

van der Waals' force. An attractive force between atoms or molecules, named after Johannes van der Walls (1837-1923). The force accounts for the term a/V^2 in van der Waals' equation. These forces are much we-aker than those arising from valence bonds and are inversely proportional to the seventh power of the distance between the forces responsible for non ideal behaviour of gases and for the lattice energy of molecular crystas. There are three actors causing such forces: (1) dipole-dipole interaction, i.e. electrostatic attractions between two molecules with permanent dipole moments; (2) dipoleinduced dipole of one molecule polarizes a neighbouring molecule; (3) dispersion forces arising because of small instaneous dipoles in atoms.

van't Hoff factor. Symbol i. A factor appearing in equations for colligative properties, equal to the ratio of the number of actual particles present to the number of undissociated particles.

Vapor. A gas formed by boiling or evaporating a liquid.

Vapor density. The density of a gas or vapour relative to hydrogen, oxygen, or air. Taking hydrogen as the reference substance, the vapour density is the ratio of the mass of a particular volume of a gas to the mass of an equal volume of hydrogen under identical conditions of pressure and temperature as 1, this ratio is equal to half the relative molecular mass of the gas.

Vapor Pressure. The particle pressure of a vapor at the surface of its parent liquid.

Variational principle. In calculation in quantum mechanics the principle that if a trial *wave function is used to calculate the energy of a system, then the energy calculated cannot be lower than the actual energy of the ground state of the system. To use variational principles effectively in quantum mechanics a trial wave function contains parameters that can be varied, with these param-etres being changed until the lowets possible energy is found.

Vector. A quantity that has both direction and magnitude, such as velocity.

Velocity selector. Used with molecular beams; slotted disks that make sure only particles with the desired speed reach the target.

Venturi tube. A pipe with a narrow constriction; if it has an opening at this constriction, it will tend to pull a vacuum through it equal to the vapor pressure of the liquid; a consequence of Bernoulli's principle.

Verdigris. A green patina of basic copper salts formed on copper. The composition of verdigris varies depending on the atmospheric conditions, but includes the basic carbonate $CuCO_3$, $Cu(OH)_2$, the basic sulphate $CuSO_4$, $Cu(OH)_2$. H_2O, and sometimes the basic chloride $CuCl_2$, $Cu(OH)_2$.

Vibrational relaxation. A process in which a poly-atomic molecule in an excited vibrational state returns to a lower vibrational state in the same electronic state by colliding with other molecules.

Vicinal (vic). Designating a molecule in which two atoms or groups are linked to adjacent atoms. For example 1,2-dichloroethane (CH_2ClCH_2Cl) is a vicinal (or vic) diha-lide and can be named vic-dichloroethane.

Victor Mayer's method. A method of measuring vapour density, devised by Victor Meyer (1848-97). A weighed sample in a small tube is dropped into a heated bulb with a long neck. The sample vaporizes and displaces air, which is collected over water and the volume measured. The vapour density can then be calculated.

Villiaumite. A mineral form of sodium fluoride, NaF.

Vinegar. Adilute solution of *ethanoic acid (up to 6%), used as a flavouring and pickling medium. Natural vinegar is made by the continued fermentation of alcoholic liquors, usually by Acetobacter species, which oxidize ethanol to ethanoic acid. Vinegar is also madeby diluting synthetic ethanoic acid.

Vinylation. The catalysed reaction between ethyne and a compound with an active hydrogen atom, such as alcohol, amine, or carboxylic acid. Addition takes place across the triple bond of ethyne to produce an ethenyl compound, containing the group CH_2=CH-.

Viscosity. The internal friction of a liquid

Visible spectrum. Radiation of wavelength 400-750nm.

Vitamin. One of a number of organic compounds required by living organisms in relatively small amounts to maintain normal health. There are some 14 generally recognized major vitamins: the water soluble *vitamin B complex and *vitamin C and the fatsoluble *vitamin A, *vitamin D, *vitamin E, and *vitamin K. Most B vitamins and vitamins C occur in plants, animals, microorganisms; they function typically as *coenzymes. Vitamins A, D, E and K occur only in animals, especially vertebrates, and perform a variety of metabolic roles. Animals are unable to manufacture many vitamins themselves and must have adequate amounts in the diet. Foods may contain vitamin precursors (called **provitamins**) that are chemically changed to the actual vitamin on entering the body. Many vitamins are destroyed by light and heat, e.g. during cooking.

Vitamin A. A fat-soluble vitamin that cannot be synthesized by mammals and other vertebrates and must be provided in the diet. Green plants contain precursors of the vitamin, notably carote-nes, that are converted to vitamin A in the intestinal wall and liver. The aldehyde derivative of vitamin A, **retinal**, is a constituent of the visual pigment rhodopsin. Deficiency affects the eyes, causing night blindness, xerophthalmia, and eventually total blindness. The role of vitamin A in other aspects of metabolism is less clear.

Vitamin B. A group of water-soluble vitamins that characteristically serve as components of *coenzymes. Plants and many micro-organisms can manufacture B vitamins but dietary sources are essential for most animals. Heat and light tend to destroy B vitamins.

Vitamin C. A colourless crystalline water-soluble vitamin found especially in citrus fruits and green vegetables. Most organisms synthesize it from glucose but man and other primates and various other species must obtain if from their diet. It is required for the maintenance of healthy connective tissue; deficiency leads to survey. vitamin C is readily destroyed by heat and light.

Vitamin D. Group of related components involved in calcium uptake in the body. Deficiency can cause rickets; humans exposed to sufficient sunligjht can synthesize sufficient vitamin D.

Vitamin E. Essential for fertility and reproduction. Occur in seed embroys and their oils and green leaves. Have antioxidant properties.

Vitamin K. Group of naphthaquinone derivatives derived from manadione. Of importance in blood clotting. Found in leafy vegetables.

Vitellin. The chief protein of egg yolk. It is a phosphoprotein and can be obtained as a yellow powder, insoluble in water, neutral salts and dilute acids.

VOC (volatile organic compound). Term used particularly in respect of paints, polymers.

Volhard method. Titration of Ag^+ with NCS^- in the presence of Fe^{3+}. A deep red colour is formed at the end-point.

Voltage. Potential difference between two electrodes; a measure of the chemical potential for a redox reaction to occur.

Voltaic Cells. Electrochemical cells in which spontaneous chemical reactions produce electricity; also called galvanic cells.

Voltammetry. Study of electrode processes through the current whilst potential is varied.

VOM. Woltohmmeter; a multimeter that measures voltage, current and resistance.

Vulcanization. The process of conferring more cross-linking upon a plastic (generally rubber) and so altering its structure that it becomes less plastic and stricky, more resistant to swelling by organic liquids and has enhanced elasticity. The rubber is heated with a vulcanizing agent, generally sulphur although other compounds, e.g. S_2Cl_2. tetramethyl thiuram disulphide, Se, Te, organic peroxides are used with additives to affect the rate of vulcanization.

W

Wacker process. A process for the manufacture of eth-anal by the air oxidation of ethene is bubbled through a solution containing palladium(II) chloride and copper (II) chloride. The Pd^{2+} ions form a complex with the ethene in which the ion is bound to the pi electrons in the C=C bond. This decreases the electron density in the bond, making is susceptible to nucleophilic attack by water molecules. The complex formed breaks down to ethanal and palladium metal. The Cu^{2+} ions oxidize the palladium back to Pd^{2+}, being reduced to Cu^{+} ions in the process. The air present oxidizes the process. The air present oxidizes Cu^{+} back to Cu^{2+}. Thus the copper(II) and palladium(II) ions effectively act as catalysts in the process, which is now the main source of ethanal and, by further oxidation, ethanoic acid. It can also be applied to other alkanes. It is named after Ale-xander von Wacker (1846-1922).

Wagner-Meerwein rearrangement. A rearrangement in which an alkyl group moves from a carbon atom to an adjacent carbon atom during a reaction. It often occurs to stabilize a carbocation formed as an intermediate during the reaction. Rearran-gements of this type have been extensively studied in terpene chemistry.

WAHUMA. A pulse sequ-ence in *nuclear magnetic resonance (NMR) used to reduce linewideth. The WAHUHA sequence (named after its inventors Waugh, Huber, and Haberlen) effects an averaging procedure by twisting the magnetization vector in various directions.

Walden reductor. A metal reduction column filled with silver.

Walsh diagram. A diagram that shows the variation of orbital energy with molecular geometry

Warfarin.3-(alpha-acetonylbenzyl)-4-hydroxy-coumarin: a synthetic anticoagulant used both therapeutically in clinical medicine and, in lethal doses, as a rodenticide.

Water Equivalent. The amount of water that would absorb the same amount of heat as the calorimeter per degree temperature increase.

Water glass. A viscous colloidal solution of sodium silicates in water, used to make silica gel and as a size and preservative.

Water of crystallization. Water present in crystalline compounds in definite proportions. Many crystalline salts form hydrates containing 1, 2, 3, or more moles of water per mole of compound, and the water may be held in the crystal in various ways. Thus, the water molecules may simply occupy lattice positions in the crystal, or they may form bonds with the anions or the cations present. In the pentahydrate of copper sulphate, for instance, each copper ion is coordinated to four water molecules through the lone pairs on the oxygen to for the *complex $[Cu(H_2O)_4]^{2+}$. Each sulphate ions has one water molecule held by hydrogen bonding. The difference between the two types of bonding is demonstarated by the fact that the pentahyd-rate converts to the monohydrate at 100°C and only becomes anhydrous above 250°C. **Water of constitution** is an obsolete term for water combined in a compound (as in a metal hydroxide $M(OH)_2$ regarded as a hydrated oxide $MO.H_2O$).

Watt. Symbol W. The SI unit of power, defined as a power of one joule per second. In electrical contexts it is equal to the rate of energy transformaton by an electric current of one amphere flowing through a conductror the ends of which are maintained at a potential difference of one volt. The unit is named after James Watt (1736-1819).

Wave function. A function appearing in *Schrodinger's equation in wave mechanics. The wave function is a mathematical expression involving the coordinates of a particles in space. If the Schrodinger equation can be solved for a particle in a given system (e.g. an electron in an atom) then, depending on the boundary conditions, the solution is a set of allowed wave functions (**eigenfunctions**) of the particle, each coresponding to an allowed energy level (**eigenvalue**). The physical significance of the wave fu-nction is that the square of its absolute value, at a point is proportional to the probability of finding the particle in a small element of volume, dxdydz, at that point. For an electron in an atom, ths gives rise to the idea of atomic and molecular *orbitals.

Wave mechanics. The electronic theory of matter is confronted by certain difficulties which have only been overcome by assumptionsof a very arbitrary nature. To overcome these difficulties by a general theorem, de Broglie and Schrodinger independently devised systems of wave mechanics which are essentially mathematical, and may only be very approximately described in terms of physical pictures. Wave mechanics give allowed energy levels. Transitions between these states give rise to various forms of electromagnetic radiation. Wave mechanics had led to a considerable ciarification of many difficulties inherent in the older quantum theory and in the electronic theory of matter, but it is still necessary to use these concepts because of their more concrete nature.

Wave number. The reciprocal of wavelength, i.e. the number of waves in a given length. Often referred to as frequency 1000^{-1} cm = 12.5 kj mol^{-1}.

Waxes. Formally fatty acid esters with monohydric fatty alcohols having was-like properties but now arbitrarily extended to any orga-nic material having similar physical properties. Waxes are water repellent and have plasticity. They are used in paper coating, polishes, electrical insulation, textiles, leather, pharmaceuticals. Typical examples are cetyl palmitate in spermaceti and melissyl palmitate in beeswax. Synthetic waxes include some forms polythene.

Weak Electrolyte. A substance that conducts electricity poorly in a dilute aqueous solution.

Weak Field Ligand. A Ligand that exerts a weak crystal or ligand field and generally forms high spin complexes with metals.

Weedkillers. Herbicides used to control selectively unwanted vegetation on agricultural land.

Wedge prism. Used for beam steering.

Welsbach mantle. A gauze mesh, similar to the one in gas lanterns, impregnated with ThO2 and a small amount of CeO2 which is heated by either a burning gas or electric charge. It gives off IR radiation between 10-100 microns.

Wetting agents. Water, because of its powerful intermoleclar attractive forces, does not readily spread over many surfaces. The addition of surface-active agents, which decrease the contact angle between the water and the other surface, thereby lowering the surface. Such surfaceactive agents, e.g. detergents, surfactants, usually consist of molecules which have an oilattracting hydrophobic group and a water-attracting (hydrophilic) group (e.g. a negatively charged carboxylic or sulphonic acid group).

White oils. Oils used in medicinal and toilet preparations obtained by drastic refining of lubricating oil stocks.

White spirits, mineral solvents. A mixture of hydrocarbons, usually from a petroleum source, b.p. 130-220°C. White spirits are used as paint thinners and as solvents for a variety of purposes.

Whiting. A form of $CaCO_3$ made by grinding chalk and collecting the finer sediments from water. It is extensively used in the chemical and many other industries.

Wilkinson's catalyst. An important catalyst for homogenous hydrogenation which also catalyses oxidation by O_2 and CO abstraction from organic derivatives.

Wiswesser line notation. A method for expressing the more usual graphical structure of a chemical compound as a linear string of symbols. The resulting alternative notation is unambiguous, short and suitable for computer processing and retrieval.

Witherite. $BaCO_3$. The white mineral form of ba-rium carbonate. Used as a source of Ba compounds and in the brick and ceramic industries.

Wood. Wood is a complex substance with cell walls containing carbohydrates and lignin together with some inorganic and many organic materials. Wood is used in construction, in the pulp and paper industries, for charcoal, rayon and for various chemicals.

Wood flour. Finely ground timber used as filler in plastics, linoleum and also in sheet metal work.

Woodward-Hoffmann rules. Orbital symmetry rules relation to ring formation and ring opening.

Wool. A natural protein fibre (keratin) mainly from the fleece of sheep.

Work. Work is done when an object is moved against a force or, e.g. a chemical reaction drives a current thro-ugh a resistance when a surfae is formed.

Work function. The energy required to remove a electron from the highest occupied level inside a solid to a point in vacup outside the surface.

Work hardening. Increase in strength and hardness, decrease in ductility and toughness of a metal alloy resulting from plastic deformation at a temperature below its recrystallization temperature. Beneficial in production of high tensile wire by cold drawing and spring strip by cold rolling. Results from mutual interference of dislocations moving on interse-cting slip planes and also of grain boundary obstruction of dislocations.

X

Xanthates. Salts or esters containing the group-SCS(OR), where R is an organic group. Cellulose xanthate is an intermediate in the manufacture of *rayon by the viscose process.

Xanthene. A heterocyclic compound having three fused rings with one oxygen atom, $C_{13}H_{10}O$; m.p.

101-102°C. b.p. 310-312°C. The ring structure is present in a clas of **xanthene dyes.**

Xanthine. A purine base, $C_5H_4N_4O_2$. found in many organisms.

Xenobiotic. Ay substance foreign to living systems. Xenobiotics include drugs, pesticides, and carcinogens. Detoxification of such substances occurs mainly in the liver.

Xenon. Symbol Xe. A colo-urless odourless gas belonging to group 18 of the periodic table; a.n. 54; r.a.m. 131.30; d.5.887 gdm^{-3}; m.p. -111.9°C; b.p.-107.1°C. It is present in the atmosphere (0.00087%) from which it is extracted by distillation of liquid air. There are nine natural isotopes with mass numbers 124, 126, 128-132, 134, and 136. Seven radioactive isotopes are also known. The element is used in fluorescent lamps and bubble chambers. Liquid xenon in a supercritical state at high temperature is used as a solvent for infrared spectroscopy and for chemical reactions. The compound $Xe^{+}PtF_6$ was the first noble-gas compound to be synthersized. Several other compounds of xenon are known, including XeF_2 , XeF_4, $XeSiF_6$, XeO_2F_2, and XeO_3. Recently, compounds have been isolated that contain xenon-carbon bonds, such as $[C_6H_5Xe]$ $[B(C_6H_5)_3F]$ (pentafluorophenylxenon fluoroborate), which is stable under normal conditions. The element was discovered in 1898 by Ramsey and Travers.

XPS. X-ray photoelectron spectroscopy.

X-ray crystallography. The use of *X-ray diffraction to determine the structure of crystals or molecules. The technique involves directing a beam of X-rays at a crystalline sample and recording the diffracted X-rays on a photographic plate. The diffraction pattern consists of a pattern of spots on the plate, and the crystal sructure can be worked out from the positions and intensities of the diffraction spots. X-rays are diffracted by the electrons in the molecules and if molecular crystals of a compound are used, the electron density distribution in the molecule can be determined.

X-ray diffraction. The diffraction of X-rays by a crystal. The wavelengths of X-rays are comparable in size to the distances between atoms in most crystals, and the repeated pattern of the crystal lattice acts like a diffraction greating for X-rays. Thus, a crystal of suitable type can be used to disperse X-rays in a spectrometer. X-ray diffraction is also the basis of X-ray crystallography.

X-ray fluorescence spectroscopy (XRF). Measures the energies of the inner electrons of an atom by knocking them off with X-rays; good for about 35 elements. Handy because it is not a destructive method of analysis - the electrons are simply elevated to outer orbitals and the relaxation to the inner orbitals is measured.

Y

Yeasts. A group of unicellular fungi of the class Hemiascomycetae and phylum Ascomycota. They occur as single cells or gas groups or chains of cells; yeasts reproduce asexually by budding and sexually by producing ascospores. Yeasts of the genus Saccha-ramyces ferment sugars and are used in the baking and brewing industries.

Ylide. A chemical species derived from a onium ion by loss of a hydrogen.

Yocto. Symbol Y. A prefix used in the metric system to indicate 10^{-24}. For exam-ple, 10^{-24} second =1 yocto-secon (ys).

Yotta-. Symbol Y. A prefix used in the metric system to indicate 10^{24}. for example, 10^{24} metres = 1 yottametre (Ym).

Young's modulus (E): the ratio of longitudinal stress to longitudinal strain.

Ytterbium. Symbol Yb. A silvery metallic element belonging to the *lanthanoids; a.n. 70; r.a.m. 173.04; r.d. 6.965 (20°C); m.p. 819°C; b.p. 1194°C. It occurs in gadolinite, monazite, and xenotime. There are seven natural isotopes and ten artificial isotopes are known. It is used in certain streels. The element was discovered by Jean de marginac (1817-94) in 1878.

Yttrium. Symbol Y. A silvery-grey metallic element belonging to group 3 (formerly IIIA) of the periodic table; a.n.39; r.a.m. 88.905; r.d. 4.469 (20°C); m.p. 1522 °C; b.p. 3338°C. It occurs in uranium ores and in *lant-hanoid ores, from which it can be extracted by a ion exchange process. The natural isotope is yttrium-89, and there are 14 known artificial isotopes. The metal is used in superconducting alloys and in alloys for strng permanent magnets (in both cases, with cobalt). The oxide is used in colour-television phosphors, neodymium-doped lasers, and microwave components. Ch-emically it resembles the lanthanoids, forming ionic compounds containing Y^{3+} ions.. The metal is stable in air below 400°C. It was discovered in 1828 by Friedrich Wohler.

Z

Zeeman effect. This is the effect of overcoming the normal degeneracy of electron spin states by applying a magnetic field which can interact with the magnetic moment of the electron. This is observed when atoms are subjected to a powerful magnetic field resulting in the spectral lines being split into a number of component lines.

Zeise's salt. A complex of platinum and ethene, $PtCl_3$ (CH_2CH_2), in which the Pt coordinates to the pi bond of the ethene. It was the first example of an enyl complex, synthesized by W.C. Zeise in 1827.

Zeolite. A natural or synthetic hydrated aluminosilicate with an open three-dimensional crystal structure, in which water molecules are held in cavities in the lattice. The water can be driven off by heating and the zeolite can then absorb other molecules of suitable size. Zeolites are used for separating mixtures by selective absorption-for this reason they are often called molecular sieves. They are also in sorption pumps for vacuum systems and certain types are used in ionexchange (e.g. water-softening).

Zepto. Symbol z. A prefix used in the metric system to indicate 10^{-21}. For example, 10^{-21} second = 1 zeptose-cond (zs).

Zero-point energy. The energy remaining in a substance at the *absolute zero of temperature (0 K). This is in accordance qwith quantum theory. in which a particle oscillating with simple harmonic motion does not have a stationary state of zero kinetic energy. Moreover, the *uncertainty principle does not allow such as particle to be at rest at exactly the centrepoint of its oscillations.

Zeroth law of hermodyamics. If A is in thermal equilibrium with B and B is in thermal equilibrium with C, then A and C are in thermal equilibrium

ZSM-5 zeolites: Commonly used zeolites which are extremely good at removing NOx. Used in auto emissions control and direct composition of NO to N2 and O2.

Zetta. Symbol Z. A prefix used in the metric system to indicate 10^{21}. For example, 10^{21} metres = 1 zettametre (Zm).

Ziegler process. A industrial process for the manufacture of highdensity pol-ythene using catalysts of titanium (IV) chloride ($TiCl_4$) and aluminium alkyls (e.g. triethylaluminium, $Al(C_2H_5)_3$). The process was introduced in 1953 by the German chemist Karl Ziegler (1898-1973). It allowed the manufacture of polythene at lower temperature (about 60°C) and pressures (about 1 atm.) than used in the original process. Moreover, the polythee produced had more straight-chain molecules, giving the product more rigidity and a higher melting point than the earlier low-density polythene. The reaction involves the formation of a titanium alkyl in which the titanium can co-ordinate directly to the pi bond in ethene.

In 1954 the process was developed further by the Italian chemist Giulio Natta (1903-79), who extended the use of Ziegler's catalysts (and similar catalysts) to other alkanes. It particular he showed how to produce stereospecific polymers of propene.

Zinc. Symbol Zn. A blue-white metallic element; a.n. 30; r.a.m. 65.38; r.d. 7.1; m.p. 419.88°C; b.p. 907°C. It occurs in sphalerite (or zinc blende, ZnS), which is found associated with the lead sulphide, and in smithsonite ($ZnCO_3$). Ores are roasted to give the oxide and this is reduced with carbon (coke) at high temperature, the zinc vapour being condensed. Alternatively, the oxide is dissolved in sul-phuric acid the zinc obtained by electrolysis. There are five stable isotopes (mass numbers 64, 66, 67, 68, and 70) and six radioactive isotopes are known. The metal is used in galvanizing and in a number of alloys (brass, bronze, etc). Chemically it is a reactive metal, combining with oxygen and other nonmetals and reacting with dilute acids to release hydrogen. It also dissolves in alkalis to give *zincates. Most of its compounds contain the Zn^{2+} ion.

Zincate. A salt formed in solution by dissolving zinc or zinc oxide in alkali. The formula is often written ZnO_2^{2-} although in aqueous solution the ions present are probably complex ions in which the Zn^{2+} is coord-inated to OH^- ions ZnO_2^{2-} ions may exist in molten sodium zincate, but most solid 'zincates' are mixed oxides.

Zinc blende. A mineral form of *zinc sulphide, ZnS, the principal ore of zinc.

Zinc chloride. A white crystalline compound, $ZnCl_2$. The anhydrous salt, which is deliquescent, can be made by the action of hydrogen chloride gas on hot zinc; r.d. 2.9; m.p. 283°C; b.p. 732°C. It has a relatively low melting point and sublimes easily, indicating that it is a molecular compound rather. Zinc chloride is used as a catalyst, dehydrating agent, and flux for hard solder. It was once known as **butter of zinc.**

Zinc group. The group of elements in the periodic consisting of zinc (Zn), cadmium (Cd), and mercury (Hg).

Zincite. A mineral form of *zinc oxide, ZnO.

Zinc oxide. A powder, white when cold and yellow when hot, ZnO; r.d. 5.606; m.p. 1975°C. It occurs naturally as a reddish orange ore **zincite**, and can also be made by oxidizing hot zinc in air. It is amphoteric, forming *zincates with bases. It is used as a pigment and a mild antiseptic in zinc ointments. An archaic name is **philosopher's wool**.

Zinc sulphate. A white crystalline water-soluble compound made by heating zinc sulphide ore in air and dissolving out and recrystalling the sulphate. The common form is the heptahydrare, $ZnSO_4$. $7H_2O$; r.d. 1.9. This loses water above 30°C to give the hexahydrate and more water is lose above 70°C to form the monohydrate. The anhydrous salt forms at 280°C and this decomposes above 500°C. The compound, which was formerly called **white vitriol**, is used as a mordant and as a styptic (to check bleeding).

Zinc sulphide. A yellow-white water-soluble solid. ZnS. It occurs naturally as *sphalerite and wurtzite. The compound sublimes at 1180°C. It is used as a pigme-nt and phosphor.

Zircon. A naturally occurring silicate of zirconium, $ZrSiO_4$, used as a gemstone. The colour depends in small amounts of other metals and may be red, brown, yellow, or green. Red gemquality zircon is sometimes called **jacinth**; gem-quality zircons with other colours are called **jargoons**. There is also a naturally occurring colour-less variety. Zircon gems can be given other colours, or made clourless, by heat treatment. The colourless, varieties (either natural or treated) are sometimes called **Matura diamonds** (after Matura in Sri Lanka). The name 'zircon' is often erroneously applied to a synthetic form of the oxide *cubic zircona, which is used as a diamond substitute.

Zirconium. Symbol Zr. A grey-white metallic *transition element; a.n. 40; r.a.m. 91.22; r.d. 6.49; m.p. 1852°C; b.p. 4377°C. It is found in zircon ($ZrSiO_4$; the main source) and in badd-eleyite (ZnO_2). Extraction is by chlorination to give $ZrCl_4$ which is purified by solvent extraction and reduced with magnesium. There are five natural isotopes (mass numbers 90, 91, 92, 94, and 96) and six radioactive isotopes are known. The element is used in nuclear reactors and in certain alloys. The metal forms a passive layer of oxide in air and burns at 500°C. Most of its compounds are complexes of zirconium (IV). **Zirconium(IV) oxide (zirconia)** is used as an electrolyte in fuel cells. The element was identified in 1789 by Klaproth and was first isotaled by Berzelius in 1824.

Zone refining. A technique used to reduce the level of impurities in certain metals, alloys, semiconductors, and other materials. It is based on the observation that the solubility of an impurity may be different in the liquid and solid phases of a material. To take advantage of this observation, A narrow molten zone is moved along the length of a specimen of the material, with the result that the impurities are segregaed at one end of the bar and the pure material at the other. In general, if the impurities lower the melting point of the material they are moved in the same direction as the molten zone moves, and vice versa.

Zwitterion. An ion that has a positive and negative charge on the same group of atoms. Zwitterions can be formed from compounds that contain both acid groups and basic groups in their molecules. For example, aminoethanoic acid has the formula $H_2N.CH_2.COOH$. However, under neutral conditions, it exists in the different form of the zwitterion $^+H_3N.CH_2.COO^-$, which can be regarded as having been produced by an internal neutralization reaction (transfer of a proton from the carboxyl group to the amino group). Aminoethanoic acid, as a consequence, has some properties characteristic of ionic compounds; e.g. a high melting point and solubility in water.In acid solutions, the positive ion $^+H_3NCH_2COOH$ is formed. In basic solutions; the negative ion $H_2NCH_2COO^-$ predominates. The name comes from the German zwei, two.

OOO